Gym Shoes and Irises

(PERSONALIZED TZEDAKAH)

Danny Siegel

THE TOWN HOUSE PRESS

Spring Valley, New York

ACKNOWLEDGEMENTS

Grateful thanks are extended to the following magazines and periodicals wherein a number of these pieces have appeared (occasionally in a different form and with a different title): *Moment, the Baltimore Jewish Times, The Reconstructionist, Achshav, Sh'ma, The Pedagogic Reporter* of the American Association for Jewish Education, *The Jewish Exponent,* and *Response.*

"19 Occasions for Giving Tzedakah" appeared in *The Jewish Almanac,* Bantam Books, 1980, editors, Richard A. Siegel and Carl J. Rheins.

Biblical translations, other than those by the author, are taken from the Jewish Publication Society's *The Torah, The Prophets,* and *The Book of Psalms,* and are included by the courtesy of the Jewish Publication Society of America.

This book was made possible, in part, through a grant from the Gimprich Family Foundation. I am particularly grateful to that foundation for allowing me the time to prepare these essays.

I would also like to thank Ms. Judy Kupchan of Washington, DC, for her assistance in preparing this volume.

To Beth Huppin, *Edele Neshama,* devoted Jew, wise in her giving, wise in her teaching, deep gratitude from a Tzedakah-colleague. Ali VeHatzlichi!

Above all, my gratitude to Arthur Kurzweil, formerly a student and friend, now a teacher and friend, for allowing me to print his study of giving to beggars. He has cited many sources previously unfamiliar to me and thereby provided the greatest joy for a teacher—to see a student surpass himself and his teacher. His skill with traditional Jewish texts, and his own extraordinary insight, give guidance to many who seek wisdom in our sacred books. I am privileged to be among those who have found instruction in his words.

Cover by Jay Wolke

For Ordering:
The Town House Press
28 Midway Road, Spring Valley NY 10977 (914) 425-2232

Seventh Printing, 1988   ISBN: 0-940653-00-1

FOR MY HEROES

Myriam Mendilow, Hadassah Levi,
Reb Osher Freund, Uri Lupoliansky,
The Rabbanit Bracha Kapach,
Si Levine, Dr. David Weiss,
Eva Michaelis, Curt Arnson,
Meyer and Hannah Bargteil,
Daniel and Charlotte Kuttler,
Uri Cohen, Miriam Itzkovitch,
Avital Shcharansky,
Rachel Guron,
Dr. Kurt Meyerowitz,
and for the many others I have met
in Israel, the United States, Canada,
—wherever Tzedakah brings hope and comfort—
heroes, all of them.

And to the Memory of
Two of The Righteous:
Irene Gaster, זכר צדקת לברכה
and
Ya'akov Maimon, זכר צדיק לברכה

אין עושין נפשות לצדיקים
דבריהם הן הן זכרונן

"We need not make elaborate gravestones
for the Righteous.
Their words and deeds
are their monuments."
(Talmud, Shekalim 2:5)

BOOKS BY DANNY SIEGEL

Essays

1980 - ANGELS (out of print)

1982 - GYM SHOES AND IRISES
(Personalized Tzedakah)

1987 - GYM SHOES AND IRISES - BOOK TWO

Poetry

1969 - SOULSTONED (out of print)

1976 - AND GOD BRAIDED EVE'S HAIR (out of print)

1978 - BETWEEN DUST AND DANCE (out of print)

1980 - NINE ENTERED PARADISE ALIVE (out of print)

1983 - UNLOCKED DOORS
(An Anthology)

1985 - THE GARDEN:
Where Wolves and Lions Do No Harm
to the Sheep and the Deer

1985 - THE LORD IS A WHISPER AT MIDNIGHT
(Psalms and Prayers)

1986 - BEFORE OUR VERY EYES
Readings for a Journey Through Israel

Midrash and Halachah

1983 - WHERE HEAVEN AND EARTH TOUCH
(Book One)

1984 - WHERE HEAVEN AND EARTH TOUCH
(Book Two)

1985 - WHERE HEAVEN AND EARTH TOUCH
(Book Three)

1985 - WHERE HEAVEN AND EARTH TOUCH
SOURCE BOOK
(Selected Hebrew and Aramaic Sources)

Humor

1982 - THE UNORTHODOX BOOK OF JEWISH
RECORDS AND LISTS
(With Allan Gould)

I am about to deliver a talk on Tzedakah. The local United Synagogue Youth group has invited me to their synagogue, and the flyer mentions that we are looking for wedding dresses to send to Israel, to lend to brides who cannot afford to purchase them.

Before the talk begins, a young woman comes up to me outside the sanctuary. She is carrying a long white gown in a plastic casing. She explains, "I can't stay for your talk, but here is my wedding dress."

It is a magnificent dress. By now—almost a year later—no doubt it has been used by a number of different brides. The lending-library of dresses is supervised by certain Mitzvah people I have met in Jerusalem.

I cannot even remember the woman's name, but the radiance of her face has left a strong impression on my memory. I think about her frequently, about her enthusiasm as she handed me the dress. I believe that women are entitled to keep their wedding dresses—that all of us should be allowed to preserve things that hold great sentimental value for us. It is a part of life, an attachment, a hold on meanings and memories—and yet —this woman gave hers away, with an open hand and full heart.

Our conversation lasted only a minute, perhaps two.

"Here is the dress."

It was a magnificent gown.

Author's Note: The photograph on the front cover has been retouched. No destruction nor desecration of United States currency is intended.

TABLE OF CONTENTS

APPENDICES

Introductory Selections

Outside the sauna at the Concord Hotel. It is the Rabbinical Assembly Convention and one of the rabbis is telling me a Tzedakah story:

One of my friends, another rabbi, told me this story about his mother. . . . She was in Florida for a few months, for the sunshine, the rest. She is in her seventies, a long-ago immigrant from Europe. There, in Miami, she stops someone she sees and says, "You are the son of Mr. So-and-So from Such-and-Such a town in Europe." The man is astounded and wants to know exactly how she might know that.

The elder woman explains, "Your father was a woodchopper in Europe. He used to chop wood and leave it at night behind the houses of the poor, so they wouldn't be embarrassed to take it. As soon as I saw you, even though it has been years since I knew your father — as soon as I saw you, I recognized your father's face."

Written on the back of a check sent to me for Tzedakah:

In honor of my husband's recovery. He needs God's help desperately.

Summary of an article from the Jerusalem Post *entitled "Lunch at the Gingi's"*

Mitbach Yitzchak is a small eight-table restaurant on Montefiore St. in Tel Aviv. It's owner is a small, red-headed, red-bearded man — a "gingi," as they say in Hebrew slang. And a survivor of Auschwitz.

From noon until two o'clock the restaurant serves nice-sized portions of home-cooked Jewish food. After two, the customers leave, and others come in. They choose from the same menu and eat exactly the same food as the other customers, but for them it is free.

Shabbat afternoon it is open only to this non-paying crowd: the poor, the lonely, the troubled.

Helga Dudman, the writer of this article, calls Mitbach Yitzchak a "little eight-table Kingdom of Righteousness."

A man from an organization called "Hatzilu" is presenting a slideshow:

Hatzilu — it means "Save!" — works with old Jews in the run-down parts of New York: Bedford-Stuyvesant, tough parts of the Bronx, other neighborhoods. He explains that some Jews have to eat dogfood. They can't afford anything better. He continues, "One lady used to go out and the neighborhood kids would throw stones at her."

A while later we send a check. Hatzilu writes back that it helped to take care of an elderly couple that was mugged in their own apartment.

Again we send a check. This time it is for food for the holidays. Hatzilu explains over the phone, "One lady kissed my hand when she received the food."

After a speech about Tzedakah:

A man approaches and begins to talk to me; he speaks with a thick

British accent. I expect the usual — some unusual story about Tzedakah.

The man explains that he was in the Australian Navy during World War II. His boat was torpedoed and the survivors were picked up by an American ship. By the time they reached port in Charleston, South Carolina, a member of the Jewish community was waiting for him and any other Jewish crew members on board who had been picked up at sea. The man from Charleston explained to this sailor, this stranger, that he was welcome to come down to his store as soon as he wanted, to pick up some new clothes. The Australian told him that it would take a while for money to be wired to him. No matter, the merchant explained. That would not be necessary — the clothes were free.

Lakewood, New Jersey, home of the Great Yeshiva:

There is a local service called Dial-a-Meal. Anyone who is sick, having a baby, or for some other reason unable to make his own meals can call. Members of a committee will prepare a meal and bring it to that person's home.

The Garden at Life Line for the Old:

As the teenagers and I are about to enter the workshop where people are in wheelchairs, I pause to point out the lovely garden. I explain that it was planted by and tended by a man whom I knew, a man in his late seventies and early eighties. I reconstruct for them fragments of a conversation I had with that man, in broken Hebrew and broken German.

"I was wounded in World War I and left on the battlefield to die."

That event took place more than sixty years before I met the gardener. Two years ago I learned that he was no longer well enough to work at his flowers. Someone else waters them now. They are his legacy to all who pass by.

INTRODUCTION

I became involved in Tzedakah work quite by accident. On a trip to Israel in January of 1975, I found myself unexpectedly graced with nearly $1000 in Tzedakah money my friends and relatives had given me. I was to distribute it as I saw fit, to whichever worthy projects and individuals I might discover during my stay. The first essay, "Gym Shoes and Irises," describes the specific circumstances that led up to that pilgrimage. The details are unimportant for this introduction, but what is significant is that everything else in this volume is a result of that one trip.

These essays represent my personal reflections about this Mitzvah. The book neither pretends to be systematic nor exhaustive, nor is it meant to be used as a sourcebook, since I have included little historical or developmental material. Some of the articles are theoretical, others deal with practicalities, including suggestions for teaching Tzedakah in the schools. After six years of listening to students and audiences, I feel compelled to bring the Mitzvah home on the most elementary level. I wish no more than that others might enjoy the same great benefits I have enjoyed through my many experiences.

I see my role as that of a *Shadchan*, a Matchmaker. I want to link willing donors to worthy recipients . . . and I want the recipients to know that there are Jews and non-Jews everywhere who believe in their work. I have chosen to be a part-time Matchmaker, rather than some other functionary in the Tzedakah world, for two reasons:

1. I have carefully made an accounting of my own emotional limits. I am unable to manage too much emotional intensity, and I would therefore be unable to carry out day-to-day work with the elderly, the deaf, the retarded, or the socially disadvantaged as so many others are able to do. I am also impatient, unable to see the victories in small victories. I have taken note of the immense quantities of energy required to keep an Akim program for the multiple handicapped functioning, and I realize that I am incapable of summoning such inner resources, no matter how great the need. The Talmud justifiably warns people with hypersensitive tendencies that they may not be able to remain stable in the face of so much suffering. I, personally, have a low threshold for absorbing the pain of others, and I take the Talmud's warning very seriously. In a short time I would become spiritually exhausted and dysfunctional, were I to attempt to accomplish what my heroes are doing.

Still, there is room for me — and for others who find themselves confined to certain emotional boundaries — to play a part within this framework: by making use of our Tzedakah money, we can still assist in bringing about great acts of kindness, striking changes in our environment. I do not offer this suggestion as an excuse to avoid our responsibilities. To the contrary, using our personal resources as extensions of ourselves is a sanctioned Jewish method of improving the quality of life in our society. By distributing our Tzedakah money judiciously, we are not freed thereby from other personal Mitzvot such as visiting the sick, comforting the mourners, burying the dead, providing hospitality to wayfarers, and bringing joy to brides and grooms at their wedding. Cer-

tainly, we are still obligated to perform those acts. But our money extends
our reach: while we are bound to our occupations as writers and teachers
and students and physicians and children, we can still make it possible for
others — no matter where they might be — to do their work, work which
we ourselves are unable to do.

2. As a Matchmaker and resource-person I am able to remain committed to the principle of The Easy Mitzvah. The complexities, contradictions, and paradoxes that life brings to my attention are beyond my range
of comprehension. I do not know where to begin to make sense of the
total accumulated pain and tears in the world. I neither wish for myself,
nor for others, to suddenly and singlehandedly take on these sorrows —
to hammer away at them, all of them, and bring the Messiah. As I understand it, that burden is relegated to Abraham, and Moses, and Jeremiah, and
Levi Yitzchak of Berditchev, the Chassidic Rebbi who could plead with
God, could sing to Him, could coax Him to be gentle. It would be blatant
arrogance to assume that I or my friends would be able, or even want, to
do such a thing.

Rather, I encourage others to take some small space in life, and
some small prescribed percentage of money and time, in order to carve
out a reasonable perimeter for their Tzedakah work. My only rule is this:
that they (and I) carry out this work with passion. We are not automatons,
but people. We are supremely capable of making use of our passions for
right-doing. One of the ancient Jewish texts expresses this succinctly and
eloquently: a poor man approached a certain rabbi and said to him, *"Zaki
Bi* — Assume your right, your privilege, to do this Mitzvah of Tzedakah
through me." The poor man has equalized the situation. He is not speaking of a helper-helpee frame of reference, and we should not understand
Tzedakah as some have explained, "I am fortunate. You are a woeful soul.
I will take pity on you and help you." No, this is not Tzedakah. Rather, in
its deepest meaning, Tzedakah is doing what is right — not because we are
Grand Generous Dazzling Righteous People — but because that is simply
what people must do for each other.

Again and again I focus on two themes in this book: money and
heroes. The idea is simple: money (and encouragement) from us, placed at
the disposal of Tzedakah-heroes can bring about awesome changes in the
lives of many people. Discovering the heroes and gathering the money are
the main tasks at hand . . . but there is a danger: we must not fall into the
trap of thinking that we, too, can accomplish all that they can do. We
must protect ourselves. I do not mean to imply that we should not strive
to accomplish more and more in this field of human endeavor. By no
means. I merely state that many of these exceptional people, these heroes,
live such high-powered lives that, were we to venture the same, we would
burn out quickly, perhaps irreparably. There is an aura that surrounds
them, a *"Ziv,"* a reflection of God's immediate Presence, that inevitably
attracts us. But they are *so* extraordinary, we must be careful. While we
may pattern some of our actions by the shape and flow of their lives, we
must remain within our own limits. The story of another Chassidic Rebbi
comes to mind — a tale of Susya of Hanipol. On his deathbed he explained

to his students that he was not afraid that God would ask him why he was not Moses or Isaiah or Maimonides. He was afraid of only one question, "Susya, why weren't you Susya?"

If some of these heroes are saintly, then we must remember that they are not perfect. We must also remember that the Jewish ideal of a *Tzaddik* does not necessarily imply someone who denies all benefits and pleasures to himself. I have met Tzedakah-heroes who appear quite "normal." As we enjoy movies and basketball games, so, too, they enjoy movies and basketball games. As we take pleasure in a hike through the Hills of Judea, so do they. As we enjoy the benefits of a stable family life, so, too, do they. To save the world and destroy one's relatives and friends is a contradiction in Jewish thinking. And for ourselves, we must understand that to whatever degree we may choose to devote our time to Tzedakah, it does not preclude, in any way, the living of a full and joyous normal life.

I have other reasons for writing this book — beyond a study of the power of money and the grandeur of heroes. I see how a growing remoteness from our European roots is shattering our connection to Tzedakah. No longer may we assume that every home has a *pushka*, some Tzedakah-box on the windowsill. No longer can we think that high percentages of Jews give regularly or that it is an accepted value in their lives to share all good things that they have acquired. My hope is that more and more people will make Tzedakah a daily concern. I would like it to become for all of us a way of looking at the world, and not just as an occasional act of check-writing, if that. In the gradual process of personalizing this Mitzvah, I would hope that it will help us to see more clearly the many other high values Judaism considers to be of critical importance.

There are no guarantees: the contradictions and paradoxes in life will probably not disappear. The place and meaning of suffering and sadness may be somewhat better understood, but certainly not fully comprehensible. There are no assurances that we will emerge from this Mitzvah-adventure as upright, Menschlich people. We, as people, will remain contradictory creatures, confusing to ourselves because of our complexities. But at least we will have focused our vision on the issue of Menschlichkeit, smoothing certain rough edges of our personalities in the process. Perhaps we will have become gentler people.

But there are no guarantees.

Tzedakah does not *automatically* change anyone.

And a final reason: we are late, late about Ethiopian Jews in particular. I would be remiss if I did not state clearly that this book was written with a sense of urgency. I see slides of black Jews caught up in a life-and-death struggle and I flash visions of Germany, 1939, 1940, 1941. Because of this book, I *do* want millions and millions of dollars more poured into Tzedakah projects to save their lives — and to buy overcoats for poor Jews in Chicago, and to make sure every Jew's Seder overflows with an abundance of wine and food, and to assure our elderly that they shall live the rest of their lives with dignity and peace of mind.

Since so much of the material in this book describes Tzedakah work in Israel, I do not want to give the impression that Tzedakah may only be done over there, or that Israel is our "poor cousin." While the needs are great in the Land of our Ancestors, needs also exist everywhere there are communities to be served. In the Syrian ghettoes, in the underground Hebrew classes in Leningrad, in our own synagogues and neighborhoods. Whether the demands of the hour are greater or less than at other times in Jewish history I cannot say. That the present demands *are* great no one will deny. If this book motivates more of our people to open their resources to others, *Haray Zeh Meshubach* — then I will have considered my work well done.

A recent Jewish Law Code magnificently expresses the ultimate meaning of Tzedakah. In a passage referring to providing money to assist poor orphans in getting married, the *Aruch HaShulchan (Yoreh De'ah 249:17)* states:

> There is no greater Tzedakah than this:
> to be forever bringing joy to those whose souls may be sad.

Danny Siegel
April 9, 1981
Rockville, MD

GYM SHOES
AND IRISES

*Where, Why, and How
the Revelation Belted Me*

Last fall friends and acquaintances began gathering for Israel; crisis, again, as usual, was hanging in the air. It seemed apparent that millions of new pages would be written in papers and analyses about whatever chunk of History was going to come crashing down on the Holy Land, any day. For myself, the Urge began to tear away at me, the Psalm-craving to go back to *Aretz*, though I had just finished a year in Jerusalem that previous August. I would go, I decided, *stam* — just because I wanted to go (or had to, or should go, or whatever). To me this was Kosher Jewish thinking . . . the more reasons given for the trip, the less chance of gathering the aromas and sounds and stirrings of Holiness waiting to be ingested in the Holy Land.

My tenth trip. You know how you feel when people tell you, "Oh, I've been there 18 times. Just last year I was over for Sukkot, Purim and the summer. Ho, hmmm, hum." It is the Repetition Syndrome which teachers, assembly-line workers, and secretaries suffer from (to say nothing of occasional neurosurgeons, Professional Fundraisers, and other assorted busy individuals). What I would do while in Israel was unclear to me, though a month in Jerusalem, if correctly unplanned, could be awesome, enjoyable, or at the least, fun.

As was my custom, I visited my well-wishers, telling them to "Give me a buck for Tz'dakah." I would give it out *somewhere* as the occasion presented itself *somewhere* in Israel. Apparently some friends adjusted their palms to the cost-of-living index, as $5's and $10's and $20's and $25's began inundating my pushka. I usually consider $10 a nice sum to take with me, but by the time this occurred to me for Trip #10, I was rated by Dun & Bradstreet at well over $150. So I decided to steamroll a little, making the rounds of aunts, cousins, parents, in-laws, friends, and passersby, saying, "I'd really like a thousand."

I left with $900-plus, and counting what arrived while I was there, we reached $955, or 5730 Israeli pounds.

Except for three people who specified where I should give their money, I was on my own, the Chevrah's *Shaliach* (messenger) to the Holy Land.

I assured them I would stretch every bill and coin. I would try to sanctify their money by giving exclusively to those who were reliable, hated bureaucracy, and could use it as directly as possible to bring some assistance, joy, and the sense of *Mah Rabbu Ma'asecha*, How great are Your Creations, O Lord, to the recipients.

No one I asked felt that he was being "hit." Each considered it a privilege to take part in the Mitzvah with me. No receipts, no questions of income-tax deductions, no hesitations like "Well, I already did my 10–20 percent for the year."

A family of eight in Oklahoma spent the better part of a late evening working out how much they could send me.

Some never let me finish my description of "The Plan." My wallet fattened before I could say, "I'll send you a report."

Oh there might have been one or two who play-grumbled. But I assured them (taking the last $7 from their hand) that even the most grumbly giver with the most obnoxious intent is moving Heaven and Earth. And I threw in a quote and some trumped-up page number from the Talmud to bolster my argument.

Reviewing my preparations, I see that the friends and relatives and strangers created a *Mitzvah-Chevrah* that would go wherever I would go, speak with me, and give me some insight into the work at hand.

So it was I, Dan Quixote, the 35 or so of them, and a few others against the Montefiore Windmills. The "few others" included my rabbi, my forebears, and some Russian Jews.

My rabbi: When he was in love and had found the woman with whom he chose to live his life, my rabbi gave $1,000 to Israel in place of buying his fiancée an engagement ring. I think it was in the late '40's. He told me that story, I think. (I was, fifteen years ago, his favorite, his hope, his most intimate prayer to God.) I remember that: his ring of love was a gift to Israel.

My forebears: Sometime in the last century, Usher Zelig Siegel took to wife a certain Sarah Golda, whose family name is forgotten. They begot a multitude of children, among them Zev Dovid, called Velvel, my Zeyde. I once pilgrimaged to Keansburg, N.J., to supplement the old pictures and conversations with my father and aunts and cousins. His drygoods store is now a gun and ammunition shop, but the cop who grew up with my father said, "He would take a nickel on a pair of gloves, and let them pay the rest whenever they could. He was a kind man." I remember that.

His son, my Abba, has carried on where Velvel left off. It is fit and proper to praise his generosity. Now that I am past the age of rebellion and crankiness towards my parents, we can sit and recall and work out insights into Tz'dakah, because he is my Rebbe-Master in this domain of *Menschlichkeit*. I am his child and again and again return to childhood when I wonder how his vision and foresight have been acted out by me, whether I am worthy of him and his parents and grandparents, all the way back to Abraham. When I bring to mind my years of knowing him, a constant flow of Tz'dakah acts-and-intimations gushes forth.

Some Russian Jews: Crossing into Russia from Finland, the border guards took half, more than half, of our Siddurim and calendars and Mezuzot and Magen Davids. They were entitled to them — they are Russians and we are Jews, 64 Jews with a pittance of thing-gifts for our friends in the Soviet Jewish Community. Stripped to the bare heart. I remember that feeling of being scared: 20 Yiddish phrases and a few *tchatchkes* to give. Over There, you give someone a $3 prayerbook, and your thanks are in tears. Whoever gave me a $3 gift that moved me so much? *That* question has stuck in my kishkas.

These thoughts and questions are everyone's, I thought.

I thought, as the plane approached Lod, *Ki tireh arom v'chisito!* When you see the naked, clothe them! Isaiah, I hear you, we hear you. The thousand one-shot Tz'dakah-slams that had whipped by Big Think brain over 30 years were waiting to explode.

Being a *Shaliach* is an ego-safeguard. Wherever you go and however you choose to distribute your funds, you are constantly aware of the fact that you are just the representative of those who sent you. When speaking to the recipients, you simply say, "It's my friends."

What Happened to the Gelt

It immediately became clear to me that there are two distinct psychologies of giving out Tz'dakah money: BigGelt and SmallGelt. If you have $500,000 to distribute, you go to different places, talk to different people and give out different proportions and quantities than if you have $955. With Smallgelt, you are constantly aware of the fact that $50 too much here means next week there may not be anything left to give, just when you are discovering that the next week's encounter is the one that needs the $50 the most. As a result, I determined to watch carefully each grush, and to proceed with a sharpened sense of spontaneity vs. overprudence.

Just as I had chosen to collect the money through straightforward, friendly means, so, also, I decided to search out the people and places of my mission through my friends, by word-of-mouth and suggestions from whomever I knew or got to know well enough to be touched by his or her grasp of what I was trying to do.

I started with flowers at Life Line for the Old. Life Line (*Yad LaKashish*) was discovered by my mother about five years ago. During one of my previous visits, she, the Mitzvah-Searcher-Outer *par excellence*, put her JewishMotherly foot down and declared that I *must* go — in the tone of voice of "No questions, no wise remarks, kiddo!"

"Tell Mrs. Mendilow I sent you," she said.

Life Line is workshops for the elderly. It is food for invalid-old people who are unable to get out. It is a choir and tree-planting, and a Chevrah of Dignity. None of the pathetic foolishness of basketweaving is to be found in its precincts, and, indeed, the handiwork that they produce has won awards in various countries, not because a bunch of doddering old fools made them, but because they are joy-forever things of beauty. The American custom of stashing away aging parents in (ugh) Convalescent Homes to let them die out-of-the-way, stripped of their well-deserved majesty and treated like infants — all this is foreign to Mrs. Mendilow. He who would wish to learn what *Menschlichkeit* is, would do well to visit her and the Old People of Life Line.

My Shabbas tablecloths are from their workshops, as are my sweaters, and a few of my toys.

So me and my friend, see, we marches in with a flower for each one to take home for Shabbas.

Big man, you say! A flower! Tzaddik! Righteous One! Ten lousy bucks and he thinks he's turned the world on its ear! One lousy rose or chrysanthemum or iris per person. Whoopidoo!

And to spite my cynic-self, the next day (Friday; Thursday at Life Line
. . . closed Friday) I did the same for my Chevrah at Hadassah. There is a
certain woman on the staff of Life Line who for the last seven years has
made the rounds of the soldiers at the hospital, bringing fruit and cigar-
ettes and candy and other things for anyone there from the Israeli Army.
After being introduced to the people in the Military Office and obtaining a
list of who was in what ward, the lady, my friend, and I, bundled in
flowers, began to walk the corridors.

It couldn't hurt, could it, fellas? I know they're soldierboys, and
tough, and Israelis, and this is sort of twinkie, but the lady said, "Don't
worry. It's all right."

Big Man — Tzaddik, with a wad of gelt in his pocket, doing cheap-
ticket-to-Paradise Mitzvahs. Flowers for everyone!

Until you talk to the boy (that's all he is, a boy) in the eye clinic, with
a bandage, and he tells you he writes and you say, I write too. And he tells
you he wrote a story about a soldier who was badly wounded, the only
survivor in his tank, and his girlfriend comes to see him in the hospital.
But he dies. And she never makes peace with it all. And cracks.

And then he says, "It's the other way around. My girlfriend died in a
car crash, and I don't know what to do."

Big Man!

And the mother, who is all War Mothers, standing over her son (the
one with the head wound, the paralyzed one), trying to feed him.

Here.

Here are some flowers for your son.

See, Shimon, she says, they brought you flowers (who? oh just some
friends from America). See, Shimon, say thank you.

Is there anything we can do?

Pray.

Tears.

Hers, I think.

Big Man. A dime's worth of flowers!

I decided then not to do any of these Mitzvahs alone. I wanted others,
preferably three or four others, standing with me, because I am not so
sure I can stretch that far — even for the Chevrah.

By Sunday I had called my friends and flipped through the note cards
of Recommended Tzaddikim, adding here and there a few names suggested by my people in Jerusalem. Spontaneously (I would try spontaneity
again and see how far it would go) I picked Mrs. Eva Michaelis. It was a
name my mother had given me, because she knew she was *edel* — refined,
devoted, kindly, a decades-long crusader for the retarded. Her most recent project is *Magen*, making a home for older retarded people whose
parents are too old and too ill to take care of their children. I began to like
one-way conversations: "Speak to me, Mrs. Michaelis. Say anything." And
she would take up her evangelical theme, displaying verbally her struggles
with the government and Welfare Department to get the proper funds,
then passing to some miracles, saving children from the Nazis at the out-

break of the War, meeting Eichmann (you mean Eichmann's henchmen? No, Eichmann.), and stepping out to get me coffee and cookies.

"I cannot give to your building fund," I explained. "My Chevrah wants more direct, more immediate results, and they want the funds to be under your personal control." We gave her 250 pounds for anything she liked, like cab fare for Irene Gaster, 77, who is a little shaky on her legs. Nevertheless, she personally went to interview the 40 candidates for *Magen*.

Ms. Gaster: founder of almost everything in Israel having to do with the retarded, denouncer of psychiatrists who are too quick to label, thereby condemning someone to retardation, anathema-hurler at agencies and institutions-gone-bad. Lover of Children Class-A with four Oak Leaf Clusters. When a child would be sent to her who could not learn to feed himself, more likely than not she taught the child to feed himself. If the child was a bed-wetter at age 10 (and therefore disturbed), she stopped the bed-wetting. More miracles. s.v.p., G'veret Gaster. Oh, here's another one, and another, and another (with absolute humility and a tinge of modest pride). And I never took a penny from anyone. And this is all I own (hand sweeps the air around the apartment on Ramban St.). And Miss (Henrietta) Szold said I would never get anywhere — that was when I first arrived. And now we have this *Magen* (take some more tea) project.

I was doing well. In the course of less than one Jerusalem-week I had discovered three of the 36 Righteous People. If I could just find another two or three, I would have fulfilled my mission. I had seen with my own eyes and the eyes of the Chevrah the all-the-time Holy People, rubbed my hands in theirs, and felt warmth and hope and the mysterious glory of what it is to be a Creature of God. There were two kinds: the quiet, soft-spoken, unannounced Tzaddik, and the other — overpowering, energetic-to-exhaustion, piling adrenalin on adrenalin, fighting and shouting where necessary to actualize their vision, not shying away from the Obstreperous of the Earth, convinced and justified in their Rightness, because it was for the sake of others. They are formidable, and for the unprepared, more difficult to be with, these Tzaddikim, because they are so right. You wonder how you ever thought of the million million wrong ways to do this thing, Living. And *they* know they are converting you to *Menschlichkeit*, and that you might not be able to keep up their pace. But they also know you will make something of the encounter, and that is enough for them. They are reliable, trusted individuals, and you become willing and inspired to give them anything they want, even if they won't tell you what they will do with your gift. Their wisdom and understanding of what is happening in the hearts of men is sufficient. And since they have revealed themselves to you entirely and unabashedly, there is, thank God, never any room for doubt.

Back to the stories. I will skip around, including and selecting and excluding, since there are too many, and not every one involves a Tzaddik. I planted trees, eight of them, for births and deaths and friends, and for my 82-year-old Zeyde Shmuel who last planted one for his 80th birthday, when I prayed I would do the same on my 80th. There was also a *bris* my friend Mickey said would be nice, but there would only be cookies and juice and soda and some wine, though a bottle or two of schnapps would go really well. So 50 Israeli pounds became some fancy-schmancy schnapps, though I don't know whose *bris* it was, and the parents certainly never heard of the family in Oklahoma.

I also Tz'dakah-alchemized 100 pounds into gasoline. Boris is my only friend in Jerusalem who has a car. I said, "Here's 100 pounds for benzene — put yourself at Bracha Kapach's disposal till the gelt runs out." Rebbetzin Kapach (or as the Sefardim would say, *HaRabbanit*) is the Utmost Yemenite, the woman I was looking for but didn't know was true until I saw her and watched her walk around Jerusalem doing her acts of gentle-loving-kindness. Four of the Chevrah had asked me to find someone to whom they could send clothes, so this was a priority. This Rabbanit-Rebbetzin gives clothes, Shabbas food, love, weddings, a jar of hotsauce and Yemenite bread, books, or whatever is needed all over Jerusalem and into the boondocks on the Hillsides of Judea . . . the most extensive far-stretching private Mitzvah-Matchmaker I was to meet, coordinating the Givers and the Receivers with enthusiasm and uplift as I had never seen before. Mickey and I went Shabbas-flowering with her, into the homes of large-families-in-two-rooms that are around, if you look for them. On the way back to her house she saw some children she knew who should have been in school. Why not? she asked. No gym shoes, the two girls said. I don't know if they needed gym shoes for gym class or whether it was teen-age fashionable to wear the casual style and, therefore, embarrassing to come to school in some other shoe. Either way, the 25 newly-arrived dollars were searing the seams of my pockets, and I understand that within two days as if by magic, they were transformed into sneakers for the girls.

I didn't see, but I heard about a person she found who goes with an elderly blind lady to the hairdresser on Fridays, to fulfill the Old Woman's wish of being presentable to the Sabbath Queen.

Through another lead I entered the bowels of Israeli bureaucracy (just once, to see what it was like): The Department of Welfare. An assistant director understood me and the Chevrah immediately, and with 350 pounds from the fund assured me that it would be used individually, directly, and personally for anything that might come to him that would not be taken care of by the Red Tape Machine.

A widow needed a loan. OK. The money will be recycled when she has finished with it.

Sara Pearl, Mother of the Soldiers all over Galilee. I couldn't get to Safed, but I called and told her husband the Chevrah believes in her. The check is for whatever she wants.

Hadassah Levi's daycare center for young retarded people in Ramat Gan. Swings for them. Let me call her The Most Loving Person in the World. Take my word for it.

Ya'akov Maimon, inventor of Hebrew shorthand, recorder for the Government, 72½, short, dressed like out of a movie, rumpled hat, thick glasses, shlepping me up and down and up and down steps visiting families (Iranian, Indian, Algerian, Moroccan) to whom he brings tutors in English for the children. For over 20 years he has been doing this, bringing truckloads from the University and other parts of town, dropping them off, picking them up, remembering each name and making sure each one is working well, becoming a part of the family. I would have wished him "ad meah v'esrim — may you continue your work till you are 120 —" but it seemed a shade insulting. He will no doubt do this much longer, with the same vigor and grandheartedness.

Mickey's cousin, Rabbi Mordechai Gimpel HaKohen Wolk, scion of great rabbinic houses, devoted to children, particularly of large families, placing them in good yeshivas, throwing weddings and simchas and worrying for their welfare. He is the full embodiment of the Life of Torah. Listening to his tales, his quotes, following his hands, you understand a hint of Hillel.

The list is longer. This is not a lyrical exposition or high falootin' dissertation. If you want more, you'll ask, or you'll go.

Getting Your Jollies and Shaking Your Kishkas

Everyone should be a Shaliach-Messenger sometime. Even if you will be in Israel only a week. Even if you won't be in Israel for a while but want to do it in Minneapolis, L.A., or Aberdeen, S.D. The moral insight and imaginative investment will be proportional in at least a 100 to 1 ratio to the quantum of money put in the pot. By giving your own money, you treat yourself to the feeling that you are not as tight-fisted as you thought you were, Recession or no Recession. You will become more aware of the privilege of Mitzvah-doing and of allowing others to join you. As the Talmud informs us: He who encourages others is even greater than he who does it himself.

So you will say: Well, I'm not all that good. I'm only part time, and Wolk and Kapach and Maimon and Levi and Gaster and Michaelis are too much . . . I'm not those people. Which is exactly right, and exactly the point. Part time is good enough.

You can play disguises: in one place you can assume such-and-such a name, and in another (wearing a different hat, sunglasses, and shirt) you can be someone else from Norman, Oklahoma, instead of Chicago. It is a Purim-play of the highest order. Your bravado, naïveté, and flair for romance that lie latent can come out to your heart's desire, and you can swagger and swashbuckle your way into a Grand Old Time of It for the Sake of Heaven. It is a real zetz in your soul, a kick in your spiritual life, and you are entitled to feel good about it.

And you may never consider despair again.

The next step is to do BigGelt projects. To raise $1,000,000 to be put at your disposal, all you have to do is convince 200 people to throw a $5,000 wedding for their kids, instead of a $10,000 job, or 400 people to throw a $2,500 bar mitzvah instead of a whopper for five grand. With the remaining money, you take them, their wives, their sons and daughters, and all their dear ones to Israel for a Tz'dakah-junket, a spree of Tzaddik-touching.

Next: find yourself a local millionaire and surprise him with a $10 proposal. Tell him you are not a foundation, institution, or home for anything, but on the contrary, think you can get a lot of Mitzvah-mileage out of $10. If you get $1,000, don't panic. Just check your Matchmaking files and start asking more friends about more people.

Heavy Conclusions

The risk and emotional drain are immense. You are in unaccustomed touch with those who suffer from circumstance, misfortune, or the Will of God in its less pleasant manifestations — and with those whose lives are hour-by-hour tied to these people. Spiritual exhaustion is a possibility to be considered. So, too are the dangers of surprise. In distributing irises and gym shoes, you are never certain who will be there to meet you in the next house, or corridor, or on the park bench.

For nine trips I loved wandering the streets and alleys of Jerusalem. I used to watch the sun throw different shadows and light-cartoons on the buildings and street corners and trees. I believe I saw an entirely different city on this, the tenth visit, a city shimmering with an extraordinary glow of Holiness I would have missed without the Chevrah's help.

When we at long last re-curriculum our Sunday schools and Hebrew schools and day schools, we must include — aside from courses on risk, joy, fear, loss, uncertainty, failure, BigThink, and death — lectures and labs on *Menschlichkeit* and Tz'dakah. By the very fact of having reached bar or bat mitzvah, a Jewish child becomes obligated to fulfill the Mitzvah of Tz'dakah. Why should we spiritually orphan our children, sending them insensitive as the cattle of Nineveh into the world, only to have them discover at age 25 or 33 or 41 that they have missed out for years on this most unique privilege? Let them begin with their 10–20 percent from the earliest age, and let us teach them the ins-and-outs of finding the Righteous Ones and the creativity of giving. Too few people consider that a hat, a hand gripped firmly on someone's arm, or a cheap $3 prayerbook can give a sense of startling and sublime joy to another person. *Menschlichkeit* should be a word in every Jewish child's vocabulary.

According to the Torah, each Jew is required to write his own Torah. By doing these acts, by conscientious and energy-charged consideration of the swirl of people around us, we can do just that. By being a Shaliach-Messenger or Mitzvah-doer or just plain old part-time giver.

And of course, by retelling the signs and wonders of the people we meet along the way.

THE FIRST TZEDAKAH REPORT: 1975

To: Those who gave me Charitable (Tzedakah) funds for my trip to Israel, and others interested in pursuing some of the people and projects I discovered during my stay.

From: Danny Siegel, your Shaliach-Messenger

I would like to report on my activities on your behalf in 3 parts: (1) a summary of where, when, and how much I contributed, (2) follow-up notes and addresses for your future reference*, and (3) general comments I have to make, having just recently rearrived in the States.

1. At my disposal was a total of $955, or 5730 Israeli Pounds (6 Pounds = $1), which was distributed in the following manner (all stated in pounds):

Flowers distributed to Yad LaKashish for Shabbas	1/9	60
Flowers for soldiers at Hadassah Hospital	1/10	40
To Chayah Pe'er for a sweater for "Batya"	1/12	150
To Mrs. Michaelis — Magen	1/12	250
8 trees in the Peace Forest	1/13	144
To Chayah Pe'er for additional clothes for "Batya"	1/14	50
Flowers for soldier at Hadassah	1/14	5
Rabbi Wolk for needy children	1/16	500
Yitzchak Almagor for Russian Immigrants	1/16	450
Flowers for Shaare Zedek & Bikur Cholim Hospitals	1/17	62
To Hadassah Levi for Meon HaYeled children	1/19	600
To Mickey Shur for refreshments at a bris	1/23	50
Flowers for Hadassah Hospital patients	1/24	69
Rachel Zafrani for poor families	1/26	450
To Aharon Langermann for private fund at the Welfare Department	1/26	350
Dr. Pesach Schindler — private charitable fund	1/26	200
Rabbi Simcha Kling for the Central Library for the Blind	1/26	250
Aviva Goldberg for the Mesillah girls	1/27	250
Lisa Schwartz for Mossad Ahavah (as instructed)	1/27	90
HaRabbanit Bracha Kapach for poor families	1/28	600
Sara Pearl for soldiers	1/29	150
Adina Geller for Mitzvot in Tzefat	1/30	150
Yeshivat HaKotel (as instructed)	1/30	60
Flowers for distribution by HaRabbanit Kapach	1/31	44
A beggar in Jerusalem (as instructed)	1/31	6
HaRabbanit Kapach for shoes for children	1/31	150
Amy Eilberg for a widow (a loan)	2/2	175
Boris Fiman for gasoline to drive HaRabbanit Kapach around	2/3	100
Ya'akov Maimon for essentials in poverty areas	2/4	150

*Many of the addresses and phone numbers on this report are now out of date.

Marc Goldman — books for tutoring	2/4	25
Bennet Spungin for an orphanage	2/4	100

2.   Notes and addresses (assume the addresses are Jerusalem, unless otherwise indicated):

A. Yad LaKashish (Life Line for the Old) 12 Shivtei Yisrael, 287-829, Mrs. Miriam Mendilow, Director. An extraordinary collection of projects, mainly workshops for old people. Mrs. Mendilow is a Righteous Woman (there will be about a half-dozen of the Righteous on this list) occupying and helping the old to retain their dignity as human beings and to continue productive living. Buy gifts for your friends at their gift shop instead of at the local merchants.

B. Flowers at hospitals: at Hadassah there is a military office (called Ram 2) as you go in the main gate. They are very helpful in pointing you to soldiers who are lonely and would like visitors. Channah Jacobsen (20 Bar Kochba, 221-902) works in Pediatrics and can help you around the hospital. For the other two hospitals, the people in the P.R. offices were kind and helpful on our pre-Shabbas rounds.

C. Chayah Pe'er, 19 Sokolov, 32908, knows specific people who are in need of assistance, none of whom would seek help through other channels. Her husband, Aryeh, also does this sort of work, but with different people. I would start with Chayah (she also makes dynamite chocolate cake). As with all these other people, use my name as reference. "Batya" is a young girl in a mental institution (she has been in more than one for a number of years). She is really alone except for the Pe'ers.

D. Mrs. Eva Michaelis, Shlomo Molcho 6, 32148, a genteel, sensitive Righteous One who has worked with retarded people of all ages for years. Her present project is Magen, a place she wants to set up for older retarded people whose parents are either too old or too sick to care for them. There is a real need for substantial sums of money here. She, as in the case with most of the others, suffers grief from the inefficiency of governmental agencies and has to carry on much of the battle herself. My contribution was made to a small, private "Birthday Fund" which is at her immediate disposal for whatever emergencies or needs may arise. I felt the money would stretch better this way (rather than trying to give it to the building fund). Mrs. Michaelis directed me to Irene Gaster, 44 Ramban, 31185, a 77-year-old incredible human being, wonder-worker, who is involved with Magen, and is, indeed, the founder of most of the institutions in Israel having to do with the retarded. Her house is always open and when you go to Israel, you must stop by and have her tell you the stories of people she has helped (and include questions about her work and that of Mrs. Michaelis saving children from the Nazis), and her recollections of Henrietta Szold. Just let her talk about anything.

E. Trees planted for various individuals in honor or in memory of people with whom I am acquainted. Over 115,000,000 trees have been planted by JNF since its inception, and it is still a critical priority. Besides, if my Zeyde at age 80 can bend down in the dirt and plant trees, we all can.

F. Rabbi Mordechai Gimpel HaKohen Wolk, Alfasi 25, Rehavia, in charge of HaVaad HaArtzi Lema'an Hatzalat HaNoar BeYisrael (roughly: the National Committee for Saving Children in Israel). My contact was his cousin, Mickey Shur, who may be reached at Yeshivat HaTefutzot on Mt. Zion 68667, who will be happy to take you to him. He is a scholarly, religious man of distinguished rabbinic lineage who embodies the best of what orthodox Jewish living can bring about. He seeks out children, particularly those from large families who could do better in Yeshivahs or who need clothes, shoes, food, care, weddings, whatever.

G. Yitzchak Almagor, Ma'avar HaMitla 3, Ramat Eshkol, 288-752, Chairman of Agudat Akadamaim Olay Brit HaMoatzot Birushalayim (Jerusalem Organization of Newly Arrived Professionals from the Soviet Union) (Contact: Boris Fiman, see entry below.) Mr. Almagor is himself an immigrant from Russia some 15 years ago. He visits new immigrants, helps them adjust to Israel, and generally provides them with the intangibles that don't come within the official purview of immigration work. At least twice a week he is out at Absorption Centers visiting the immigrants. He and his wife are sweet, devoted people, energetic and loaded with power to get things done (= PROTEKTZIA.)

H. Hadassah Levi, 21 Herzl, Ramat Gan (72 22 40) (Contact: Marcella Zion, 7 Palmach, Jerusalem, 66557), Supervisor of Meon HaYeled. No doubt the most full-of-human-love individual I have ever met. Her place, a house, is a day center for young retarded (up to age 10?), just doing great, great things. I believe my contribution was transformed into a set of swings for the children. You have to meet her. You must!

I. Rachel Safrani, Palmach 49, 69066 (Contact: Mrs. Shmuel Ben-Naeh, 71 Herzog St.), provides on a small scale for various families, similar to the work of Mrs. Pe'er.

J. Aharon Langermann, Assistant Director of the Department of Welfare, 8 King David St., 234-481. I expressed my negative views about the department work to him; he was sympathetic. I then asked for some way of directing personal funds to needy people that Welfare doesn't get to. He came through nicely, explaining his private activities for helping. He also agreed to find places for people coming over who want to do the most good according to their talents and desires, with the least bureaucratic garbage . . . which is a big order for Israel. I trust him, despite his official position. He was recommended by Eli Cohen (see below.)

K. Dr. Pesach Schindler, 2 Agron, 226-386 or 227-463, Director of the United Synagogue of America in Israel, involved privately with similar human situations. He is a good resource-man for finding situations to be involved in, with no overtones or hangups having to do with the organization. All private and personal. He is a Grayser Mensch.

L. Rabbi Simcha Kling, 66 Azza, 35764 (till June, then returns to his position as rabbi of the Conservative synagogue of Louisville, Ky.) He informed me of a project he is involved in for the past number of years: a center for providing and preparing materials for the blind all over Israel (not a school). On his word (he is a most reliable, sweet Motek of a man), I decided it would be nice to make us a part of this, also.

M. Aviva Goldberg, 29 Mem Gimel, Apt. 12, 527-324), social worker at Mesillah (415-690, 413-571), a diagnostic way-station for girls who have been in scrapes with the legal authorities. The director is Eli Cohen, 6 Chopin, 38289 (contact: Marcella Zion, 66557), who is one of the Unbelievable People, though my private conversations with him were limited. Aviva will tell you all about him.

N. Lisa Schwartz was my Shelichah to deliver 90 IL to Mossad Ahavah near Haifa, since I was unable to go.

O. HaRabbanit Bracha Kapach, 12 Lod St., 231-296. Unbelievable. The Rabbanit is an immigrant (years back) from Yemen, and for the last number of years has discovered and helped more families and individuals all around Jerusalem (and into the Hills) than anyone I met. For those of you who asked about *CLOTHES:* she is the one. She knows the most and most needy, and does everything from clothes to Shabbas candles and food for people. Clothes instructions: to be mailed to her, in packages no larger than 22 pounds each (otherwise there are payments involved). They should be clean and in decent condition, and children's clothes are especially needed (sweaters, too). She is one of those people you should make a point of meeting when in Israel (her specialty is dynamite hot sauce for good Sefardi food). She will introduce you around to members of the Sefardi communities at your request.

P. Sara Pearl, Herzliah Hotel, Tzefat, 067-30007 (contacts: my mother, Joel Kamsler, Yitzchak Jacobsen, etc.) — spoken of as a mother to all the soldiers of the entire Galilee. I did not get to see her, but her work is praised with overwhelming enthusiasm by all those who know her or of her.

Q. Adina Geller will attempt to use the funds for something to do with the children of the Ma'alot Massacre.

R. Yeshivat HaKotel, according to the wishes of one of the contributors.

S. A Beggar in Jerusalem, according to a contributor's wishes (I picked one who was standing at the gates of the forest.)

T. Amy Eilberg 536-701 (till June) had heard of a widow who had not received some sort of compensation payments on time. She was in dire need of assistance, and so I handed some funds over to Amy, who believes the woman will pay the money back, so I instructed Amy to then recirculate the funds in some Tzedakah-fashion as she saw fit.

U. Boris Fiman, Hartman Yeshiva, The American College, Shedeyrot

HaMeiri, Kiryat Moshe. Boris was an all-around assistant in many of these projects, shlepping me and others around in his car. We felt it would help the Rabbanit Kapach if she had a driver and a tankful-plus of gas available for her work.

V. Ya'akov Maimon, 39211, 34451 (Contact: Marcy Goldman, Shikunay HaElef, Givat Ram, Hebrew U. 4/3/4) — another one of Those People. Ya'akov Maimon is 72 +, the inventor of Hebrew shorthand, Recorder of the Knesset, and Tzaddik of the First Order. His project (among others) is to take volunteers (usually, though not always, students) to tutor children in English in the poorer areas of town (like Katamon Tet), and to have these volunteers become part of the family. He goes to Hebrew U. and other places with lorries and takes the people to the homes then picks them up a few hours later. I walked up and down more steps with this man in 2 hours than I normally would do in a month: each place he entered he was treated with deference, and he reacted with humility (often characteristic of the people I am listing). He will make use of the funds as he sees fit. Marcy tutors for him, and I gave her some funds to purchase books she and her friends might want to get for their students.

W. Bennet Spungin, 10 Palmach, 31630. Through a friend I heard of an orphanage for girls which I did not get to visit, but on his word I entrusted him with 100 IL for the purpose of doing something personal for the girls. By this time it was abundantly clear to me that my contacts would recommend to me places and people who were of the highest order of Menschlichkeit, so while I do not even know the name of the orphanage, I am sure the money will go to good use.

Two additional notes:

Rabbi Robert Hammer, the Pnimiyah, Neve Schechter, 31121, has lists and ideas of similar projects if you want to get involved.

Micha, Reading St. #23, Ramat Aviv, 415-146, Director: Ethel Cohen (better to talk to Tviah Ma'ayan, one of the teachers) is a fine, modern, well-equipped school for the deaf, recommended to me by Seymour Goldberg. I did not contribute because the place looked well-enough funded from people in the States, but it is a thrilling place, and should be included in your itinerary.

3. General Remarks

This entire Mitzvah-month was a privilege for me, and I wish all those who contributed a Yashir Koach — continued strength to carry out similar work on their own. The month was also very difficult, in that most of the people pointed out in Part 2 were very high-powered, devoted people who, when you sit in their presence and watch their work, cause an emotional drain in the observor. Somehow in the presence of suffering or "unfortunateness" they are capable of rising to sublime heights, day in and day out. For someone not used to such intensive contact, it is particularly difficult to adjust, though ultimately rewarding. My thanks to you for entrusting me with the responsibility-turned-pleasure of discovering these people for myself and for you when you go to meet them.

I found that there are 2 distinct psychologies in distributing funds: Big-giving and Small-giving, neither being easier than the other — just different ways of thinking. While I may have mis-evaluated on some of the contributions, each person and place was carefully considered on the merits of the absolute directness to people and the reliability and devotedness of the person doing the work. While I would not advocate withholding funds from Bonds and UJA, I am firmly convinced that we should all set aside some money from our normal Tzedakah funds for these types of work, which guarantee Menschlichkeit-Humanity with a minimum-to-zero of red-tape and woe that we associate with institutions and government. I am also convinced that to some extent, everyone's future trips to Israel should include visits to these people. These are, indeed, the people who make the Land holy.

I am exhausted and evangelical: Exhausted after being your representative to works which I believe move Heaven and Earth, and evangelical about spreading the stories of these people.

If you want more information or want to comment to me, do write.

Perhaps this is what the essence of Chevra-Friendship is: sharing a month such as this and making something of ourselves through the grandeur and splendor of other people.

Na'Aleh V'Natzliach — may we continue to do more of the same in the future.

THE 1980 TZEDAKAH REPORT

September 1, 1980

To my Tzedakah-Chevra of friends and relatives, and to other interested individuals, once again I say Shalom and Yashir Koach! The summer's work is now over, and this report will clearly show how our work has expanded — more people contributed, more read the Tzedakah reports, and a greater number and wider range of recipients have been reached. This year, as your Shaliach-Messenger, you allowed me to distribute $12,720.00, a substantial sum, even with disheartening inflation. In the past, as you may recall, we have distributed $955.00, $1667.00, $2930.00, $6396.00, and $9102.00, bringing our total contributions over the past six years to $33,770.00.

As is customary with this report, I will begin with the details of this summer's distribution of money. An asterisk (*) indicates people and projects that have been mentioned in previous reports.

I. *Four Major Projects: Places that Absolutely Must Be Visited in Israel*

*A. Ma'on LaTinok: Hadassah Levi's home for infants with Down's Syndrome continues to provide warmth and hope for almost forty children. A visit here can become, by far, the most powerful experience of any trip to Israel — she, fighting for the dignity of the retarded, they, living the lives of children free of cares, as is the right of all children. Almost all the infants were abandoned by their parents in the hospital; one, in fact, was brought in named Revav (רבב), meaning "a stain". . . . that is the name the parents gave the child. Hadassah has changed that, and the child grows, gorgeous, lively, enjoying the happiness of a child to the fullest extent. The ten United Synagogue Youth Pilgrimage groups visited this summer (600 teenagers, plus staff), and were deeply moved. They themselves contributed over $1000 of their own money. We contributed $2000 from this summer's money, (and added $500 more which was available from a free loan we had made last year.) Among other things, Hadassah bought a new floor in one of the rooms — the neighbors had been complaining of the noise the infants were making rocking their cribs! Hadassah needs supplies of infants' clothes, which I hope our Tzedakah-Chevra will help send over. Eventually she hopes to found a Kibbutz for retarded people somewhere in Israel. (Hadassah Levi, Ma'on LaTinok, 4 Ma'alay HaTzofim St., Ramat Gan, 03-721-565. Contributions to "Yediday Ma'on LaTinok" ["Friends of Ma'on Latinok"], 45 Rambam St., Givata'im, ATTENTION: HADASSAH LEVI.)   Total of $2000.00.

*B. Yad LaKashish (Life Line for the Old): Mrs. Myriam Mendilow's array of workshops for the elderly and disabled of Jerusalem functions at full strength, despite the evergrowing economic hardships. The meals-on-wheels program and afternoon activities (such as the choir) also continue to function. They hope to open a bakery and café in the near future, a lovely addition to the work she has carried on for nearly 20 years. One point I have always forgotten to mention: *this is not an old-age home.* No

one lives at Life Line. Everyone comes from his or her own home to work
at the bookbindery, needlecrafts, metal shop, and other workshops. They
— these Elders of Jerusalem — are part of society: I see them frequently in
the streets, shopping, on their way to meetings, wherever people as people are supposed to be going. The number and variety of products they
make grows each year (each week I would say): from stunning tablecloths
to the finest dresses, to the cleverest of toys. This year, and the past 4
years, the USY'ers visited — some 3,000 teenagers taking a grand tour of
the workshops. The disappointment is that more adults do not visit with
their group tours. Whatever we can do to change that will be of the utmost importance. We bought two knitting machines ($320 and $240) for
one workshop, allowing two more people to be retrained to do fine clothes-
making. Furthermore we spent $92 to buy products from their store,
which I gave to two USY'ers to circulate and show around whenever they
or others speak about Life Line. (Yad LaKashish, 12 Shivtei Yisrael St.,
Jerusalem, 287-829. Tax-exempt contributions may be sent to American
Friends of Life Line for the Old in Israel, 1500 Palisade Avenue, Fort Lee,
NJ 07024.)   Total of $652.00.

*C. Yad Sara: Uri Lupoliansky, the director, is a מלאך, an angel. His
unassuming manner, his nobility, devotion, and intense sweetness sweep
you into the highest realms of Judaism and Tzedakah. He supervises 300
volunteers in 20 centers around Israel, lending out medical supplies at no
cost to people who (for bureaucratic or economic reasons) cannot get the
wheelchairs or oxygen or vaporizers or walkers or crutches they need. A
prime example, explained by Uri: a child breaks his hearing aid. During
the two weeks it takes to get it repaired, what will the child do in school?
Yad Sara supplies one immediately, until the other is fixed. In four years
the project has grown extraordinarily — meeting a real need within Israeli
society . . . without a single salaried professional. Our Chevra contributed
$350 towards part of an expensive emergency alarm system they are set-
ting up in people's homes, with a central receiver and print-out at Yad
Sara and Magen David Adom. We also gave $80 for a large sign in English,
so passers-by will take notice. (Yad Sara, 49 Nevi'im Street [around the
corner from Bikkur Cholim Hospital], 244-242; Uri's home: 813-777.)
Total of $430.00.

*D. Yad Ezra: Reb Osher Freund's extensive network of projects ex-
pands each year — Passover, more than $115,000 in food distributed to
more than 5,000 families; 250 families receiving free food each week; hundreds more buying food at discounts; clothing at discounts; dental clinic;
X-ray clinic and other medical services; daycare center; free-loan society;
birthday parties for mental patients in the institutions; lending of dishes
and kitchen facilities for simcha-catering . . . the list is very long. My interest has focused on the printing presses and sewing workshop. Mental patients
from institutions and disturbed individuals from their homes come to
work during the day making dresses, challah and matzah covers, tallis and
tfillin bags, and producing a variety of printed items for commercial pur-

poses. O to visit, to see people who might otherwise be damned to a labelled life of "mentally ill" — to see them at work, piecing their lives back together under the most loving guidance of Reb Osher and his people! Our contribution was given specifically for the sewing machine workshop. (Yad Ezra, 15 HaRav Sorotzkin St., Jerusalem, 526-133. Shmuel Katz will arrange visits and tours. His home phone is 817-767. You may also contact Yehoshua Lendner, Ron Hotel, Zion Square, Jerusalem, 223-471.) Total of $400.00.

II. Scholarship for a Couple to Continue our Work in Israel during the Year

During the past year, Beth Huppin, a close friend of mine, spent the year in Israel introducing a variety of people to our Tzedakah work. A summary of her work is included in this report. There is no question in my mind that we need people in Israel year-round to carry on this work. For the coming year, Gordy and Sharon Fuller will be there, beginning work sometime in late October. They will take individuals and groups to these places, and will serve as our Shelichim-Messengers for other Tzedakah-Mitzvot that might arise. They are our שדכנים, the Matchmakers, bringing our people together. Until mid-October, they may be reached c/o Matti Harris, Kibbutz Ein Dor, Doar Na Jezreel, 19335. After that, through Dr. Pesach Schindler, 2 Agron St., Jerusalem, 226-386. They will be based, of course, in Yerushalayim, and welcome any calls and letters. Please try to convince your synagogue, AJC, Hadassah, or Federation tours — any tours at all, to avail themselves of this service we are offering. We left $2000, which was matched by another $2000 from someone in Israel. We have possibilities of additional, limited funding for this scholarship, and would welcome any supplementary contributions towards this part of our work. We anticipate a total budget of $6500– $7500 for the year. Gordy and Sharon may now be reached at 1604 Brummel, Evanston, Il, 60202, 312-328-2707. Total of $2000.00.

III. Individual and Specific Contributions — The Guts of the Matter

Following our pattern of seeking out situations of immediate need, we arranged through a number of friends to provide a variety of goods, services, and educational materials for people who have direct contact with families who need these things. There were seven allocations: $79, $100, $100, $100, $120, $125, and $150. For one — a seriously ill woman, money towards purchase of a washing machine; for others, materials for a household budgeting class, books and games for children, scholarship money for a kindergarten student for next year ($14! Fourteen dollars is all that was needed for that one.) And teeth. One young lady was having serious dental work done, when budget cuts brought about an immediate halt in the treatments. For $120, the work could be finished, without long-term delays and serious consequences. Total of $774.00.

IV. Soviet Jews in Israel

Avital Shcharansky, a woman of presence, gentle, soft-spoken, genteel. Beth arranged for both of us to meet her. In her apartment are posters of Anatoly Shcharansky — posters we have seen everywhere, except that there, in her home, it is her husband, not just a cause or a bunch of slogans. Her husband, suffering in a Russian prison. We gave her $500 to use as she would determine best for her personal contacts with Soviet Jews in Israel and in the Soviet Union.

Beth also introduced me to another Soviet Jewish activist in Israel, to whom we gave $250 to assist her in organizing activities and maintaining contacts with her family and other refuseniks still unable to leave.   Total of $750.00.

V. People on the Personal Look-out for Tzedakah-Mitzvot to Perform

We gave four contributions ($150, $150, $250, and $300) to individuals to use at their discretion as their contacts bring Tzedakah-situations to their attention during the year. One elderly woman cares for others, bringing milk, other food, and some human contact to another. A young woman, a friend of hers, had been in a mental institution for years, but is now living independently and holding down a job. Some of the money will go for clothes for her. Over the years, this older woman has brought her conversation and things and friendship through the Dark Times in the Institutions, and now she is back in the world, functioning, readjusting.

Three of these four wish to remain anonymous, but the fourth, *Si Levine, is available when you come to Israel to take you around: 23 Horkania St., #8, Jerusalem, 666-864. He informed me that each of five or six first-class hotels in Jerusalem (the Plaza and Hilton among them) provide a once-a-week buffet, with entertainment, for groups of twenty elderly Jews. He says it is done with great dignity and style. Just one more variation on the Mitzvah!   Total of $850.00.

VI. For the Handicapped: Services and Materials

*A. Micha-Jerusalem (מיח״א = מחנכי ילדים חרשים-אלמים):   My friend Toby Wolinsky continues to do fine work at this school for pre-school deaf and hearing-impaired children. We gave $200 to Micha for books and materials and $350 to Toby for whatever she felt was necessary for her work. (Micha, Director, Brenda Eichler, Akiva St., Jerusalem, 232-021.) Total of $550.00.

*B. Akim (אקי״ם = אגודה לקידום ילדים מפגרים):   Curt Arnson's branch of Akim (which is the national organization for retarded people in Israel) is the dumping ground for multiple-handicapped children. He does wonders, and fights tooth and nail to achieve his goals with the children. Our contribution helped him continue his summer programming throughout August. (Akim, 4 Ben Shimon St., Jerusalem, 232-633.)   Total of $400.00.

*C. Magen — The Irene Gaster Hostel for Retarded Adults: nearly twenty adults are now living at the home, and a few more come in during the day for various activities — substantial, creative programs. Lewis Warsaw, an American who has made Aliyah, is back supervising the program. They will still have to move from the neighborhood, because of pressure from the neighbors, and the ultimate irony is that the building used to be a house of prostitution. In those days — less than four years ago — apparently no one complained about the noise and goings-on. Our contribution was used for sports equipment and summer activities. (Magen, Mrs. Eva Michaelis, Honorary Chairperson, Lloyd George St. 4a, Jerusalem, 665 -945). Total of $200.00.

*D. Alumim (עלומים) School for Retarded Children: My friend, Lorraine Lemberger, informed me that there were 55 children involved in the summer program. Our contribution was used towards summer activities, and other needs Lorraine may find. She gave me a good example of inflationary costs: the rental of a bus for a daytrip has skyrocketed in the recent past. (Lorraine Lemberger, 51 Shachal St., Jerusalem, 669-378.) Total of $300.00.

*E. Ilan (אירגון ישראלי לילדים נפגעים = איל"ן): Ilan is the national organization for the handicapped. Rachel Guron's workshop for people with cerebral palsy, located next door to Life Line for the Old, is functioning well. Our contribution was also used for summer activities, specifically towards a day trip to Kibbutz Tzor'ah — just for everyone to see what a kibbutz is like. (Ilan, 16 Shivtei Yisrael St., Jerusalem, 286-555.) Total of $100.00.

*F. The Central Library for the Visually Handicapped: Uri Cohen, the director, supervises the preparation of braille books and tapes for the entire country. Our contribution will be used to add to the library of books and tapes. (Central Library for the Visually Handicapped, 4 HaHistadrut St., Netanya, 053-25321 or 32422.)   Total of $125.00.

Each of the people listed above demonstrates the qualities we have always looked for: devotion to others, a sense of caring, and insight into the nature of people . . . and an ability to keep the stultifying forces of paperwork and administration from standing in the way of their specific vision of what is right and Menschlich.

VII. *Interest-Free Loans* (גמילות חסד)

A. Our fund supplied $300 in free loans this year ($200 and $100) directly to two individuals.   Total of $300.00.

*B. Gomel L'ish Chessed (גומל לאיש חסד): Dr. David Weiss, Jew *Extraordinaire*, continues to work with this free-loan society (over 20 years without a default). He is Chairman of the Department of Immunology at Hadassah Hospital, a Torah scholar, and one whose sense of Judaism and Judaism's profound insights into the nature and ways of human beings is a great joy to discover. Our contribution went into his fund. (Dr. David Weiss, 20a Radak St., Jerusalem, 669-363 or 428-726.) Total of $300.00.

C. Free-loan society in East Talpiot: Miriam Itzkovitch, an older Russian woman, works with immigrants and the elderly (and nearly everyone else in that part of town) . . . a real miracle-worker. She has set up contacts with over 300 old people, 78 of whom are all alone, with 32 meals-on-wheels delivered every day. She organizes volunteers, clinics, block committees, and homemakers (much like Project Ezra, Dorot, and Hatzilu in New York), to allow these elderly people a dignified lifestyle. *Not a single one of them has had to move into an old-age home.* She wanted to start a free-loan society. Beth had $300 available, and we added another $200. (Miriam Itchkovitch, 12 Alfasi St., Jerusalem, 630-350.) Total of $200.00.

D. Another $900 was available from free loans from last year's work, which was turned over to another person as a free-loan.

VIII. Additional People and Projects — New and Old

A. Isha L'Isha (אשה לאשה): This is a refuge for battered women in Jerusalem. Two such centers already exist, one in Haifa and the other in Herzliya. The women involved in establishing this center are (unfortunately) filling a great need in Israel . . . a place for battered women to go until reasonable solutions can be reached in each individual domestic situation. As we become more aware of domestic beatings (wives, husbands, and children), we must realize that Israel has not been spared. Our contribution was used for the barest essentials — cleaning materials, paper goods, toiletries — all the unglorious things they will need to function well. [They have also received funding from (among other places) The New Israel Fund, contact Jonathan Cohen, 22 Miller Avenue, Mill Valley, CA 94941, 415-383-4866, an important project to learn about.] (Isha L'Isha, Joan Hooper, 62 Shimoni St., Jerusalem, 639-740.) Total of $300.00.

*B. The Rabbanit Bracha Kapach: Every conceivable Mitzvah — help with families, help for Pesach (1300 families this year, almost $12,000 worth of food), outings for mothers, camping for children, family problem-solving, and, of course her warehouse of clothes for distribution. To send clothes: packages must be clearly labelled "Used Clothes." She also takes wedding dresses and lends them to brides who cannot afford to buy their own. Send them the same way. (The Rabbanit Kapach, 12 Lod St., Jerusalem, 249-296.)   Total of $439.00.

*C. The Daniel Kuttler Charity Fund: Daniel and Charlotte Kuttler continue their work lending out wedding dresses, along with a number of other individually-oriented Mitzvot. If you send dresses to the Kuttlers, they must have long sleeves and a high neck. Bridesmaid's dresses are also of use to them and the Rabbanit. Beth's sister and cousin in Spokane organized a Wedding-Dress Tea, complete with dresses, dress-contributors,

tea, cake, explanations of the project (Hachnassat Kallah- הכנסת כלה)
and packaging materials. One item they sent — a corsage of silk flowers —
arrived just in time for one bride. The Kuttler's say she soared with joy
when she saw the corsage. (Daniel and Charlotte Kuttler, 7 Keren
HaYesod St., Jerusalem, 233-991.)   Total of $100.00

*D. Americans and Canadians in Israel (AACI) Jerusalem Scholarship
Fund: Mr. and Mrs. Bargteil informed me that their program assisted 224
junior and senior high school students last year (textbooks, school supplies, field trips, etc.) — scholarships for relatives of people who have died
in Israeli wars or terrorist attacks. They hope to reach 300 students this
year. It has been our good fortune, through our Tzedakah work, that we
have encouraged others to contribute sums totalling $20,600 (beyond our
own small contributions) to this fund. The supervisors of this project are
devoted and careful to take individual interest in each student's progress.
(Contributions from the United States may be sent to: P.E.F. Israel Endow-
ment Funds, Inc., 342 Madison Ave., NY, NY 10173. In Israel: Meyer and
Hannah Bargteil, Nili St. 7, Jerusalem, 664-278.)   Total of $100.00.

*E. Committee for Families of the Fallen Paratroopers: The central
committee of 15 paratroopers oversees this group that reaches about 120
wives and 300 children of paratroopers who have died since the 1956
Sinai Campaign. Everything from summer camping and field trips to bar
mitzvah presents, legal assistance — even plumbers and contacts for car
repairs are supplied, through personal contact. One member of the central
committee came to Jerusalem to show me a film of some of their activities
— a crude, non-professional film filled with the easy pleasures of a few
days out in nature, laughter, joy. I was very much moved by it — as all of
you would be — when I realized that what ties them all together is the loss
of a husband or father because of The Wars. (Contact Motka Weissbord,
P.O. B. 3499, Jerusalem.)   Total of $250.00.

*F. Zahavi (זהב"י = זכויות המשפחה ברוכת ילדים): Dr. Eliezer Jaffe
explained to me that Zahavi, the Israeli grassroots organization for families
with four or more children, continues to fight legal battles as well as provide immediate services to large families. Most amazing was a visit I made
to a development town for a book ceremony. Piles of books were distributed to carefully-selected children for use for school: dictionaries,
atlases, Jewish books of all kinds — to keep. Half of our contribution went
to the book project, half to the general Zahavi fund. (Dr. Jaffe, 37 Azza
Rd., Jerusalem, 661-908 or 637-450.)   Total of $200.00.

*G. Keren Pe'ulat Ya'akov Maimon: As with the three previously-
mentioned contributions, this group is also working to give Israeli
children a decent chance to integrate into society. Maimon, who died
three years ago, had reached thousands: teaching English and a battery of
other subjects to immigrants, students, and anyone else who needed his
personal touch — through a corps of volunteers he personally supervised.
Now, his followers have concentrated on Mevaseret Yerushalayim, an ab-

sorption center, and Ma'oz Tzion, a tough neighborhood, where the volunteers continue their work with enthusiasm and great energy. If you have friends in Israel who wish to do this kind of volunteer work, please have them be in touch. (Contact Dr. Kurt Meyerowitz, Keren Kayemet LeYisrael St. 21, Jerusalem, 639-970.)   Total of $250.00.

H. Keren Nesi Yisrael — The President's Fund: President Navon is personally involved in many Tzedakah projects, large ones, and also those of a personalized, individual nature. Both he and Mrs. Navon have established a reputation for Tzedakah-work, and I felt it was important that we share in his work. It is critical for Jews to know that all Jews, whether Presidents or truckdrivers, should be actively involved in this mitzvah. (Contact Ruth Shaul, Mishkan HaNassi, Jerusalem, 668-231.) Total of $100.00.

*I. Alyn (אלי"ן = אגודה לעזרת ילדים נכים):   Through a friend I found a woman working in the summer program for crippled children — a volunteer — who brought games and arts-and-crafts materials with her from the States. She was well aware of ways to stretch our dollars, buying materials at discount prices, knowing exactly what and how much to purchase, etc. We added to her supplies, and allowed her greater leeway in her programming for the summer. (Brenda Hirsch, Alyn, Olsvenger and Shemaryahu Levin Sts., Jerusalem, 412-251.)   Total of $200.00.

*J. Matav-Homemakers (מט"ב = מטפלות בית):   This is a service, similar to that in the States, where people come into the home to assist others with household work, during periods of illness and other stress situations. Budget cuts have taken away payments for Matavi-workers to continue their work if their clients go into the hospital. We gave our contribution specifically to continue that hospital service for some specific clients Mrs. Rivka Jaffe knew of through her work. (Same address as Dr. Eliezer Jaffe, VIII, F.)   Total of $150.00.

*K. Gemillut Chessed Fund: A general Tzedakah fund supervised by Dr. Pesach Schindler, director of the United Synagogue in Israel, set up to take care of needs that would arise within his purview during the year. Dr. Schindler also informs me that they are setting up a small Holocaust lending library at the Conservative Center — particularly periodicals with articles on the subject. (Contact: Dr. Pesach Schindler, 2 Agron St., Jerusalem, 226-386.)   Total of $200.00.

IX. *Miscellaneous: Trees, a Little Cloak-and-Dagger Work, and Flowers*

A. To one USY'er to encourage him and others in his USY group to avail themselves of Tzedakah opportunities in Israel.   Total of $10.00.

B. To one person on this report for expenses to investigate matters concerning a large grant for the blind in Israel. We are not certain if this will succeed, but the investment in time and effort, and the few dollars, is well worth it if someone can free some thousands for the blind. Total of $25.00.

*C. Flowers: A sum of $10 to a USY'er (he and others would add more) to make the rounds in some hospital on a Friday afternoon, giving out flowers and wishing the patients a Good Shabbas. The rest was used by a friend and myself near the end of my trip, for a similar visit to Hadassah Hospital on Mt. Scopus.   Total of $35.00.

*D. Trees: Six gum trees in the Jerusalem Peace Forest, adding to the already breathtaking view.   One tree was planted for each year of our work — in honor of us. One certificate was given to Rabbi Ron Hoff-berg of Cranford, NJ,   for his assistance in making preparations for the work this summer, and another to Bea Dickstein for her help with the bookkeeping and mailing. The others— well, I am keeping them here for myself. Total of $30.00.

Now JNF can count 150,000,006 trees to its credit! It was a beautiful morning: most of the money had already been distributed, and, gazing at Yerushalayim in the distance, I thought — next year the Tzedakah-Chevra should come and plant for themselves. (Ah, it's the romantic in me com-ing out!)

X. *A Report from Beth Huppin on the Year's Tzedakah Activities in Israel*

With the aid of grant money received from Dr. Abram Sachar's Dis-cretionary Fund, USY's Tikun Olam Tzedakah Fund, and the Samuel Rosenthal Foundation, I was free to spend this past year in Jerusalem seek-ing out Israel's Tzadikim, as well as groups and individuals whom I could bring to meet these Tzadikim. The idea was simple and exciting: to teach the true meaning of Tzedakah and Gemillut Chassadim through the peo-ple on the Tzedakah Report, and through others I would find during the year. The experience was both exhilarating and inspiring. As a result of the work this past year, I have reached several conclusions:

First, although it is difficult to find funding for a project such as this (it doesn't fall into any "category" and isn't "academic" enough), the fund-ing *is* available. Though Gordy's and Sharon's scholarship is already largely provided for, some additional funds are necessary, and we should consider the possibility of guaranteeing continued money for subsequent years.

It is important that this be an ongoing project, for I found that there are many people interested in seeing various places on the Tzedakah list, but, almost without exception, unless I took them, they did not go. It follows, then, that, if those who *are* interested will not go on their own, those who *are not* initially interested certainly will not go unless they have a gentle push. (I tried to explain Life Line for the Old, and all they could imagine was a depressing old-age home. It is all they know. Of course, this makes it even more important for these people to see Life Line.) The exciting thing was, however, that those whom I was able to convince to join me inevitably felt that their few hours spent observing and hearing of the Tzedakah work were among their most stirring and productive times in Israel.

For example — this summer I took many Jewish Agency student groups to Life Line for the Old. At first, most did not want to go. Afterwards, however, all of them agreed that it was among their best experiences in Israel, and that every group must see Life Line. Teenagers who were not impressed by anything in Israel suddenly came alive in this place. The educational value of such a tour is obvious, and overwhelming. Apparently, the Agency will be willing to pay someone to integrate this into their summer and winter programs.

During the course of the year, I worked with many people and groups other than those associated with the Agency. They included American students studying in Israel, parents of those students, ulpan groups, tourists, and, of course, Israeli schoolchildren and adults. Without exception, they were extremely moved by what they saw.

I cannot accurately measure how effective this program has been. Many of the individuals who came with me to these places began, afterwards, on their own, to bring their friends and families. Others offered their services as volunteers at various places. The person who works on this full-time only serves as a spark to interest others. The network of contacts grew very quickly this year. By making this an ongoing project, the network will inevitably continue to expand.

For the next two years, I will be at the University of Judaism in Los Angeles, and will be happy to give talks and slide presentations on my experiences this year, to tell the story of the people on the Tzedakah report.

XI. *Some Summary Comments from your Shaliach-Messenger*

Over and over again, and yet again, I am dazzled by "our people." The old ones we know from past years, and the new ones. They hammer at the hearts of all who meet them, and then soothe and baby the excited soul to rest. The economy moans, the Exodus from Israel grows, distress and unease are common feelings in the streets — and yet there are all these Good People. They take money (even the smallest sums) and create monuments of hope and meaning, markers reminding us of the grandeur of the human being. Even in our failures.

Last year, and for two years before that, we paid a music teacher to give a chance to an emotionally disturbed child. Now she has been moved to another institution out of Jerusalem, and the lessons have ended. And still, the remaining money from the salary will be used for music lessons for a promising child.

The stories multiply: more people give, including a half dozen Jewish schools, more big and more small contributions ($3.17 from a child's pushka, a check for $1,000 after a program I gave); more receive, too. But the principles are the same — people must make Tzedakah a daily issue in their lives, and they must aggressively seek out the Good People. The principles apply to the Big Money — UJA, Federations, Hadassah, JNF — as well as to us. Indeed, articles about our work have been used by some of these organizations. We complement each other, though our scale of operations are vastly different. Our goals are the same: to educate Jews to take joy in turning money into Mitzvot.

I, personally, have gone beyond my bounds of time and energy. While I will continue to function as a resource person and lecturer on Tzedakah, I cannot maintain the pace and extent of the work demanded. You must make use of Beth, and Gordy and Sharon, and become yourselves resource centers for Tzedakah-work. I will, of course, continue to manage funds throughout the year: to cover mailing and phone expenses (now at 5–6%), to supplement Gordy's and Sharon's scholarship, and for other occasions that arise.

What is my main disappointment? Let me express it clearly, with a touch of anger and bitterness. It is this — that the major institutions of the North American Jewish Community — the Bureaus of Jewish Education, the national organizations such as the CCAR, and Hadassah, have not seen fit to call upon any of us — Beth, myself, and others — for our particular expertise in these matters, nor have they done the simplest of things: picked up the phone and asked to have their tours go through our places and meet our people. There, it is said! . . .

I must limit my correspondence, must hope that others who read this report will fill in the gaps, must hope (against my better judgment in these matters) that sufficient numbers of Jews will become evangelical about our work, and will pass the ideas on to others: to teachers, to businessmen and women, to children, to the many administrators and supervisors who hold so much power in their hands.

I did one teachers' seminar last year — in Providence, RI. I would hope this year to do many more. And that Beth will do the same, and you, yourselves.

Again, as always, a great, warm, heartfelt Yashir Koach to all of you. Being your Shaliach for six years has been the greatest blessing of my life!

שנה טובה ומבורכת. שנת אושר ועושר וכבוד,

שנת תחיית החיים, רגעי זיו ושגב.

בכבוד,

Danny Siegel

יזקה ינילה ה דן יתחן צעלק וזיזית נדזיי

קליפ"ץ

Publisher's Note: The addresses in the foregoing Tzedakah Report still apply for the following agencies: I:A-D; V; VI: A,C,E,F; VII:B; VIII:A-F,I and K.   All others should no longer be used.

The Essays

THE FIRST RULE OF TZEDAKAH

Awe, And wonder. That's the essence of the work. You have to be ready to be stunned, again and again — in the most positive way. That's the foundation of Tzedakah work.

Obstetricians have an advantage. They are forever delivering babies, bringing new, fresh life into this world, pausing to observe origins, innocence, a hundred miracles at a single moment: how breathing begins, how sound is made, how, emerging from the cheesy substance called *vernix caseosa*, a human being begins to grope through moments and new-found spaces.

And the electronmicroscopists have an advantage. They are forever scraping the edges of structures and shapes that send messages and mold eyes and ears and somehow, someway make for seeing and hearing and the chemistry of life.

And the poets, too, at least in the popular grasp of the word. Whether strolling through the rain or sitting at their desks, their eyes see beyond things, around things, inside dimensions of time, elements of the world that the so-called "general population" never gets the time to see. They are ever and always priming themselves to test dissimilar notions, rubbing them together, making new, wonderful combinations. They say "O, my luve is like a red, red rose,/ That's newly sprung in June" and new images explode on the consciousness of humankind. A pair of shoes is no longer just a pair of shoes, but leather from distant places, an inclosing of the foot, protection from harm, an invitation to wanderings. Life becomes a song, a shadow, a sailing ship, withering grass. All the textures of experience are in that channel between imagination and the penpoint.

Awe and wonder are daily with them.

This is the poet's verse of verses, a reflection on the essence of living:

> I praise You,
>> for I am awesomely, wondrously made;
>> Your work is wonderful;
>> I am intimately aware of it all.   (Psalm 139:14)

King David — the lyrical poet *par excellence* - and the other poets, the obstetricians, the electronmicroscopists, and some stray others have made this a pursuit of their beings — to be aware, as always as possible, that all aspects of life are more than mere curiosities to be tested and played with. They are, rather, sublime products of a divine handiwork, masterpieces to be gazed upon with absolute concentration, stared at in awe, admired not for themselves, but as a Psalm of reality in praise of the Creator.

All that lyrical phraseology sounds nice. But what of the so-called "general population," the shoppers, the insurance salespeople, the systems analysts and car mechanics? How are they to afford themselves frequent and powerful glimpses of these stunning events? If they are so preoccupied with routines and repetitive jobs, and errands — mailing their letters and writing their forms down to the last detail — how are they to be allowed the opportunities to share the joys of the Awe-struck and Wonder-eyed?

I have a simple answer: Tzedakah.

It is not the only way, to be sure. But Tzedakah-work opens doors to great distances and visions, colors of life and arrangements of the human soul which are available at any time, should the opportunity be embraced.

This is possible in a number of ways, at the very least:

1. Money: Money becomes magic. It goes through metamorphoses, becoming now food packages for Passover, now a hat that brings dignity to one who needs just that — a new hat. It buys gasoline to transport the old when they have become too old to drive. It buys sewing machines for retraining mental patients. It buys spoons for those who must be spoonfed . . . and pays salaries for spoonfeeders to do the work.

Money — miraculous, wondrous, awesome. I know a hundred dollars that bought some deaf woman a weekend at a convention of fellow Jews that brought her warmth, friends, the end to loneliness.

I know three dollars that last year bought a tree that comforted parents on the death of a child. And another three dollars that bought another tree that elated other parents on the birth of another child.

And I know another sum that bought a glob of clay that let a one-eyed hunchback man rebuild his life through the fashioning of necklaces.

I also know millions of dollars that did this and that: built schools, purchased canes and crutches, made great libraries of Judaica. But we should never think that it takes only Big Money to work magic. Witness five dollars in toys to shatter a child's depression. Witness fifteen dollars to take a dying old man to dinner and Radio City Music Hall — to him, a palace, though millions of New Yorkers might take it for granted every day. Five of the fifteen dollars for a ticket to a show — and the man was a king.

2. The wonder of people (Part I): Seeking out the miracle-workers, the Patient, the Devoted and Just of our People, seeing maestros and maestras of the human soul at work restores our own sense of awe. We are reminded that we, so steeped in routine, so chained to inconsequentials, we are reminded that we, too, may be awestruck. Hands are no longer just hands, but rather the hands that bathed a neglected child; hands that wove dreams into a tablecloth that now adorns a Shabbas table in Michigan or British Columbia, hands raised in defiance at bureaucracies that refuse to see. We are reminded of hands threatening to raise hell in the streets if the retarded do not get a decent, dignified group home, if the old do not become part of the workforce of the nation, if the blind do not get budgets to have their braille-books set. Hands mold hope from depression and images of majesty from despair. Even hands that surround the shoulders of one who weeps, touching just so, yielding comfort, gentleness, and warmth. And the weeper — alone, perhaps all alone in the world, her dead, his dead, lying there on a bed, waiting for a Comforter. I have seen a few dollars buy time for a woman who does just that: com-

forts. Money bought time, liberation from the day-to-day, so that someone, at least one person, would be available to comfort another.

The principle is simple: the more opportunities we find to give of our resources, the more we shall discover those with the Magic Touch, the ones who will teach us, in turn, to touch, gently when needed, or with great unknown strengths, if that, too, might be the need of the moment.

3. The wonder of people (Part II): We will soon discover that it is not just the miracle-workers who render such services to others. We see the sister of a friend, a barbershop owner, a C.P.A., a child, bakers, toy makers, students, even ourselves, doing, to some measured degree, the same. The Magic Touch is contagious, and though we may not reach the heights of the Righteous, we are allowed a view of ourselves that says, "Just maybe, I, too, am capable." At certain moments, time permitting, energy permitting. Some wonder-workers I know sleep two hours a night, perhaps three. That is beyond me. Some live hard lives, with families sharing the deprivations with joy. That, too, is beyond me. Some are blessed with visions that only a handful in each generation may share: Henrietta Szold, for example, the diminutive Miss Szold changing the entire face of health-care in Israel. Though their lives can never be ours, still, we can set ourselves to discovering them, and the "everyday people" who at their own pace and rhythm and with their own unique style do the same . . . people we have underestimated (including ourselves) who collect furniture for immigrants, unassuming people who volunteer their day, arranging flowers for a fund-raiser for some Great Project, people as people who remember to write that specific note of concern that gives hope to the lonely, and the teenager who makes faces so an autistic baby might smile, the committee people running here and there to buy a Westminster Torah, saved from the Nazis, for their synagogue. The list is endless — the grandmother babysitting another's infant, despite her own pains and fainting fits and a multitude of other illnesses. They are everywhere. And as our money and efforts radiate outward in many directions, we see these people, listen to them, either through words or silence, and learn wisdoms unique to this world of Tzedakah.

4. Finally — the stories: When Tzedakah is done, we have exchanged worlds. We no longer hear chatter of weather reports, ball scores, the latest murder or mugging in the park. Suddenly we hear of some individual who has chosen a Mitzvah — to take the blind woman of Jerusalem to the beauty parlor on Fridays, for one queen to greet another in appropriate style. We hear offers — a car at the disposal of young people too distant from home for Pesach, unable to pay air fares — a chance to drive all night and through the next day from Chicago to Boston, New York to Miami, for a Seder at home. We hear of this aunt who worries that unemployed immigrants from Russia and Iran should have work — and hires and hires and hires them beyond her means. And a lady so far away from us we may never live to see her, a lady called the Mother of the

Soldiers, smashing loneliness, and exhaustion, be it with tea or a sandwich or a warm bed and roof on a drizzly night. We hear of her wonders.

That is the first rule of Tzedakah work: never to lose our sense of wonder, of awe. There really is no danger of that, once the involvement begins. It seems that, as we open ourselves (the money, the time to think it out, the summoning of powers of wisdom), then the opportunities, and people, and stories present themselves to us in great number. The first move is ours, though. Once we have done that, we discover infinite possibilities.

I often quote a particular passage in the Talmud, concluding my Tzedakah thoughts with the hope that centuries of Jewish tradition offers. It is as true as any truth I have encountered:

> Whoever runs to do Tzedakah, the Holy One, blessed be He, will find for that person both the money and the appropriate recipients for all his Tzedakah-desires. (Bava Batra 9b)

Surrounded by the chaos of our world, bombarded with truths from varied sources, some sublime, some moronic, it is time to reflect on our own truths, to consider this wisdom that transcends time and place and reaches into the deepest recesses of the Jewish heart.

THE GIANTS OF JERUSALEM

The kids and I are sitting in rows in the courtyard. We are reviewing our morning tour. Inevitably, Mr. Wolf will appear, howling, cracking bad (but not embarrassingly bad) puns. He will most certainly ask the kids, "Do you want to hear a song I learned at camp?" They begin to cheer, and Mr. Wolf, our Hero of the Day, breaks into some ditty about a froggy and his girlfriend. He motions for us to sing the chorus with him, and the kids and I go at it with gusto. When he finishes, they cheer and applaud wildly and demand to take his picture, though they have already done so earlier that day. Some shake his hand and are surprised that someone in his mid-eighties should still have a wrestler's grip. When Mr. Wolf leaves, it is difficult to hold their attention again — their minds are drifting. Neatly packaged chunks of myths they had acquired in their teen-aged years are being thrown out, life-directions are beginning to change. They have learned the meaning of "Elders," and many are surprised that they have fallen in love.

I have gone through this scene a hundred times — more than a hundred times. It has been a typical summer morning for me at Life Line for the Old in Jerusalem. Just me, a few friends perhaps, and most important of all, thirty teenagers from the United Synagogue Youth Israel Pilgrimage. Three thousand teenagers over the past five years.

And I love it.

And they love it.

When I lecture on Jerusalem and the Righteous of the Land of Israel, I tell everyone that more than half my friends in Jerusalem are in their sixties and seventies and eighties.

My personal salvation is there, somewhere in the courtyard and workshops of Life Line. There is a call, despite the drag and chaos of the Big World, a call to some shred of idealism, of a far-reaching vision. Of dreams I may have dreamed when I was younger but gave up because some uninspired, cynical *momzerim* erroneously convinced me that life just doesn't work the way I want it to work.

Let me describe the morning's program — it is rather simple: The kids and I walk or ride to Life Line, to a part of Jerusalem that used to sit right on the border with Jordan. I give them a brief introduction, right in the courtyard, in the thick of things, with elders of every stature and origin passing by. Then, Myriam Mendilow, founder and director, prophet, hell-raiser, and seventy-year-old miracle worker, comes out and speaks to them from a bench. (She stands on a bench because, even in thick-soled shoes, she is at best five feet tall.) After her passionate talk (we are amazed at her energy. "What a giant!" we are thinking), after her blazing words, we divide into two groups and walk through the thirteen workshops, then to the store to buy things, then back to the courtyard to discuss the guts of Tzedakah and to talk about the people we have met. We think about Old Age, make resolutions, search recesses of our hearts we had forgotten to look into. It is rather like Passover: Life Line is the candle we use to exam-

ine corners and nooks of ourselves, seeking out the chometz — the artifi-
cially leavened pieces of our minds that have spoiled our dreams.

That's where Mr. Wolf comes in — to tie things together in his own
fashion. To remind us not to forget the Persecution of Elderly Jews.

*A few years back, Mr. Wolf told my aunt, "If I had stayed in New York, I'd
be in an old age home. I'd be dead by now."*

Life Line for the Old, or Yad LaKashish as it is known in the City of
Cities, is *not* an old-age home. It is workshops. People come from their
own homes, on foot, by bus, by two buses, to work Sunday through
Thursday mornings. They complain of Shabbas and Yontiff because they
can't come to work.

They are happy. Well, I can't lie about this. Some complain, but I also
complain — and my life has been easy, very easy. Still, they are happy,
and they more than impress us . . . they wow us (including an old-timer
like me who has been there a hundred times and more), making wondrous
things with their hands: tableclothes, sweaters, toys, wall-hangings, more
toys, new bindings on schoolbooks, booties for infants, more toys. Each
day there is something new.

Look, the formula is simple. A lady in her late forties, this Myriam
Mendilow, quits her job of twenty-two years as a teacher because she is
disgusted with taking her students to the streets and showing them
decrepit, dying old people begging, sitting in misery and loneliness. She
quits — just like that — begs for a teacher from the Ministry of Labor, and
drags beggars and abandoned elders to her first workshop — a bookbindery. She says, "Let the old rebind the books of the young, and let the
young see who has done the job so well, so carefully and lovingly. Let
them rediscover the meaning of Grandfather, Grandmother."

That's how simple it is. I have been over it again and again in my
mind, trying to convince myself that there is some element I have missed,
some complicating factor. But there are no hidden ingredients, no classi-
fied information. Everything is out in the open: a visionary, love and devotion, tenacity, a bullheaded will, and a Jeremiah-voice screaming at society.

*Mr. Wolf tells the kids, "When I came to Jerusalem a few years ago, I went
around looking for a job. No luck. I was told I was too old. Too old. Then I came
here and they put me to work the same day I came."*

Myriam Mendilow is a myth-breaker, an iconoclast of the first order.
These are some of the myths that have been shattered before our eyes as
we walk through the workshops:

1. You can't retrain most old people. (Neither the kids nor I will use
the phrase, "You can't teach an old dog new tricks." Perhaps that works
for dogs. But people — well, people are people, not some strain of collie
or dalmatian.) "Lies!" Mrs. Mendilow would say. Almost everyone we saw
is doing things they had not only never done before, but things they had
never considered possible for them to do. As Myriam the Giant explains,
"Some of them never had a tradition of work. We often start with nothing."

2. Laxatives, good denture glues, and Geritol (as the commercials would lead us to believe) are the true source of happiness for the elderly. (Scanning the medical journals:) Anti-hypertensives, bypasses, and tablets of every shape and color ease pain better than anything. We see, quite to the contrary, that high expectations, caring, and love bring smiles, songs to the people at work.

3. Heart attacks and strokes kill most old people. Every kid sees that this is not so: loneliness and uselessness are greater killers.

4. Begging in one form or another — welfare, handouts from all sorts of sources — will solve the problems of the elderly. Again — no! The old people work for far less than they could make with their palms extended in the streets, trembling hands stretched out to Israeli and tourist alike, playing on their heartstrings. Myriam Mendilow shows us her photograph of The King of the Beggars (now deceased) and tells us how she fought to get him to come to work, despite the very respectable sums he could bring home from his streetcorner perch with a cup in his hand. "But where was his self-respect, his sense of Kavod?" she shouts at us. The little lady, who is our Rebbi for that day, and for long into the future, reminds us that dignity is the ultimate source of the will to live.

Mr. Wolf tells us his granddaughter in Maryland just had triplets. The kids take pictures, recite a mile-long string of mazal tovs. They wish him well, "Biz Hundert Und Tzvantzig . . . May you live to be a hundred and twenty!"

What strikes the kids right away, as soon as they walk into the courtyard is No Stink! No medicine, no urine, no stench of fecal matter. Now, I have to ask — with all the possibility of protests I will hear from This Great Nursing Home and That Grand Senior Citizens' Residence — where did these teenagers ever smell such smells? Somewhere they must have visited the old and been overpowered by it. The smell of medicine is easy to answer. Almost to the last teenager, they have been inside a home, or heard stories, and the smell of antisepsis pervades each visit, each tale. Medicines, drugs. (All those lectures they have heard on drug abuse! They know what it means.) They recall memories of a similar phenomenon, "One Flew Over the Cuckoo's Nest." Mental patients, old people, hyperkinetic children on Ritolin. Here they know that people are weaned from many of their drugs. They see pain change when the reason for living changes.

The kids say, "No zombies!" They've entertained in old-age homes for Purim and Channukah and led Seders and Shabbat songs with their youth groups. Most mornings at Life Line, someone brings up the zombies. They know that in many cases (not all cases: why should I exaggerate when the truth stands so well on its own?) — in many cases they drug the old just to keep them under control. The kids are outraged. They would never let someone do that to them. They *know* what drugs can do to you. They have heard the sermons, seen the notices of overdosing in the papers, know every word for dope in the book. And yet they see how society condones drug abuse among the elderly and they are shattered.

There are no white coats at Life Line for the Old. No nurses, no doctors, no medical personnel circulating among the workshops. The cure-alls from the pharmacy are totally absent, and the teenagers are gloriously surprised. I share their joy. I feel their hearts take heart. "Kol HaKavod!" I want to say. "Well done, Myriam Mendilow!"

The kids are not stupid, nor are they blind. They have been great teachers to me over the past five years. They know. They see through things very quickly and readily spill out their guts:

"My grandfather . . . I screamed at my parents. Take him out of the home." (The old-age home, a prominent one at that. I, too, had been there once.)

One young woman weeps near-hysterically after leaving a workshop. "Why is there nothing like this in the States? Why wasn't there one when my grandmother needed something like this?"

"Wonderful!"

"Incredible!"

"What can we do to start something like this back home?" (I reply, blind to rational thinking, stunned again by Mendilow's dream, "Start with the synagogue. Invite the old down one night a week. Begin with the needlecrafts — you don't need heavy equipment for that. Sell the products and give the money to Tzedakah. But don't start by storming the community old-age home. Some professionals have already told us they do not want you meddling in their schedules.) (I see the outcries, the letters of protest coming to my mailbox. "Who are you to criticize? You are naive. Of course we welcome the teenagers' help." Composing this article at the typewriter, I admit to myself some doubt, even fear. Perhaps Mendilow is wrong, perhaps she really doesn't understand how things really work out there. I am scared.)

Now I am rewriting the article. Fear grows in me. I realize, of course, that there are some wonderful old age homes, many doing fabulous work of dignified caring for their people. Many do have workshops and programs that raise up the souls of the elders in their care.

But I have to ask myself, "Where does all the kids' anger come from?" All those cries of Bingo, card playing, hours and hours of television, miles of endless walking around a track, second-rate borscht-belt comedians doing their bits. How is it that so many of them know that old people die sooner if they go into an old-age home (often against their wishes), than if they had stayed in their own homes, with outside care coming in when necessary?

By no means do we (I and the kids) denigrate the skills of professionals in the field of gerontology. (I, myself, am a professional poet and lash out frequently against critics who would call me moody, effete, spacy, effeminate, and inconsiderate — besides their attacks on my professional skill with words.) But I have to ask myself again, "Where do these kids come to be so amazed at a place where social workers and geriatric specialists are absent? Strikingly absent. How do *they* (the teenagers) conclude "love, caring, devotion," rather than "group techniques, senior citizens' activities, and tranquilizers?" How is it that they know that jargon is lethal if it is used as a euphemism for failing to care?

We enter the carpentry shop. Avraham Ermosa, seventy-five-year-old Sabra, begins his talk, sometimes in Spanish, sometimes in French or Hebrew — depending on which language the kids want to translate. He tells how he takes old, dead wood and brings it back to life. He is in the Resurrection Business.

He says he uses the sander for scratching his back — it is more efficient and effective. One minute and you'll never have to scratch again!

He explains that the buzz saw is for multiple brisses — 2,000 boys at a time. The kids howl. (The males squirm a little.)

He shows us pictures of his family and tells us how he chases his wife around the house for a kiss. Then we step outside for pictures. Ermosa with his arms around the girls (always the girls), cracking jokes.

I ask questions:

1. How many of you live 1500 miles or more from your grandparents? Hands and more hands go up.

Ermosa was sick last year. He has a bad heart . . . a bad physical heart, that is. I was worried I would leave Jerusalem last year and come back ten months later and hear sad news. Ermosa explains to the kids, "They took me to the cemetery. I didn't like it. No sunshine, no air. So I came back to work."

I ask questions:

2. How many of you left for Israel afraid you would get a telegram that one of your grandparents died while you were gone? Many hands. Even worse, I ask how many were afraid their parents wouldn't tell them until they got back. Hands, more hands.

Ermosa recalls, from fifty years ago and more, a girlfriend who was mad at him. She called to say she wanted her picture back. But he couldn't remember which one she was. So he sent her his whole album of girlfriends' pictures and told her to pick out the right one.

I ask questions:

3. How many of you have a grandparent in an old age home? A great uncle or great aunt? A great-grandparent? Many hands, some with good stories to tell of their forebears' sojourn, some with sad stories. Some strike out at me for slandering all old-age homes. "What about Baycrest in Toronto?" they say. "What about the Shalom Home in the Twin Cities?" I say, "You are right. I overdo it." But then I ask myself why this is the reaction of only a handful of the kids.

The Old Yemenite in the wheelchair has died. God, I miss him. He married a Polish woman decades ago. She went back to Poland with the four children to visit her family. Then the War came, and he was alone.
The hunchback in the ceramics workshop has died. The one with one good eye. Others I never got to know well enough also died, while I was in exile.

I ask one more question:

4. How many of you have an older relative who was forced to retire

because he or she reached mandatory retirement age? Hands, maybe four or five out of thirty. How many of you had an older relative who folded up and died shortly after being forced to retire? Two or three hands. Then there is silence, a distinct, crushing silence.

I tell the kids about Miriam Itzkovitch, another half-mad woman in Jerusalem. They laugh at the name. (Itzkovitch laughs at "Lincoln" and "Washington" — she's Russian and speaks Hebrew with a thick Russian accent.) I tell them that among her far-reaching and varied Mitzvot are programs to take care of the old, more than three hundred of them, seventy-five of whom live all alone. She brings them help and friends and visitors and people to clean and shop and talk and open windows. *Not a single one of them has had to move into an old-age home.*

The kids feel good about that. I feel good about that. Caring triumphs for the day! Jewish caring.

And then I confess to them that I do not know how I could manage caring for someone day in and day out, someone with multiple problems, physical and psychological. I tell them I just don't know, but I tell them I know more options now. I know there are other options besides Death Row. In New York alone I know Project Ezra and Dorot and Hatzilu: visits, food packages for the Jewish holidays, shopping, a touch, a cup of coffee and conversation, a phone call in the middle of a long week.

One Hatzilu worker says to me, "When we brought the food for Rosh HaShana, one woman kissed my hand."
My God, I think. What have we done?

I am quick to blow holes in my self-righteousness. I remind them, and myself, that, I, too, am slow to learn, and slower to act. I tell the kids that they are our hope. Mrs. Mendilow loves them more than any millionaire who might walk in and throw stacks of big dollars on her desk. "Raise hell," she says to them. "Raise hell," I chime in, and hope that they will be less insecure than I. I can only expose them to this Magic Kingdom of Life Line for the Old. They can't always count on me — I tell them that. But somewhere in that long stream of three thousand kids are new Myriam Mendilows, Miriam Itzkovitchs, Henrietta Szolds. My idealism is satisfied when I think of their potential. The thought fires me nicely for months on end.

I like to end my articles with stories, tales of the way life is, despite what the experts and cynics proclaim in their official statistical studies and carefully calculated commission reports. Jews know from the rabbis of the Talmud and the Chassidic Masters that sometimes a story carries more meaning than a chart of figures and pages of analysis.

I am blessed with heroes — these teenagers. When I arrive in Israel before they have even packed their bags for the trip, the first question from the Elders of Jerusalem is, "When are the kids coming?" The workers at Life Line have been waiting for their return.

So here are two stories about my heroes:

It is 8:30 in the morning in Jerusalem. I am standing on my bench in the courtyard of Life Line, the kids facing me in semi-circles. As usual, I ask the teenagers, "Who speaks French?" (They will want to use their broken, halting high-school French to speak to the Elders from French Morocco and Algeria.) "Who speaks Spanish?" (For Bulgarian Jews, the South Americans, the one from Hungary who moved to Argentina before coming to Israel.) "Hebrew? Hungarian?" (We had one who spoke a good Hungarian.) "German? Rumanian?" (No one for Rumanian.) And down the long list of languages Jews have had to learn to speak to survive in their wanderings.

This morning was different:

"Spanish?" Many hands.

"Russian?" Some hands, including one teenager who had just raised his hand for Spanish.

"Yiddish?" The same hand as for Spanish and Russian. All the other kids cheer. It's their boy — they call him "The Rabbi." He spoke them all, fluently, and he sang.

He sang Yiddish songs for the Elders. God, you could have burst from the joy on their faces (and mine). Unabashedly standing there singing "Mein Shtetele Belz" while the Old Ones beat rhythms on the tables with their hands.

My hero.

And the second tale:

It is the last day of summer, the last group. After the tour and the buying and our discussion, some kids still want to have their picture taken with Mrs. Mendilow. The last kid of all — he must have been six feet three or four inches tall — stands next to Mrs. Mendilow under the big Life Line sign. After the picture is taken, he turns to her and hugs and kisses her. I thought he would crush her — she barely reached his shoulder.

This is my greatest joy: the memory of those two giants, standing in the Jerusalem sunlight, embracing.

THE GIANTS OF JERUSALEM: II

Additional Principles I Have Learned at Life Line for the Old (in no order):

1. Laughter and goofing-around are permissible in the presence of the old.

2. Calling old people "senior citizens" does not necessarily solve their problems. Many take offense at the term.

3. Drugs used purely to make the old more manageable are an invasion of privacy, a violation of their rights, and a travesty of the medical profession's power to use such drugs.

4. Silliness is debasing: treat the old like silly old people and they will themselves fulfill that image, unless they are incredibly strong-willed.

5. One person can change hundreds of worlds. (Mrs. Mendilow has done it. Thousands, perhaps, over the years.)

6. Money is important to the old: they must be paid for their work. They must also pay for their services, if even a symbolic amount. Handouts humiliate them no less than we would be humiliated by receiving the same.

7. The Cult of Youth put forth by American culture is a pack of lies.

8. Adoptive grandparent programs should work the other way: the Elders should go out into the community to seek out grandchildren they can adopt and spend time with. Community organizations should encourage such programs.

9. If you expect more from the old, most likely you will get more from them in return.

10. Professional training is important, but not everything. Devotion and intuitive skills sometimes (but not always) compensate for lack of formal training in gerontology.

11. Busy work is not the solution to keeping the Elders active and creative. *Real* work — within whatever limits a specific Elder has defined — brings about renewed enthusiasm, hope, a will to live.

12. One need not always believe the doctors or relatives when they estimate how long a certain elder will live. I sometimes think Life Line extends lives even beyond God's Own estimates.

13. Shouting and anger are good for the Elders. It is a sign that they are alive and have retained their self-image. (Life Line is often noisy, excited verbal exchanges are not infrequent. It may be momentarily unpleasant, but ultimately it is glorious.)

14. Breaking bones in a fall does not necessarily mean that Death is waiting around the corner. (Many of the Life Line Elders have diseases and maladies and deformities that would kill an ox — but not a human being. My great-grandmother Chaya, blind and nearly ninety, fell down the steps one Sukkot years and years ago. She broke her arm — the bone thrust out through the skin. But the doctor fixed that, and it healed nicely. She died a considerably great while afterwards from some virus.)

15. The old and the young, the healthy and the physically and mentally handicapped, the eccentric and the "straight" can work together well.

(All these varieties of people are to be found in abundance at Life Line.)

16. Vision and dedication come before money. Projects such as these need not begin with $1,000,000. (Life Line began with nothing.) (One teacher to teach the old how to re-bind books.) High-financed projects have failed. In the end this kind of unique, devoted madness prevails, by sheer brute force of the Mitzvah of Tzedakah.

17. Not everyone who is in an old-age home should be in an old-age home. Not everyone who is in an old-age home should be living outside an old-age home. But many who are there shouldn't be within institutional walls. I leave those interested in refining these statistics to go to Life Line. Listen to the ravings of a madwoman, screaming to make us see.

THE SECOND RULE OF TZEDAKAH:
BE USEFUL

Make sure you count.

Even if the job you work at is frustrating and you feel locked in a rut, you're underpaid, overtrained, the market is ever-tightening, and your bosses show no appreciation whatsoever for the hours of effort you put in.

Even with all that, there is still a chance for personal re-appraisal. If you pick a place where you can send part of your Tzedakah money, where you know it will make a difference, there is that chance that you may restore your self-image to its proper place. As the Book of Genesis informs us, self-image is really a reflection of God's image.

Let us assume you are a lawyer, and you are being taken away from your family week after week for long-distance trips, working on a mammoth case that doesn't interest you in the least. Let us further assume that the case will drag on for another few months, and you feel that — other than the fact that you are earning a living — you are wasting your time. The opportunity presents itself to you (on the plane trips back and forth to the trial-site) that you may allocate some of your Tzedakah funds for a university scholarship in Israel for a graduating senior who is similarly locked in: tough family, tough neighborhood, stagnating influences stabbing from all sides. Someone has discovered a lead for you, a specific individual (perhaps an immigrant from the Soviet Union). He lives in Tel Aviv, has finished the army, and hopes for a college education. The Russian-Israeli — say, Bronovich — never met you (and will never meet you), doesn't even know someone is thinking about him. And you, 7,000 miles away in Kansas City, gather some friends and put the money together, transfer quietly and anonymously the funds to an organization that will inform Bronovich that the door is open to him.

This will not get you off the case in San Francisco or Phoenix. It will not prevent your law partners from overworking you. But it will remind you who you are — a person who is ultimately in control of his or her own life, capable of rising above the immediate whirling activities and projects, capable of bringing about changes, immediate, striking changes.

Just so long as you make it count.

It is refreshing, encouraging. And it does not have to interfere with your other Tzedakah work. You may still continue to contribute to UJA, ORT, Hadassah, and other large organizations, taking your place in Tzedakah schemes on a larger scale. Your $100.00 as part of a multi-million will continue to play its important role, but, by this additional act, somewhere in your overall Tzedakah budget, you will have made a *specific* difference. It may well be that you have asked your "contact" not to tell you the recipient's name — you wish to keep the anonymity solid on both sides — so that there will be no formal thank-you's, no constraints as to whether or not this student gets 90's on his exams at Bar Ilan or Tel Aviv University. You will only know that somewhere, in the midst of 3,000,000 Jews in Israel, you will have done just that much more to make the reborn country live, and live well.

Here is another variation on the theme: say you have just graduated law school. You are in that six-month interim period where you find you just don't have a job (you didn't go to Harvard, Yale, Columbia). Your funds are limited and you can't, by any means, buy a year's worth of college education for anyone Over There. You have only $50.00 to work with.

The problem and the solution are still the same: pick something where it will be useful, direct, of immediate consequence. A sum of $50.00, properly placed, will bring five Rosh HaShana meals to Jews who wouldn't have a decent Yontiff dinner — were it not for you. The same $50.00 will buy two small libraries for schoolchildren in Israel: dictionaries, atlases, elementary encyclopedias. It is not hard to find *Zahavi* (37 Azza Rd., Jerusalem), the organization that seeks out the students and the students' needs, buys the appropriate books at a discount, and gets the books into their homes, on their bookshelves.

And $50.00 will buy enough cloth and materials for five elderly Jews to get back to work, needlepointing, crocheting, knitting, crewel-working, embroidering wonderful pieces of craft-art that will adorn other people's homes. They can begin again to use their hands, to sell their products, to regain their own sense of usefulness. All this while you are still out of work, still searching for a job. All that is needed is the $50.00, and locating the right people who will get a project rolling, or who will, because of you, continue to carry on projects already successfully functioning. (Try Life Line for the Old, 12 Shivtei Yisrael St., Jerusalem.)

Only be certain to choose some place where a portion of your Tzedakah money will have an impact.

And what if you have only $10.00 to spare — the rest having been pledged to other Tzedakot, or because you are only fifteen years old and have only $10.00 to give . . . and you share that locked-in feeling, the grind of schoolwork and papers and exams and debate practice, which bores you? What of this $10.00? That money you may take by yourself to the local hospital, or wherever the lonely lie in bed or sit in wheelchairs, and with those few dollars you bring some refreshment, some flowers, and you sit for an hour and ease a little pain. I remember the Gray Ladies my mother used to speak of — the volunteers in the hospitals, filling in where the doctors might not go, with conversation, with patience, with a touch. You can be a Gray Lady, even if on only one occasion. You are entitled to the satisfaction of having made a difference, of coming home, the memory of the flowers' fragrance still in your mind, and saying to yourself, "It was good." (The phrase echoes back to Creation.)

How much does it count?

An example: the cantorial students at the Jewish Theological Seminary of America go to the Montefiore Hospital cancer wards a few times a week. They sing, entertain, talk, teach, relax with the patients. I would imagine it is the most unpleasant place on the face of the earth, a place any right-minded person would least likely want to go with time of his or her own to manage. But the stories are more than just heartwarming. I will retell one I have heard, in brief . . . A woman says, "They have tried every kind of drug and therapy on me, and nothing helps. I am always in pain.

But after the cantors come, I feel no pain for a couple of hours."

That is how much it can count.

The same can be done with money, or time. Money can be so versatile; you can make things happen. You can give the Cantor's Institute a small sum and tell them to buy cantorial records, to set up a record library in the bowels of the cancer ward, so that in between the visits the melodies will always be on hand. The tunes bring soothing moments of respite from agony; let the patients have more access to them.

The variations are infinite, with just a few dollars.

And with time — though there was an outcry a while back that Volunteerism Is Dead, I do not see it as being so absolutely true. There are still so many who offer one afternoon a week, or an evening, or a Sunday morning, tutoring a learning-disabled child in Hebrew, walking an old Lower East Side resident to the store, to the park, to the pharmacy, to a minyan. See what the dentists do . . . an ever-growing group of them, committing themselves to an unpaid summer in Israel, volunteering on kibbutzim up and down the country. And from what they tell me, the simple dentistry they are doing has saved many a painful, complicated mess in future years. This one needs a filling, that one a lecture on sugar consumption, another a good cleaning. The dentists are needed, and they choose to take care of that need. Everyone benefits, because they are useful.

Think of the thousands of Pioneer Women, Brotherhood Men, the Shriners, the Knights of This and That Order, extending themselves to some limited time-commitment, raising not only funds, but spirits . . . to make fun for the crippled children, to make sure there are enough eyeglasses and hearing aids for whomever needs them, to handle tons of rice shipments to distant lands where starvation is all too well-known. Not full-time, and not encompassing all their Tzedakah money, but still, in their own lives, a most significant aspect of their self-definition. If some part of them cannot be free to be of service to others, then, they ask themselves, just what are they, who are they?

Let us leave the complex overall problems of Tzedakah to the experts. There are a few who, with the assistance of demographers and statisticians, social workers and economists, can lay the general plans for the needs of our people, for the world. Sometimes they are absolutely right, sometimes slightly off-direction, and occasionally dead wrong. But they are the experts and can usually predict trends and cost-analyses better than we. When they say there are such-and-such number of elderly Jews on the South Beach of Miami committing suicide each year — they know. They have the means for determining such figures and can formulate reasonable plans of attack. But if you live in Houston or Greensboro or El Paso, you cannot help immediately, directly. You can only take the larger picture and carve out your small part of it, work with it energetically, with your own personality, your own unique elements of individuality. That is how the Small Ones complement the Experts in their work.

Only be useful, even in the face of staggering statistics.

A concluding example — the Classic Example — of which I speak frequently:

Ya'akov Maimon, (Zichrono Livracha, May his memory be for a blessing). He died a few years ago, but while he lived, this was his method: approaching a perfect stranger on the street or on a campus or army base or at a gathering at someone's house, he would say, "Shalom, my name is Maimon. I want to bring Jews closer together." He would then explain that he needed volunteers, tutors, to be more specific. For whatever expertise the listener might have, Maimon had a ready student waiting for those talents. He was the Ultimate Shadchan, the Matchmaker, connecting people from different social strata and backgrounds all over Israel, one teaching music, another tutoring English, a third making Hebrew something less than terrifying to a new immigrant. There were thousands of Maimon volunteers. He knew the names of every one of them, to his dying day when he was well into his seventies. Up and down the steps of run-down apartments, taking the volunteers into the homes. On the road, riding his circuit in the Galilee, taking volunteers, taking lorries full of Hebrew University students to scattered streets in Jerusalem where some other Jew was waiting to learn something new about physics or geography or the syntax of our ancient Mother Tongue. Most of all, waiting to learn the greatest meaning of the word "Jew."

Maimon was unique. Perhaps no one else established such a network of volunteers. But there are others, everywhere, doing their variations on the same theme: organizing teams of volunteers to read for the blind, finding drivers to bring the disabled to community functions, making phone calls upon phone calls to make preparations for a festive dinner in honor of local Soviet Jews, cooking, setting tables, uncorking wine bottles, and pouring vodka all around. They are not hard to find, because they are everywhere to be found.

Set your own pace. Select your own money-and-time budget. Only make some portion of that money and time useful. Making it count for the beneficiaries of these gestures can only make it count for us, too.

I suppose, if we were perfectly honest with ourselves, we might find doctors who would write on certain documents, "Cause of Death: Inflated Ego." I do not recall from my few years of contact with the Maimons, the Gray Ladies, the scholarship-givers and flower-distributors any high mortality rates, nothing higher than the general population. If anything, I have noticed a brightened countenance, a certain radiance that surrounds their presence, a vigorous speech pattern. Even among social workers who day-in and day-out share uncountable aches and troubles with their clients — unfathomably varied and depressing human problems (torn families, abandoned households, slow deaths by all manner of disease) — even they, on the forefront of the battle to make life decent and full of hope, demonstrate a lively affirmation. That is brought about by giving of themselves *outside their jobs.* They, of all people (and the oncologists and the hematologists reading too many truncated leukemic lifelines, and the pathologists seeing too much in the lab, too many malignancies too late) — this community should, by all rights, be overwhelmed with despair. But some of them have succeeded in going beyond their work, achieving a certain calm, a peace of mind. Clearly, as I listen to them unravel their stories, it is a result of their wisely-distributed Tzedakah money, the extra time outside of their jobs that restores their vision to a renewed clarity.

A quote from Dante comes to mind: over the Gates of Hell is this inscription, "All hope abandon, ye who enter here!" I think of the Montefiore cancer wards, the hell of our modern society, and I think of the cantorial students, engraving, instead, some less august, less forboding phrase. Something modest like, "By all means, be useful."

Singing Yiddish melodies, Hebrew folksongs, making even Hell itself a livable place.

Who can believe it?

THE STORY OF THE
FIVE-DOLLAR MITZVAH
OR TZEDAKAH À LA ATHOS,
PORTHOS, AND ARAMIS

Money fascinates me.

How $100,000 can purchase a mansion in El Paso and yet not buy a bungalow in Los Angeles gives me pause. How the cost of a suit has doubled in the course of a year or two. How 25¢ can still buy you a cup of coffee in some truckstops, while two miles up the road Howard Johnson's charges twice that much (not counting tax). It makes no difference to me if you are talking millions of dollars or one thin dime — the way money works (or no longer works) carries my mind great distances.

And it makes no difference to me if you are talking money in the marketplace or Tzedakah money. In either case, I am astounded.

I have met people who easily give away a million dollars a year, and others who contribute a thousand, though they are in debt up to their ears, and beyond. And then there are multitudes just beginning to be touched by a sense of substantial giving, people on $25,000-30,000-a-year incomes who are enjoying that first $1,000 sent away, knowing it will buy a small machine that will allow someone to work again, or pairs of crutches, or an English-language teacher for Russian immigrants. Nowadays, however, I most frequently encounter children eight, nine, ten, eleven years old, with only nickels, dimes, and quarters, wondering how their coins could possibly redirect the broken world away from despair into a glowing joy. From a dollar-a-week allowance they may have only ten or twenty cents a week to give away. That is scarcely earthshaking when even they are aware of the starvation of millions, the cold that oppresses down-and-outers without overcoats, the abandoned thousands in mental hospitals and flophouses. It is a very real problem for them.

How have I gained entrée into this World of Our Children? The procedure is simple: when I come to speak at a synagogue, I often go into the Hebrew school and play Tzedakah Musketeer. I imagine myself clothed in a flowing cape and broadbrimmed hat (with feather), and sweep into the classroom and say, "Let's talk about money and Tzedakah." I tell the Short People of Our People that my friends give me money to give away. I stun them, saying that I had $12,720 to distribute last summer in Israel. That scares them. So many dollars are beyond their realm of experience. They have never physically seen so much money, let alone given it away.

So I do this: I take a $5.00 bill from my wallet and announce, "Who would be willing to take this $5.00 and buy flowers some Friday afternoon . . . to take the flowers to people at hospitals or the local Jewish old-age home, to wish people a Good Shabbas?" There have been several, varied reactions, some of which have been stark revelations to me. I have sometimes said, taking the money from my pocket, "Who would like $5.00?" It is shocking to see how many say they would just take it. Even after the joking is over and the giggles die down, there are still a few who would take it — money out of the clear blue, from a stranger. So I tell those few, "If your parents say it is all right to take it, I will leave the $5.00 with the rabbi. If your mother or father agrees, it is yours." I made that deal once, but, when the child asked his parents, they told their son it was all right to take it — if he used it for Tzedakah. (I was grateful. I had been *very* worried.)

When things have settled down, and I make it absolutely clear that the money is only for flowers, reactions fall into patterns.

One child returned the $5.00 to me after the class, thinking it was a game, a joke, or some educational trick.

Most are reluctant to take the money. (I only offer one or two $5.00 bills per class.) They may be frightened by the responsibility, or just not interested. I have rarely heard afterwards from the teachers, which is my fault. I shall have to inquire in the future about the follow-up discussions, to try to understand their reluctance.

In class, though, most usually the kids are dumbfounded and suspicious. Why would anyone give away money, just like that? That worries me. Even after I reassure them that it is not my own money, but rather money my friends give me specifically for this type of project, there is still that look on their faces. It is a tinge of Early Cynicism. I am very troubled by that. I theorize that the source might be the bombardment of phony sales and specials they see in stores, or toy advertising that is made to look too good, or conversations overheard from their parents about being "ripped off." Whatever the source, though, many have acquired a suspicious mood, even at this young age.

But for the ones who take the money — it is a delight. You can see their faces brighten from the opportunity offered to them. They seem eager for Friday to come, so they can set out on their Mitzvah-adventure. That very much pleases me, though I rarely have enough time to ask the teachers why a particular child took the $5.00.

I give them encouragement, telling them how much they will mean to the people they visit — young, fresh-looking, hopeful Jews coming by to wish them a Good Shabbas. I tell them they have the power to move people more than any adults, even the friends or family of the sick or elderly they will meet. This is their part in the Musketeer Mitzvah — they, perfect strangers, come dashing into the room offering a carnation or rose, saying, "We wanted you to have this, to brighten your Shabbas. We know it is not easy being away from the family for Shabbas."

It is all so very simple.

A LETTER WITH COMMENTARY

I do not require the children to write me a letter afterwards, though occasionally I do get a report on their excursions. One such letter very much moved me, and I reproduce it here (with names changed), so that we might understand more completely the potential impact a little money-turned-Mitzvah can have. It was written by a young woman in grade nine, age fourteen:

Dear Mr. Siegel,

I am writing to you to tell you about the exciting afternoon I spent today. I went to the Roselawn Rehabilitation Center for the Aged with two friends of mine, Shari Krauss and Michael Levinger.

With your five dollars and fifteen dollars of our own money, we bought twenty dollars worth of carnations (60 flowers).

At the home for the aged we wished each resident a Shabbat-Shalom.

I found it an experience I will never forget. For instance, I gave one gentleman a flower and his son told me it was the first time he smiled today. I also met a man named Max Lowenfeld, who I really got to know. When it was time to leave, I really didn't feel like going, I found our conversation so very interesting.

The visit to the nursing home has been one of the greatest experiences of my life.

Seeing people in wheelchairs in the hallways with a flower in their hands and a smile on their faces gave me a certain satisfaction I never had before.

I was asked by the nurse in charge before leaving the home, if I could volunteer my time when there was no school to work several hours at a day-care center for the elderly. I set some dates on my calendar to do so.

I want to thank you for coming last Sunday morning to talk to my Sunday School class and challenging me to participate in this new experience.

Thank you,
Sincerely,
Karyn Mendelsohn

At first reading, the cynics will say, "That's nice . . ." — meaning it is sentimental, all-too-simple, perhaps a little too much oozing with emotion. I do not agree. I believe this ninth-grader has taught us a number of great principles in Tzedakah work, which I would now like to review:

1. Karyn took two friends along, thereby creating a Tzedakah-Chevra. I have often mentioned in the classroom that such experiences might be too emotionally charged for someone to do alone, so I recommend that they go with a friend. (I do not recall whether or not I made such a recommendation in this particular class.) Karyn took two friends, and added a new element to her old friendships — a sharing of a new understanding of human interconnections.

2. The three of them added $15.00 of their own money. Karyn realized that doing Mitzvot exclusively with the money of other people is not sufficient. Every Jew must participate with his or her own resources. This is an important standard for all professionals in the field of Tzedakah work. Federations stress this: unless you, yourself, have given to a reasonable extent, you cannot expect others to do so — even if your job entails disbursing hundreds of thousands of dollars of communal funds.

3. Karyn calls one old man a "gentleman." That one word alone makes the entire experience worthwhile. Perhaps she will never be tempted to use the ugly Yiddish term "Alta Kocker" for the Elders of our

People. It may be she will spend her entire life never once thinking, "rotten, bothersome, pain-in-the-neck old coot."

4. For the cynics, the worst is this: Karyn is moved by the old man's smile, as is the son. "Superficial tripe," the armchair grouches will say. "Quite to the contrary," Karyn would reply. "If a smile and warmth can be negotiated with such little effort and money, let us, then, proceed at full tilt to bring more smiles and warmth. Let us seek out more and more varied ways to bring about the same in others." That is what I believe she would answer.

5. Karyn misses Max Lowenfeld. I would suspect she called him sometime afterwards, or went back to visit again. Yearning is a sublime human quality, and it is hoped that teachers and parents everywhere will pass on to their students and children constructive, healthy, Jewish yearnings of this nature.

6. Finally, Karyn committed herself to additional hours at a day-care center for the elderly. She did it on her own — I had not suggested this in class. Frankly, I am unwilling to make greater demands on people. There are always extenuating circumstances I can never understand — each person lives his or her own life so differently from how I do. I can never hope to grasp their constraints, their fears and dreams, the tenor of their souls. Nevertheless, I am convinced that, once people are opened to these experiences, they will develop their own individual style, carrying the Mitzvah far beyond any preconceived bounds. That is, I believe, the essence of the creativity of people.

One fourteen-year-old has now become my teacher. I speak of this letter frequently in my lectures on Tzedakah. I have asked her permission to use it, and she has graciously consented. She has taught me new sensitivities, and I am grateful.

IN CLOSING, A STORY

This summer's $12,720 came from contributions in many sizes: a check for $700 Canadian (which was then worth $604 American), two $500 checks, and a few at or around $200. There must have been ten or so for $100, with many others at $18, 25, and 50. Reviewing the books, I also note $1, 2, 3, and 3.17. It's that $3.17 that keeps me thinking. With $100 here and $200 there, I kept reminding myself not to forget the $3.17 from a pushka from some child in the Midwest. I didn't want it to be swallowed up by the Big Money. I discovered that, in some ways, it was worth the same as a $500 check — as long as I preserved my sense that it was an individual's Tzedakah money. I felt obligated to stretch every penny, nickel, and dime, making the Small Money do things only Small Money can do. No hospitals will be built with $3.17, no Jewish day schools — that is for foundations and Federations to manage. But the $3.17 buys more than a dozen flowers in Israel, short-stemmed roses (flowers are still inexpensive in Israel). A dozen Good Shabbas wishes, a dozen moments of closeness, and the greatest fulfillment of the meaning of Tzedakah.

With some change left over for the next Mitzvah.

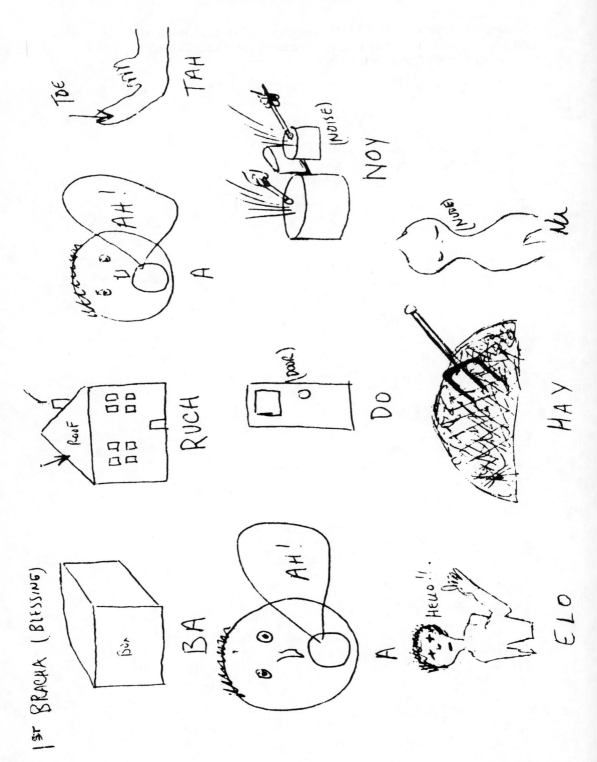

A chart one of my friends gave me:

A picture of a box. A roof.
Someone saying the word, "Ah." Picture of a toe.
Someone saying the word, "Ah." Picture of a door. Picture: Drums making noise.
Picture: someone saying hello. Picture: stack of hay. Picture: a nude figure.
From this chart Alan Teperow taught a retarded man who was unable to read how to recite the blessings for his bar mitzvah.
The pictures spell, "Baruch Atah Adonai Elohaynu. . . ."
Of course.

A teen-ager, a member of United Synagogue Youth I met at a USY convention, tells me the following story:

I am a swimming instructor, and I often work with the handicapped. I once taught a young woman who had a bad leg. She was seventeen, and it was the first time she had been in the water.
Within a short time she was swimming the whole length of the pool.
I could tell you other stories, if we had the time. . . .

The house that was a storeroom:

I know I will always bump into friends in Jerusalem. I never know which ones will be strolling towards me on Ben Yehuda Street, but I know there will always be someone.
One day it was a friend I knew from a USY convention. He is a rabbi now, and we see each other once or twice a year, in the States. But this was Jerusalem, and I was in the thick of distributing the Tzedakah money, so the opportunity presented itself for us to exchange some stories.
Moshe's story is brief. He explains, "My father's house is a furniture warehouse. Old people who have to vacate their homes or apartments because of extended illnesses leave their furniture at our house. When they recover and relocate, they pick up everything. My father has rooms and rooms of furniture. It's always been that way with him. I remember it long back into childhood."

I am with the USY'ers at Life Line for the Old. I encourage them to strike up conversations with the Elders of Jerusalem:

The morning tour is over, and we sit down in the courtyard to review our experiences. I ask them what they talked about with the Elders. They relate many interesting tales, but some of the teenagers are troubled. When they ask how many children and grandchildren the Elders have, they usually don't give an answer.
The reasons are relatively simple: In some cases they have so many they do not have an exact count — children, grandchildren, great-grand-children. Others do not wish to invite the Evil Eye by specifying the number.

But I want to hear their ideas. So I ask the kids, "Why don't you think they answer?"

They give the American and Canadian answer, "Maybe they are embarrassed. They do not want to be reminded how infrequently they come to visit."

Shoes:

The woman is old. She was old two years ago, too, but she has aged markedly in the past couple of years. Circulatory problems and other infirmities are taking their toll.

Her husband died two years ago, but now she takes out his shoes — good shoes — and gives them to me to give away. I take them to the Rabbanit Kapach who will find someone else to wear them, someone who will not know the passion behind the gift.

From Myriam Mendilow, founder and director of Life Line for the Old:

I saw a woman sitting in filth, her head surrounded by buzzing flies. I came over and started to shoo them away. The woman said, "My child, why are you doing that? It is the only pleasure I have."

CREATIVE, AGGRESSIVE GIVING

Two particularly crucial problems in Tzedakah-giving are the following:

1. Many Jews have not yet acquired the sense of joy and privilege that comes from giving.

2. Even among those who have discovered the delight and invigoration which results from giving, a certain percentage still performs the Mitzvah in a mechanical fashion. They may do it openheartedly and openhandedly, apportioning a generous sum from their incomes to Tzedakah, but all too often it is a once-a-year practice. There is no question that they have performed the Mitzvah, but some element is still lacking, some touch which can complement the act and add a unique aura to the deed.

To confront these two problems it is essential to examine some traditional Jewish texts. The most critical one is in the Shulchan Aruch, the basic Code of Jewish Law:

> The amount that should be given — if the person can afford it — is whatever amount is needed for the poor. But if the person cannot afford that much, he should give up to a fifth of what he has. That is the Mitzvah to the highest degree. A tenth is considered average, and less is considered ungenerous. (*Yoreh De'ah 249:1*)

The opening statement is important in that, for example, someone living in New York knows that he or she cannot provide for all the poor. Surveys estimate that there are between 200,000 and 300,000 poor Jews in the New York area alone. The Shulchan Aruch therefore continues that, while we cannot provide for everyone, we must not conclude that there is nothing we can do. The Law Code, based on thousands of years of Jewish history, sets a reasonable range for "doing our part."

Most Jews are aware of "The 10% Principle." Sometimes they have heard about it from other religions (the Mormons for example), and at other times, somewhere along the way in their Jewish educational experience. Here, however, it is clear that Jewish tradition does not merely advocate "10%." Rather, each Jew is offered a wider range of possibilities, from 10% up to 20%. Opinions among the commentaries differ as to whether this percentage is to be taken before or after taxes, but depending on which interpretation one chooses to follow, there are even more variations. Mathematically speaking:

A $30,000 income, before taxes = $3,000-$6,000 for Tzedakah.
A $30,000 income, $5,000 taxes = $2,500-$5,000 for Tzedakah.

This is the first opportunity for a Tzedakah-conscious Jew to use his or her own judgment. Nothing in the world of Tzedakah should be mechanical, and the decision of "which percentage" and "with or without taxes" gives each individual considerable leeway for his or her own choosing.

Furthermore, let us reconsider the opening statement in the Shulchan Aruch: besides the needs of the local poor . . . the support needed for the handicapped, for Jewish education, for Israel, for Jews in other lands is so great, the decision as to "just how much" becomes that much more important. The tradition incontrovertibly states that *something* can and must be done, but we are not required to deplete all our resources for that purpose. Self-induced poverty is not a Jewish concept, nor is it an ideal, and it would only serve to exacerbate the problem by putting one more person on the Jewish welfare rolls. That is why a range of giving is set; it is a reasonable, human compromise, preserving the personal integrity of the giver while still providing for those in need.

More Tzedakah-creativity is allowed by a different law:

> How much should one give to the poor? Whatever it is he needs. How is this to be understood? If he is hungry, he should be fed. If he needs clothes, he should be provided with clothes. If he has no household furniture or utensils, furniture and utensils should be provided . . . One who is used to warm bread should receive warm bread, cold bread, should receive cold. If one needs to be spoonfed, he must be spoonfed. (*Yoreh De'ah 250:1*)

What is most powerful in this passage is the statement about spoonfeeding. We, as concerned Tzedakah-givers (within our specific range of giving), have an infinite variety of possibilities where our money may be put to use. This selection from the Shulchan Aruch only reminds us that we must seek out these places, these opportunities. It is our money that we have acquired, through hard work, or through gifts, or interest in the bank, or wise investments, and now it is our privilege to decide exactly how to distribute a certain percentage for the benefit of others . . . according to the needs of the community and *according to our own preferences*. If, for whatever reason, we emphatically believe that every Jew should own two sets of clothing — one for weekdays and another for Shabbat and holidays — then we should search for projects that concern themselves with the proper distribution and redistribution of clothes. If we believe every Jew should visit Israel at some stage of life, then we can choose to provide scholarship funds for trips for teenagers or elders or the Jewish deaf. And, if the aftermath of disease so troubles us that we cannot tolerate the thought of anyone being reduced to spoonfeeding in the prime of life — then we must divert our Tzedakah funds to people and agencies that make certain such rehabilitation and individual care are given to all who need it. The possibilities are vast, challenging.

Once again, Jewish tradition addresses the issue:

> Happy is the one who uses one's *Sechel*, one's God-given powers of judgment, in performing the Mitzvah of Tzedakah. (*Leviticus Rabba 34*)

Maimonides states it in a more striking manner, explaining that

> giving a thousand gold coins at one time to one worthy person, and as a result, none to another, does not allow the giver the full opportunity to acquire the quality of generosity — not as full an opportunity as one who gives one thousand gold coins on a thousand different occasions . . . The repetition of the generous acts a thousand times secures for that individual the personal characteristic of generosity. (*Commentary to Mishna, Avot 3:15*)

All of us, from our first days in school, have experienced repetition as an educational method. Even before school, the "good health habits" of brushing our teeth regularly, eating regularly, learning the basics of taking care of ourselves — all this applies also to taking care of others. The Talmud states:

> One who reviews a particular text a hundred times is not as proficient as one who reviews it a hundred and one times. (*Chagiga 9b*)

Certainly in living, which is essentially a writing out of our own text — a biography, certainly applying this principle of Torah-study makes sense. As it operates successfully in the classroom, so, too, it is a meaningful axiom for the actions that constitute our way-of-living.

By no means do I wish to imply that a person who writes a check once a year, to one place, for a full percentage of his Tzedakah-money, is not fulfilling the Mitzvah of Tzedakah. Not at all. Still, extending ourselves to examine more possibilities, weighing and considering where our money will be best and most efficiently used — and then distributing it accordingly — this process offers additional benefits to the donor. Among other things, this procedure will serve as a constant reminder of the grandeur of the power of money, not as an egocentric tool for Self-building and Self-aggrandizement, but rather as a vehicle for extensive and diverse Mitzvot. It can buy a sewing machine to help rebuild the life of a psychologically broken patient in a mental ward. It can buy gasoline for a minibus for a field trip for the elderly to some place where the air is fresh, the countryside exploding with fragrances and the colors of flowers. It can buy a teacher whose hands will guide the damaged hands of a surgeon back to some meaningful form of creativity — and away from despair, the ultimate enemy in the very human life of human beings.

Yes, all giving of money is Tzedakah — whether it be once a year or every day, small amounts or mammoth sums, donated willingly or only after being pushed. Maimonides considers all of these variations in his famous Eight Degrees of Tzedakah. Many are acquainted with the highest degree: providing someone with an opportunity to become self-supporting. And the second one: giving when neither the recipient nor the donor knows the other one. But the lower ones, the less-studied rungs on this ladder — these are the ones that need to be examined more carefully:

6. When the donor puts the money into the hands of the poor after being solicited.
7. When the donor gives less than he should, but does so cheerfully.
8. When the donor gives grudgingly.

(Mishna Torah, Hilchot Matnot Ani'im, 10:12 – 14)

I am not recommending that Jews aim for the lowest levels of Maimonides' scheme, but it is important to note a number of principles that can be derived from these lesser degrees:

1. Giving less is, without a shadow of a doubt, still considered Tzedakah.

A. Conversely, not giving at all, but "thinking Tzedakah," is not Tzedakah. *Tzedakah can only be done by doing.* Pledges are only pledges, and if they remain unfulfilled, they do not qualify as an act of giving. In some Tzedakah organizations the overwhelming percentages of pledges are paid, though I imagine others manage to collect only 60-75% of what has been promised. The solicitors hear of sudden fits of forgetfulness or long tales of interim circumstances which prevent the paying off of the pledge. It is frustrating, dismaying. In the real world, "thinking Tzedakah" — whether in unfulfilled promises of gifts or just "generous thoughts" — "thinking Tzedakah" is as useless as telling someone after a long stay in the hospital, "I am sorry I did not get down to visit you, but I thought about you while you were recuperating."

B. Many Mitzvot call for a certain attitude: Shabbat and holidays should be celebrated with joy, a Shiva must preserve a somber mood — jokes and idle chatter being out of place — the Days of Awe must, naturally enough, be approached with a feeling of awe. With Tzedakah, though, the attitude, while important, is secondary. The Shulchan Aruch recommends that the act of Tzedakah be done "pleasantly, joyously, with a good heart, showing sympathy for the poor, sharing in his sense of pain and sorrow" (Yoreh De'ah 249:3), and "without arrogance" (249:13), still, the Mitzvah itself has been performed, no matter what the mood of the donor. He may be angry, disgruntled with the pushiness of the solicitor, or angry at an invasion of privacy (giving only to get the solicitor to leave him alone), but, no matter what the emotions involved, the Tzedakah that is given is true Tzedakah. The money will still be used to bring about a vibrant society of individuals filled with trust, faith, and hope. That is the meaning of Maimonides' sixth and eighth degrees.

2. In one's own personal giving, both small and large amounts need to be carefully examined.

A. Small amounts: Whether the amount is modest because it comes from children with limited available funds, or from others on frozen budgets in inflationary times, or whether it is a less-than-10% donation — in all cases the money can be stretched to the greatest effectiveness . . . or swallowed up by unwise decisions. Some people prefer spending $10.00 where $10.00 will actually buy Shabbat food for an elderly poor couple for some holiday meal. Others prefer the unifying feeling of being part of a million-dollar project, sharing the communality that "many small parts make a massive whole," a sum that can move mountains or rebuild neighborhoods. Some earmark $25.00 or $36.00 of a $500,000 campaign for some specific item, so there is an immediate feeling of having provided something real and specific. Being responsible for the purchase of six pairs of crutches in a four-hundred bed hospital complex in Israel carries a certain definite weight with the donor. All three possibilities are viable options in Tzedakah giving. All, however, demand thoughtful consideration of the value of the $10.00 or $25.00 or $36.00, whatever the relatively small amount might be. *Only let the donor be certain that the money will be well and carefully used.*

B. Large amounts: There is no escaping one fact — thousands and hundreds of thousands and millions of dollars can do things ones and fives and tens simply cannot do. For all the extremely well-considered contributions of small amounts for individual needs, there is still a pressing demand to carry out Tzedakah work on a grand scale. It is absolutely impossible to provide for a hundred handicapped Jews in a city the size of Boston or Philadelphia or Los Angeles without extensive funding. Kosher meals-on-wheels programs in Toronto and Miami (even with government assistance) cannot be managed without large sums, and even greater infusions of dollars are needed to renew and revive poverty-stricken neighborhoods in Israel.

And still, the $10,000 donor, the $100,000 donor, the $1,000,000 -a-year donor is required to allocate his own Tzedakah money with the utmost care, no less than the ones who have only a small handful of dollars to contribute. Periodically the newspapers expose The Great Frauds — professional fundraisers (shown on "60 Minutes") raising over $2,000,000 for the Southern Christian Leadership Conference, and turning over a mere $100,000. After taking out their expense money and "fees." Or a police association in New York which hired fundraisers who took 60-90% of the money raised. Those are the blatant frauds. The subtle wastes are just as significant: we must be concerned with Tzedakah buying-power no less than we worry about the shrinking buying-power of the dollar for rent or mortgages or gasoline or food.

The big givers (and the relatively small ones) are entitled to see a budget of the organization to which they are giving. They are entitled to know what percentage of each dollar goes for expenses, secretarial work, printing and mailing, and the salaries of board members. Every donor should inquire, and any organization that refuses to show a reasonable outline of its budget need not — must not — receive our money. Plain and simple. Whether it be the Girl Scouts, or Mt. Sinai Hospital, the American Cancer Society, Jerry Lewis's Telethon — whatever charity it may be. Whoever demonstrates a reasonable overhead and wise usage of the funds may then benefit from our hard-earned dollars. Those who do not — will have to look elsewhere. Again, plain and simple.

TWO METHODS FOR FACILITATING THE PROCESS OF GIVING

1. Whenever a paycheck (or any source of income) is taken in, let the individual separate his percentage, 10-20%, before or after taxes, and let that individual put it in a separate checking account.

2. Have different colored checks printed — one for the Tzedakah work, and one for the day-to-day expenses. Some might find it useful to have two different methods of signing the checks: The regular checking

account might be "Mike Hauptmann' or "Shirley Kreiner" while the Tzedakah account might be "Michael T. Hauptmann' and "Shulamit Kreiner." The distinctive contrast between the two accounts will serve as a reminder that the money in each is for two very different purposes.

These are only the first steps in understanding the nature and power of money. Other methods may be developed according to each person's individual style, but by a *regular and recurring* awareness of the power and possibilities of Tzedakah, each Jew can become more aggressive and creative in his or her own giving. It is a great leap from rare or occasional or haphazard giving to frequent, judicious Tzedakah work. Without question, once the individual is exposed to the world of traditional Tzedakah, and once that person has been offered an intelligent choice of recipients — the matter of expanding personal giving will take care of itself.

I personally disagree with those who believe that people are by nature acquisitive or cheap. I believe that pleasant, gentle, joyous exposure to Tzedakah will produce breathtaking results — breathtaking for the community, which will have that much more money for the benefit of all its members, and breathtaking to the individual when he or she realizes just how much power money has to create and maintain hope, faith, and inspiration.

The number of Righteous Ones in the world seems to have been fixed by tradition at thirty-six. I would not expect a hundred or a thousand "Hidden Ones" to reveal themselves as Tzaddikim, Righteous Jews — surrendering their businesses, medical practices, university professorships for the purpose of devoting themselves exclusively to others. Many families are torn and wrecked by such devotion, many wives and husbands and children suffer greatly from this turning-outward. No, that is for the Select Few who can balance their personalities and personal lives with the incredible accumulation of pain, suffering, and misfortune the world generates every day. I would rather see the percentages of non-givers disappear, and the lower percentages of personal income giving rise to the traditional 10-20%. I sincerely believe that the process of exposure and education can bring this about.

A CLOSING COMMENT

In the two weeks previous to the writing of this article two events of great significance took place:

1. I was informed of a will that included a provision of $10,000 for Life Line for the Old in Jerusalem.

2. I was asked to forward a check for $8.00 to the same place. I have no doubts that (a) Life Line will use the $8.00 as wisely as they will use the $10,000, and (b) both the family of the deceased and the anonymous $8.00 contributor have performed the Mitzvah *par excellence* — with judicious consideration of the many opportunities to give, they chose wisely, each party valuing its own specific contribution no less than the

other, each wishing to do the Mitzvah in a unique way, openhandedly and openheartedly.

If I were a Rabbi, I would add, "So may it be for all Jews, yea, speedily, in our own days. Amen."

19 OCCASIONS FOR GIVING TZEDAKAH

*(In addition To, Or As One Aspect Of,
A Regular Pattern Of Giving)*

19 OCCASIONS FOR GIVING TZEDAKAH:

A. *Concerning other people*

1. In honor of a birth, brit milah, baby naming, bar mitzvah, bat mitzvah, wedding, anniversary, or other joyous occasion.
2. In honor of a patriarch or matriarch who has reached a significant birthday: 60th, 70th, 75th, 80th, 90th, 100th, up to 120th.
3. To extend wishes for the recovery of someone who is sick.
4. In memory of someone who has passed away, and on Yahrtzeits.
5. In honor of a conversion of a friend.
6. In honor of friends hanging the mezuzah on the doorpost of a new home.
7. On Yom Ha'Atzma'ut (Israel Independence Day), to Israel.
8. On Yom HaShoah VeHagevurah (Holocaust and Heroism Remembrance Day), to some Holocaust research institute, or to Simon Wiesenthal (write: Dokumentationszentrum, 1010 Wien I, Salztorgasse 6, Austria).
9. In honor of major events in a person's life: graduation, new job, etc.

B. *Occasions in your own life*

1. Bar mitzvah, bat mitzvah, wedding, anniversary, or other joyous occasion.
2. Reaching a significant birthday (till the 120th).
3. Upon recovery from an illness.
4. Upon hanging the mezuzah on the doorpost of your own new house.
5. In honor of your own graduation, new job, etc.
6. Before candlelighting on Friday evening.
7. Before Jewish holidays, specifically to people and agencies providing food for the poor on those holidays.
8. At synagogue before a weekday minyan.
9. Upon arriving safely in Israel.
10. Upon receiving a foundation grant or inheriting a sum of money or receiving any money as a gift.

THE THREE-POINT TZEDAKAH PLAN

(With Two Addenda)

I write from obsession.

My latest obsession is the gap we have created in educating our children about Tzedakah. To be truthful, it is not a gap, but rather an abyss, a hole no less catastrophic to our people than a hole in a vital artery over which our blood tries desperately to leap, but fails, gushing instead into some cavity of the body, causing hemorrhage and, sometimes, death.

It is at one and the same time fashionable and old-fashioned to pour out one's heart over the disintegration of the American Jewish family, but, as I said, I write from obsession, not from fashionableness or old-fashionedness.

Two facts are absolutely clear:

1. A child's education in Tzedakah begins with Keren Ami nickels and dimes in Hebrew School — and ends there (except in the most remote cases). Conservative and Reform Jews may note that this is generally less true in Orthodox homes.

2. The home-centered Mitzvah of Tzedakah has been cast aside, disturbingly so. No less dramatically than the family Shabbat meal and the blessing of children by parents. Tzedakah is neither discussed by parents with their children, nor inculcated by role-modelling, persuasion, verbal encouragement — nor by force.

The second point is the main issue, and I believe it essentially revolves around the issue of money: the power of money, the nature of money, the taboo attached to discussing money in certain contexts. As I visit various communities, I ask again and again, "Why do you think Tzedakah is not discussed at home?" Answers are diverse, but the responses are usually burdened with the awareness that, indeed, it is rarely if ever a topic of conversation. Occasionally there is hostility on the part of the adults — I am overstepping my bounds, suggesting that they may be falling short of their parental responsibilities. I joke with the audience and tell them that it is wise for me to leave town the next day.

A fact: large numbers of children believe they can estimate how much money their parents earn, within a thousand or two thousand dollars. But only about half that number venture to respond to the question, "How many of you can guess how much your parents give to Tzedakah?"

I have pondered this point many times. And I have asked, "Can so many parents really be so cheap as to leave their children with the feeling that they really do not give much to Tzedakah?" I do not believe this is so — not at all. I simply believe that parents — younger ones in particular (the ones we most often find with children in Hebrew School) — that parents are only beginning to get the "feel" of money. Their incomes begin to stabilize, they worry about inflationary spirals, they are caught in the concepts of buying power, budgets, saving and investing wisely — all the things money can do. And Tzedakah falls by the wayside.

I am puzzled by another phenomenon of the times — the swing to old-fashioned values of parents "putting their foot down" on certain issues. It is no secret that parents "ground" teenagers for family misdemeanors or shortcomings in school achievements. They may withhold use of the car, or a night out at a movie, should this punishment be warranted. They *do* say, "No!" — and very emphatically so. Now, this is the puzzle: why can't they also be parentally emphatic and say, "Here is your allowance. You must give 10-20% away to Tzedakah, then you may use the rest for yourself." What exactly is this God-forsaken holiness of money that prevents our children from learning that once money comes into our own possession it is subject to the rules of Tzedakah? Where have we picked up the pagan value that "mine" means absolutely and incontrovertibly mine to use as I see fit, for myself?

I openly admit that generosity moves me. I receive letters three and four times a week with truly human stories of caring, consideration, giving. But the selfishness of a few dollars here and there among teenagers and younger children overwhelms me even more. I am moved in another direction, to depression, to a terrified sense that the next generation will bring about the closing down of so much that we value in Jewish life: a vibrant, creative life in Israel, Jewish education, free-loan societies, agencies for the re-settlement of Jews from oppressed lands.

The Federations are well aware of the abyss. They have developed young leadership groups because they have seen thousands of people in their twenties and thirties without any tradition of regular, thoughtful giving. They re-educate them, open them up to the joy and privilege of Tzedakah, and the professionals deserve a great deal of credit. But then I hear that 81% of the Jews in Queens, N.Y., do not give, and I realize that the dent made in this iron curtain of un-generosity is very small indeed.

I, therefore, (nonstatistician that I am, nonsociologist that I am, nonprofessional Jew that I am), I therefore make a modest, simple three-point proposal to remedy this situation:

1. Every home must install an unmarked Pushka — unmarked, that is, except for the word "Tzedakah." I do not mean they should remove the JNF blue boxes or the tins for other Tzedakot. But, rather, besides these there must be a blank pushka, and when it is full, the family as a unit must sit down and decide to which places the money must be sent.

That is easy enough. Now for the tougher ones:

2. Every bar and bat mitzvah child should be encouraged to give away 10-20% of his or her money acquired from The Great Event — to give it to any Tzedakah he or she chooses. Only let the child not be sloppy. Let it not be a snap decision to the American Cancer Society or Jerry Lewis's Telethon, just because these are the ones most publicized. Hopefully because of point #1 (The Plain Pushka), the child will be aware of a variety of Tzedakot, local and international. His or her decision-making process will be made that much easier thereby.

That one is a little harder.

Now for the one which will create the greatest antagonism:

3. Let every parent who is going to have a bar or bat mitzvah for his or her child go to the caterer for a quote. Let us say it is $2,500.00. Let

them then deduct 10-20% from that figure, ask the caterer to have a party for the lowered price — perhaps with less hors d'oeuvres and chicken instead of prime rib — and let the parents give the difference to Tzedakah.

Two addenda:

A. The parents need not give their Tzedakah money to the same Tzedakot as the child. All that is important is that the child is brought into Jewish adulthood through a shared sense of sharing — of Tzedakah.

B. I do not begrudge the wealthy their lavish bashes. I imagine that if I made $150,000 a year, I, too, would want to have a tasteful but quite splendid affair to honor my child. If they want to spend $10,000 on the party, that is fine, only let them deduct $1000-2000, and give that to Tzedakah. Let the wealthy pass on that sense of generosity to their children, and let the strugglers and dollar-conscious do the same. It will provide yet another feeling of communality for all Jews.

Having done these three things, I believe we will have reinstilled in our children (and in ourselves) a sense of the continuity of this Mitzvah throughout the years of a Jew's life. After all, Bar and Bat Mitzvah literally mean "being obligated to perform Mitzvot." All too often this has meant being counted for a minyan, and little if anything more. It appears to me that we are cutting our own throats if this is where we allow the issue to remain.

Let us do a small bit of Tzedakah-mathematics:

Take a large synagogue — Beth Shalom in Kansas City, Ahavath Achim in Atlanta, or Holy Blossom Temple in Toronto.

Assume 40 B'nai and B'not Mitzvah a year.

Assume an average of $1,000 in gifts for the child (stocks, bonds, cash).

That makes $100-200 Tzedakah × 40 = $4,000-8,000 . . . for the children.

Now, for the parents:

Assume $2,500 for party expenses.

That's $250-500 × 40 = $10,000-20,000

The total range for shuls such as these is, therefore, $14,000-28,000 in Tzedakah money. How many scholarships to Israel does this mean? How much better salaries for Day School and Hebrew School teachers? How many more children assured a dramatically life-changing summer at Ramah, Olin-Sang-Ruby, CEJWIN?

And multiply that, adjusting for size, by hundreds of synagogues.

And add to that similar customs for weddings, anniversaries, any Simcha through which more Tzedakah money may be accumulated.

The Talmud reminds us that each Jew is required to write a Sefer Torah during his or her lifetime. Some commentators state that by living our lives full-Jewishly, we are writing these scrolls. Proverbs calls the Torah a Tree of Life, and the Zohar uses the same image for Tzedakah. The metaphors merge well: Torah, Tzedakah, Life. As parents have given their children their very physical lives through the mystery of love, so, too, they should pass on to them a life that makes breath and heartbeats and flexing muscles a sublime journey of glorious and sweeping significance.

LIMITED-INCOME TZEDAKAH GIVING OR WHAT IS MINE IS MINE VS. WHAT IS MINE IS 10-20% YOURS

BY WAY OF INTRODUCTION: A LAMENTABLE CASE-IN-POINT

An article from the front page of the Washington Post, February 17, 1981, reports some pathetic facts concerning student loans:

1. For the second time in two years, the Justice Department in southern Ohio is suing defaulters on student loans. In this instance, the suit seeks to recover $663,838.46 in defaulted loans.

2. U.S. Attorney James C. Cissell states that, in that particular district, the amount in default in one loan program amounts to $23,600,000. This represents 76% more than the total money taken in all bank robberies in the United States in 1978. *That* figure was only $13,400,000.

3. Burglars averaged only $526 per burglary, while the average loan in default amounted to $947.

4. The grand total of loans in default nationwide — for this one program — is $732,000,000, which Cissell states is "more than four times greater than all robberies in the nation in 1978."

Cissell indicated that it would be erroneous to assume that those in default are destitute. Quite to the contrary. Investigations carried out by attorneys and paralegals amassed data showing that among those not willing to repay are people working in sheriff's departments, police departments, fire departments, probation departments, employees of newspaper and telephone and construction companies, and broadcasting companies, and utility companies, and on and on (among many other reasonable-salaried occupations).

It would make a wonderful sermon, "Responsibility, Self-Dignity, and New, Creative Forms of Highway Robbery." But I leave the sermons to the clergy. Rather than rant, I would prefer to present some traditional Jewish material relevant to the topic of "Just Exactly Whose Money Is Whose."

BACKGROUND MATERIAL: HOW I MEET CONTRIBUTORS LIVING ON LIMITED BUDGETS

During one winter and five summers in Israel, I have distributed my friends' money to various Tzedakah projects. Over the six years, more than $33,000 has been disbursed, an accumulation of funds consisting of contributions from many sources, and of many sizes. A great percentage of the contributions have been in amounts of five, ten, fifteen, eighteen, and twenty-five dollars, and I find many coming from students in high school, college, and graduate school, and people in their twenties and thirties who are struggling on what I would call sufficient, but hardly comfortable, incomes. Even years after graduation, many are still in the process of repaying a variety of student loans — loans which allowed them to obtain their bachelor degrees, their MSW's, MBA's, and PhD's. In some cases (still in debt), they begin social work positions or teaching jobs at $12,000 a year, or in better locales, at $15,000. There are even a few contributors who are elderly, living on limited, fixed incomes.

I have managed to protect myself against a common Tzedakah- collecting malaise: over the six years, I have never said to myself (with two or three minor slips of the mind, "He/she could have afforded to give more." Instead, I assume a number of other possibilities — they are burdened with other responsibilities, or they give extensively to other Tzedakot (UJA, local agencies, favorite particular projects), or they are being badly squeezed by the economy, or they are just beginning to feel the strength and splendor of giving their money away. Usually the opposite effect strikes me: people whom I assume are pushed down hard by financial matters send me $100, sometimes more. I am surprised, and deeply moved by their generosity — not just the fact of their giving, but the impressive amount. This is by no means an infrequent occurrence.

In the field of Tzedakah, I am known for my quiet approach. I neither wheedle nor strong-arm my friends, though I do not deny the importance of that method of Tzedakah-collection in certain circumstances. Jewish tradition allows for it, the ancient texts speak of it — forcing community members to give — and historical records clearly show that coercion has been used in the past. There is no question that, with the overwhelming needs of the Jewish people, force (pressure, arm-twisting, duress) is a viable approach in specific situations. I, myself, however, am just not that kind of person, so I leave it to others who can do it well, in a Menschlich, dignified manner. The studies substantiate this quandary — employing an exclusively soft-spoken method simply would not bring in the vast amounts of money our communities around the world desperately need.

There is one exception to my practice: I have been known to pressure a few friends who say they cannot afford to give anything at all. I push them to give me a dollar or two or five — something — so that they will be in my mind as I walk the streets of Jerusalem. I will think of them and remember that their dollar, or two, or five must be very carefully distributed. I do not want their individual dollars lost in the mass of hundreds and thousands.

As a matter of record, I am always aware of my friends as I go about writing the checks in Israel. I think of them and the raw, elemental generosity that harks back to the beginnings of our life as a People: to Abraham's hospitality, to the stories of Moses tending Jethro's sheep with the utmost care, to the common people contributing to the building of the Tabernacle in the Wilderness. Most deeply, I am struck by the simplicity of one statement in Deuteronomy:

> If there is a needy person among you, one of your kinsmen in any of your settlements in the land that the Lord your God is giving you, do not harden your heart and shut your hand against your needy kinsman. Rather, you must open your hand . . . (*15:7-8*)

In light of the Washington Post article, it is ironic that this passage specifically refers to extending loans, though the later tradition applies it to extended forms of Tzedakah. Two verses later, the Torah states, "Give to him readily and have no regrets when you do so."

So here is the blatant tension, the pain: on the one hand, anger and frustration at the gross irresponsibility of loan-defaulters (the fact that they are college graduates only intensifies the flames of despair); and on the other hand, friends, many wrestling with heating bills, mortgages, and tuition payments for Jewish day schools for their children — yet readily giving, with no regrets. Tight-fistedness and egocentricity vs. open-handedness and altruism.

SOME CRITICAL JEWISH TEXTS

Jewish tradition addresses itself to this agonizing problem. The Shulchan Aruch — the most well-known of the Jewish law codes — states:

> Even a poor person who is supported by Tzedakah must give
> from what he receives. (*Yoreh De'ah 248:1*)

I have taught this text again and again, and asked study groups of every kind of secular experience and Jewish background — young, old, wealthy, financially unstable, European immigrant and American born, friendly and hostile — I asked them what are the reasons for this law. Thus far I have received a number of substantial answers:

1. It always reminds the poor person that there is someone more destitute, someone more in need than they themselves, no matter how miserable their present condition. This is the most common answer, and usually the first one given by groups of teenagers.

2. The law implies that Tzedakah money is needed *now*. A poor person who waits may have prevented someone else from having a decent Passover, wine for Shabbat, clothes for the drizzly winters in Jerusalem, a bus ticket to get back and forth to work. Next week, next year, or whenever money comes in in greater quantities will do no good for the immediate needs. There is always this element of immediacy. Waiting invites unknown and unpredictable disasters, which we see particularly clearly now with the situation with Ethiopian Jews. Five dollars *now* may be more significant than one hundrd dollars in a year, two years, some hazy *whenever*, more valuable than a thousand dollars. We are writing history through the work of Tzedakah, and the flow of that history changes by our acute sense of the present.

This is an exquisite answer, loaded with a sharp insight into the meaning of the continuity of our lives, and the fullest meaning of Tzedakah.

3. Economic struggle sucks out a person's sense of *Kedusha*, the basic holiness of life. If the day is overtaxed with worry over where the next dollar will come from, and the burdens of bill-paying and credit, then how can we expect people to bring to mind the grandeur and glory, the gift — perhaps the loan — of being alive? Grandeur? Glory? Gift, loan?

How often does a person think in those terms at all? But the simple act of giving provides opportunities for transcendent experiences, a soaring into higher possibilities of meaning. It is perhaps our best reminder, a roadside marker showing us that we may become fully human again, Menschlich, not just struggling flesh, straining to maintain our basic needs for food, clothing, and shelter. Menschlich by giving.

4. Tzedakah is a privilege. Take a room with twenty-five people and say, "I need Tzedakah money from all of you. Except for you. Ms. Plonit. I know you are too poor to give." When we do that, we strip that individual of her dignity, embarrass her, take away her right to rise above an ego-centered Self, and to give. *Kavod* — dignity, privilege, self-respect — something a poor person is entitled to no less than anyone else. Perhaps even more so.

And yet, despite the animated responses to this centuries-old Jewish principle, few make the connection between the poor person and themselves. The underlying values do not seem to them to be transferable. Perhaps it is because few of them have ever met a poor person. To them, discussing the guts of poverty is like telling stories of "Once upon a time there was a prince . . ." They have met neither princes nor poor people. I write this without malice, and without phony self-righteousness. It is a purely analytical summary. The people find the topic interesting, but not immediately applicable to themselves. Therefore, I sometimes mention another text:

> Two poor people (who are themselves required to give Tzedakah) may exchange their contributions with one another.
>
> *(Yoreh De'ah 251:12)*

And I add that some opinions state that the poor are required to give 10-20%, while other legal experts rule that even a minimum of one-third the value of an ancient shekel is acceptable — as long as the poor give.

But this only serves to make the topic more remote. Those studying with me think "poor people," and do not extrapolate extended principles for their own lives. Again, this is not stated with hostility. I do not believe that my audiences are "cheap" (though many professional fund-raisers have told me I am wrong — dead wrong to a great extent). They do not react belligerently, nor do they take offense at my subject matter. To the contrary, they find it very interesting, but, as I said, remote. The distance between them and the poor is very great — as it is for myself, having seen the Jewish poor only on rare occasions in the ghettoes of Tehran, the Lower East Side of New York, and the rundown neighborhoods of Jerusalem. I have never lived a Shabbas in a cold apartment, nor eaten a week's poverty-bread, nor felt my body shiver because my coat was not warm enough.

So I introduce one more passage (from the Talmud), which hopefully will bring us — the students and myself — back to a more exact contact with reality:

> If one sees that his resources are limited, he should make
> use of them for Tzedakah.

(*Gittin 7a*)

This is indeed the text that relates to many of them, and to myself. This
ties us together in the discussion, and to this they address themselves with
more realistic insight. Two essential answers are suggested, both well-
grounded and powerful:

1. Give now, because on that basis you will have integrated into your
life a pattern which will remain with you, particularly should you begin to
make a more substantial living. You will then enjoy distributing greater
sums, releasing the past frustrations that you could not do enough "back
then," when there was only a little to give away. It is also a powerful antidote to the often-thought but not-often-stated feeling, "I worked damned
hard for it. Now it's all mine; I'll do with it whatever I damn well please!"
Many people have spoken to me about this specific feeling they have
about the members of their community, whether it concerns the once-
struggling merchant who started out with the little corner store and now
has fifteen outlets in three states, or whether it concerns those who spent
eight, ten, twelve years in advanced educational ventures — and only
now are beginning to make $40,000, $75,000, or $150,000 a year. The
sense is, "They suffered long, lean years, and now they want all the
goodies for themselves."

If, however, (as the Talmud suggests) the pattern of giving is never
broken — through the lean years, through the struggle — then that feeling
of self-centeredness may well be averted.

2. Giving, even under the conditions of a restricted income, means
that you are able to teach yourself that you always have enough. My audiences speak of middle-aged people making $75,000 a year, with children
already finished with college and comfortably settled in their own fields
of endeavor, people unable to give more than a hundred dollars, if that.
They are bitter at those who say, "I just can't afford it right now." They
hear this from those making moderate sums, those who can comfortably
afford it (e.g., a young couple with combined incomes of $42,000), and,
most frequently, from the Rich and Super-Rich, nickel-and-diming their
way through life. "Just plain cheap!" That's what they say, or think, even
if they don't say it.

"There is never enough." — "There is always enough." Those are
the threads of tension, and the thrust of Jewish tradition supports the latter view.

Always there is room for giving.

AT THE END OF THE TZEDAKAH STUDY SESSION

The air has been cleared. Deep-felt anger has been vented. Most of
the electricity in the air has been released, though there is still an at-
mosphere of people slightly ill at ease. The topic has touched some very

raw nerves, and a few of the people feel they may have revealed too much of their inner selves in the presence of their peers.

I am sorry for that, as I am their guest, and I promise myself I will reconsider whether or not high-intensity teaching is an appropriate method of Jewish education, particularly for the one-night stands and weekend lectures. In doubt about my whole approach, I look forward to escape, to the plane, or train, or car ride home. It is a very touchy topic, shaky. Now and again I consider this: you do it not because you are courageous, but because you are a careless fool and don't know when to keep your mouth shut. But then I consciously cut these thoughts off, finding refuge in the poet's rainbows and flowers, unable to face myself. It is touchy, tricky for me, too.

Occasionally I conclude with one last text:

> The Holy One, blessed be He, will furnish all the necessary
> resources for anyone who runs to do Tzedakah.
>
> *(Bava Ratra 9b)*

It is a message of hope for those who are willing to commit their money to changing things, to raising people from depression, helplessness, and despair, to bringing them to a reinvigorated sense of dignity. It says that individual human beings can rearrange the life around themselves, making Life more than just livable. Tzedakah can make it glorious, grand, a precious gift to wonder at, to be prized.

SOME TIME AFTER THE TALK, IN ANOTHER PLACE FAR AWAY

Later, in a week, six months, a year, I am afraid to ask if the wallets and purses and glow of people's faces have changed, if incomes have dipped or soared, if warmth and kindness have filled some empty moments. I am afraid to ask in my own life, and much more so in theirs (it is their life, after all). So much is involved in this act of giving, the grasp of "mine-yours," our common desires, fears, our failures.

My self-confessions startle me. They push me to yearnings for rest, a return to the poet's lyricism or the writing of new fairy tales, something other than the ache of revelations . . . until my vision clears or some new blindness envelops me, protecting my heart, gently.

IDEALISTS AND HEROES:
FROM HELEN KELLER
TO RAOUL WALLENBERG

Helen Keller.

Helen Keller and Anne Sullivan.

Their story not only brought inspiration to my childhood, but the previous generation thrived on their accomplishments. My mother remembers how much the two of them meant to her back in her own grammar school days. Whenever you want to talk about heroes, ideals and idealists, people to admire, you may always find a sympathetic listener when you speak of Helen Keller and Anne Sullivan.

The same is true with Albert Schweitzer, though he is a more controversial figure. About the time my mother was born, Schweitzer left Europe for Africa. World War I was about to begin, and already a year before that, Schweitzer was setting up a hospital in the jungle. Even with all the criticisms and reassessments of his life and work, there is still a strong attachment to him, a man to consider over two long generations.

Then there was Tom Dooley, laboring to bring care for thousands of refugees in Indochina in the 1950's. He died young in 1961, but his books strike deeply into the human soul. An idealist, living the life of devotion to others, the many long hours actualizing his dreams.

I even recall vague memories of someone called "The Burma Surgeon," though neither my mother nor I could remember details. When I called the Library of Congress the same was true: some unclear recollections, but no details. He must have been like Schweitzer and Tom Dooley, picking out a small space of this world and working away at making it livable, a delightful event in which to breathe and move about.

I see now that it is important to review who our heroes were as we ourselves grew up and assumed our places in society. I see how worthwhile it is to have others talk about their ideals and where they originated. Who impressed us then? Now? Who — despite latter-day critical biographies — who moved us by their heroism, and how much of that stayed with us, at least in some small degree in our own lives?

I remember that when I was a small child I owned a children's book about Mickey Marcus, the American soldier who came to the emerging State of Israel to advise Ben Gurion and the Haganah about defense, the most critical defense in the country's history. He was a real hero, commander of the Jerusalem Front in the early stages of the War of Independence. I remember from the book how Colonel Marcus was killed by accident by one of the Israelis' own sentries, and how I cried. It was so sad. I must have been six or seven years old, and many memories of that stage of childhood are long forgotten, but Mickey Marcus's heroism stayed with me. Nearly thirty years later I went to visit a monument to his memory on the outskirts of Jerusalem. I stood there considering the span of years and how one person's story could have touched me so deeply. That a terrible movie — "Cast a Giant Shadow" — was produced about his life has in no way tarnished that image in my mind. He is still a hero of mine, and will no doubt remain a hero for the rest of my life.

Once again I consulted my mother, asking which of her heroes have become my own. We reviewed the life of Orde Wingate, the non-Jewish officer in the British Army who helped train the Jewish underground in the late Thirties. He gave the fledgling corps of soldiers the necessary skills to defend themselves against the Arab attacks; he raised the future generation of Israeli military leaders. The British transferred him out of the country in 1939, with a notation in his passport, "the bearer . . . should not be allowed to enter Palestine." Wingate died in a plane crash five years later in a jungle in Burma and was brought for burial to Arlington Cemetery, not more than ten minutes' ride from the house I was raised in. We shall have to visit the grave together, my mother and I, talking as we go of this exceptional man, this nonconformist whose devotion to our people needs to be remembered.

These are the heroes of my past, at least some of them — the grand names written up in encyclopedias. Exposés and re-examinations of their biographies try to chip away at their memories, but my need for myth is stronger than any craving I might have for facts and truth. Even if I were to discover great shortcomings in their lives, the part they have played in my own life will be scarcely affected. They will still remain my heroes.

Clearly this grasping for ideals was reinforced in me over and over again. It was a strong yearning for innocence that kept itself alive despite disappointments and failures in the natural course of my own life. It became a craving for higher, broader visions that could not be torn away from me, though these desires have become somewhat muted in the past few years. Still, today, though cynics are everywhere to be seen and heard, and though I all-too-often teach with cynicism and bitterness in my voice, I am easily drawn back to the memories of these people, and other ones. My Tzedakah work has brought to the surface my predisposition to hero-searching, and I am once again confronted with considering the place of heroes and idealists in my own life and the lives of others.

There is a difference, though, between my earlier heroes and the new ones: almost no one has heard of the Lupoliankys and Gasters and Maimons and Mendilows. People are incredulous when they hear about the work of these lesser-known personalities. I understand their skepticism: they would assume that anyone living such enormously idealistic lives would be better known. If their pictures are not on the front page of Time or Newsweek, at least they should be featured prominently in the periodicals of the Jewish journals. It would be a hackneyed grumbling to complain that the media-conglomerate is "The Enemy." We are bored to hear that a politician's obituary runs a full page, while the dreamer passes from the world barely mentioned in a short paragraph at the bottom of the page. Cynicism is a very easy characteristic to cultivate.

Nevertheless, we must consider one special case from the world of television: Dr. Benjamin Franklin Pierce, otherwise known as "Hawkeye." Anyone who has watched M*A*S*H knows that he is the hotshot surgeon played by Alan Alda, the hero of the show. Inevitably, on at least every second program, there is some situation where Hawkeye expresses some profound humanitarian thought. His main theme is clear and simple: these boys — brought in with shrapnel in their backs, their legs blown to pieces — they are people, not meat, not cannon-fodder, but people, usually fresh out of high school. Kids. It is an effective, powerful message. What is astounding is how a show such as this has remained on the air for so many years. There is so much gore, and on several occasions there have been depressingly serious shows proclaiming the ghastly ugliness of war. The humor is superb — there is no question about that — and Hawkeye is the maestro of sharp repartee, but beyond the laughs of a standard sit-com, there is this one hero proclaiming high ideals. He speaks for all who would wish to maintain some shred of Menschlichkeit, and though he is surrounded by many other figures who are sympathetic characters — he alone remains The Great Teacher, the Rebbi.

I do not know whether I am happy or unhappy with this situation. I am pleased, of course, that such magnificent values are so eloquently expressed. I am happy that millions of people at one time or another have heard his tirades about evil and inhumanity, his proclamations on The Dignity of Human Beings, have witnessed his gentle bedside manner. There is nothing phony about it. One would even suspect (by reflex action) that in real life Alan Alda is divorced, remarried, divorced, outwardly kind and privately a terror. But from all accounts I have seen, this is not the case at all. Alda seems to be a decent person, very much enthralled by his role as Hawkeye.

My frustration is this: I have to ask myself, "What do we have in the field of Jewish education that could ever hope to match this message from the media?" How could we ever hope to put these values in a Jewish context, to such an extent? Our impact in the Jewish world is so minuscule compared to any single show or rerun of M*A*S*H. We should be thankful, I suppose, for TV's contribution to the literature of gentleness and devotion, of kindness and caring. At least we can build on the legend of Hawkeye, supplementing with stories of our own, presenting the Jewish values which overlap and complement Hawkeye's words of Torah.

But, still, there is this gnawing feeling: Hawkeye has become the modern-day Rebbi, and we have nothing at all of that magnitude to offer in comparison. It is a losing battle. Perhaps we should not even consider it a battle, and they, the networks, not enemies at all. Let us take M*A*S*H, encourage our students to watch it carefully (even "religiously"), and then listen to their impressions. From there we can proceed with lessons in Tzedakah. It is not such bad pedagogy: the Chassidim took drinking songs and marching songs they heard from their neighbors and transformed them into Jewish praises of God and His creatures. Let us accept, then, without anger, this Rebbi as one who can teach us well. Beginning with his words, we can proceed to search our own sources for deeper meanings.

To Hawkeye Pierce, *Lechaim!*

A POSTSCRIPT: RAOUL WALLENBERG AND JANUSZ KORCZAK

International attention has recently focused on Raoul Wallenberg. In 1980 and 1981 a number of major articles were written about him, including a feature in the New York Times Magazine. And "60 Minutes" produced an important program on his work. This single man, this non-Jewish diplomat from Sweden, was responsible for saving the lives of thousands of Hungarian Jews — personally responsible. It is an important story:

In July of 1944 he was sent to Budapest. By then over 475,000 Hungarian Jews had already been sent to the death camps. Wallenberg boldly defied the Nazis, gathering and protecting Jews all over the city from the enemy. It is known that he even pulled Jews off the trains as they were about to depart for the camps. "60 Minutes" interviewed a number of people who owe their lives to Wallenberg, and though it seems absolutely impossible that one individual person could accomplish so much, the facts are clear: he himself accomplished this feat. Unquestionably.

Wallenberg was last seen on January 17, 1945, in the company of a Russian officer and his driver. It was assumed that he was en route to the Soviet authorities to report on his activities. They were the liberators of the city, and he apparently was going to appraise them of various plans he had. Since then, the Russians have claimed that he died in a prison camp in 1947, though there have been many accounts of his being alive long after that. There are some who believe he is still alive, and committees around the world are working towards establishing that fact and securing his freedom.

Wallenberg is a late-discovered hero, the paradigm of decency who, for clearly humanitarian reasons, struggled to save Jews from destruction. I wonder why it has taken so many years for me and for others to become aware of him, of his life-saving work. I was six months old when he disappeared into the Soviet Union. Surely by the time I was seven or eight I could have been told about him in Hebrew school. While it is not too late now to keep his memory in my mind, it would have been better to know about him while I was reading my children's storybook about Mickey Marcus. The two of them together could have guided me better through my childhood.

Even now I think of another hero omitted from my early awareness — Janusz Korczak. Since 1911 he supervised an orphanage in Warsaw. When the Nazis formed the ghetto, he remained, keeping the operations of the orphanage as stable as possible under those conditions. Had he wanted, he could have settled in Israel, having visited in 1934 and 1936. But he came back to the children. There was even a last-minute offer — as he and the children marched to the trains for Treblinka — an offer to save his own life. But he would not abandon the children, choosing rather to go with them to the gas chambers.

Israel issued a stamp in his memory in 1962. (I did not know about this until 1981.) There are books and posters about Korczak everywhere, perhaps even filmstrips for the schools. I am sorry that I, too, did not know about him as I was growing up. He could have been another hero. It may be that my teachers wanted to protect me . . . they did not want me to be exposed to such grisly circumstances at such a young age — even for the sake of a lesson in heroism. They may have been right, since I am myself unsure of where and when to begin to teach about the Holocaust. I have no way of knowing whether or not the idealism of Korczak and Wallenberg could have outweighed the surrounding horror. I just don't know. But *sometime* before I turned thirty or thirty-three or thirty-four when I discovered these two people — *sometime* — *someone* should have told me about them.

Everyone keeps telling me to "stop dwelling on those things from the past." Stop thinking, "How would it have been if . . ." And yet, as a Jew, I must ask myself why I arrived at this Tzedakah work via Helen Keller and Schweitzer (and Florence Nightingale and Clara Barton and Lou Gehrig), and not through Wingate, Wallenberg, and Korczak. I need to know why the road to the Jewish heroes should have been so circuitous. I am certain this is not a fruitless pursuit. There must be some reason, and, as a result, some way to rectify the situation for the next generation of students. Someone will have to do the research. Soon.

TZEDAKAH APPRENTICES

A SCENE FROM PASSOVER

Jerusalem, a few days before Passover. Long lines of people await the distribution of flour, wine, eggs, sugar and other staples. The Rabbanit Bracha Kapach supervises, assisted by students from schools, and friends, and people enamored of her manner. One helper is a friend of mine, David Morris, an immigrant from Florida, who has brought other friends to help. He has other responsibilities in his life, but there is no place in Israel he wants to be that day other than here, with the Rabbanit, helping to perform the Mitzvah of Ma'ot Chittin — providing Pesach provisions for the needy. It is not the first time he has been with the Rabbanit. A month before, he played a part in doing the same for Purim, so everyone who needed celebration-food for the holiday should have it.

And, I am certain, my friend will be back at other times, to do more, as the occasions present themselves. He is a Tzedakah-apprentice.

AN OVERSTATED, PREACHY COMPARISON

A parent remarks that his or her child studied privately under Leonard Bernstein.

A husband says his wife, a pathologist, was awarded a post-doctoral fellowship and will be studying under the Eminent Professor Ploni Almoni at Sloane-Kettering.

A woman tells me her brother is clerking for a Supreme Court Justice.

A young man tells me he has a friend who is Rabbi Soloveitchik's pride and joy. The greatest student he has had in years.

And a mother rediscovers her artistic talents from college and earns a grant to study with X, the eminent artist in New York, The Master.

And all I have is my friend distributing Pesach food in Jerusalem, under the watchful eye of The Rabbanit Bracha Kapach. She, too, is a laureate — recipient of the Israel Prize, for her sense of devotion, I suppose. But that is secondary to her essence. Prizes are only tools for her, a matter of leverage to get more power to do more Mitzvot.

David Morris is also a musician. (Perhaps he, too, could have someday studied with Bernstein.)

THE PROPOSAL, NAIVE

1. Families should examine themselves and send their gloriously talented children, sisters, brothers, mothers, and fathers to be apprentices, Tzedakah-apprentices.

2. They need not do it with Tzaddikim — the number of Righteous Ones is limited. The Good People are good enough. There are only so many geniuses of this craft of Tzedakah in the world; it will suffice for them to work with less-than-geniuses.

3. They need not travel to distant or exotic places to become appren-

tices. They may seek out the Tzedakah-Maestros-and-Maestras in their own communities.

VARIATIONS

College students are the most obvious candidates for this work. Ever since the Sixties it has been admirable how many students take a year off for various projects: travel, six months on Kibbutz, a job. It gets their minds off the pressures of study. It makes them broader, deeper human beings. It helps their college educations make sense.

Let them switch their plans to Tzedakah-apprenticeships.

(The same can work for people who are entitled to Sabbaticals — professors, Jewish school principals, rabbis.)

(The same can apply for schoolteachers with their long summer months free.)

Three months is a good stretch. Six is better, and a year would be wonderful.

Let us concentrate, though, on the college and graduate students. We have all been troubled by the "run to the gurus" of the Sixties, and the still-threatening numbers of our children exploring the shallow promises of the cults — the Krishnas, EST, the Maharishi, Jews for Jesus. A Tzedakah-apprenticeship is only one counter-opportunity to avoid these crises. Perhaps the best one.

Sooner or later, in these vulnerable years, our children will be asking, "What is the meaning of life?" It will strike them in the middle of some course or midnight bull-session in a dorm or lounge, sometime during their schooling. Their peers will offer answers, and their professors and their bed partners, and some of the answers may very well be substantive and life-guiding. But if it were true that all these people were offering such satisfying, significant answers, why do we see so many graduates with a bachelor's or master's or PhD still swimming for meaning — and so often?

Thus, the proposal: a clerkship with the Righteous, with Menschen.

I have received letters from people, years after their contact with the Tzedakah-Masters, recalling the critical impact that experience had on their lives. Out of nowhere, people tell me, "Maimon. Ya'akov Maimon. I learned so much from him!" "Hadassah Levi — a genius!" And for the ones who knew Henrietta Szold, sharing the work of her dreams . . . there is no end to the stories that come pouring out.

Long ago I was taught the quote from Pirke Avot — The Wisdom of the Rabbis — "Sit in the dust of the feet of the *Chachamim*." I used to think that *Chachamim* should be translated as "scholars," but I was wrong. I have since narrowed my vision, become suspicious of knowledge per se (at the cost of insight). Now I understand the translation as "the Wise" (though they may be of average or less-than-average intelligence). The Wise Ones I have met are those who have acquired their wisdom through devotion to the People. Some have acquired their wisdom washing bodies for burial, or changing bedpans. There is even one of these *Chachamim* who trains his apprentices to do those things which are hardest for them to do. I may disagree with that theory and practice, but the results are striking. I might allow for a more conservative stance, permitting each apprentice to work well within safe emotional and energy limits. I would allow them — under the tutelage of the *Chachamim* — a period of intense human contact, all the possible feelings of Tzedakah in six months, a year, but within their own personality range. Burnout is a danger here, too.

There is a popular joke in Israel, "What is the greatest waste of human resources in this country? The time consumed making Israeli salads!" Tomatoes, onions, and cucumbers, chopped into the smallest of pieces, half an hour for a side dish.

The non-joke is that there is another waste of human resources: these Good People are scattered everywhere, capable of training so many others in similar work, and too few would-be apprentices avail themselves of the opportunity.

There's a blue-eyed young woman in New Jersey who did it one summer: a month at Life Line for the Old. She worked in the workshops with the Elders of Jerusalem, making wall-hangings and dolls and other craft-items, sharing conversations and listening and laughing and feeling good about herself and the Elders. She can tell us what this apprenticeship is like. She will not hide the shortcomings of such a program, but the failings certainly cannot be any more serious than the deficiencies in a typical college education. She will certainly tell the story, many stories.

They must be good stories — her parents did the same a few months later, choosing their own workshops at Life Line, sitting at their work-tables, taking their places with the Elders.

WHAT THE JEWISH COMMUNAL STRUCTURE CAN DO

There are many volunteer programs offered in every community, and an abundance of others in Israel. Sherut La'am is one program; the World Union of Jewish Students has another, and there are more. But, what I believe is essentially lacking is this link-up with the Great. The volunteers on many programs may well benefit (as I know so many have). Their self-image has grown stronger, clearer, their sense of giving more refined, their love of Israel and the Jews strengthened beyond all anticipated bounds. But there is this one other element — harking back to Leonard Bernstein, Rabbi Soloveitchik, Mr. Justice Burger — the insights of the Master.

I must clearly state that I do not believe in Rebbis. I used to. I used to be very romantic about the Chassidim, nourished at the Rebbi's table. But it was a rose-tinged vision, and while I have begun to see the greatness of The Early Masters, I have come to be suspicious of a certain Infallibility I hear so much about. "My Rebbi can do this." "My Rebbi said that." "Whatever my Rebbi says or does is right." I am not speaking only of the world of the Chassidim — I think of a broad range of other rebbis. What is irritatingly common to all of them is the thinking of the disciples. The followers in all-too-many instances have surrendered their critical faculties.

So, in this apprenticeship program, I would not wish the apprentices to be so overwhelmed by their Masters that they will lose their powers to criticize. Let them say, respectfully, "No, I cannot do that . . ." or "No, I believe that is beyond my sense of right and wrong." I do not wish to substitute the Good People for the Rebbis, with the same rules of relationship still in play. If anything, I want the apprentices to see imperfection, to study it, to gain a perspective on the nature of failure. They will be working with people who do so much good, let them not forget their shortcomings. If they wish to find perfection, they will have to journey elsewhere, outside the human realm. Still, in the overall matter of Living, I believe it is better that they attach themselves to the Mendilows, Kapachs, Lupolianskys, the Si Levines, with all their personality flaws, rather than to others who would take away their own personalities, their precious individuality. The goal recalls a moment in the life of Rabbi Akiva: He entered the Orchard of Mystical Teaching *B'Shalom*, and emerged from the same, *B'Shalom*, still whole, still himself.

The community's task would be to provide information about where to find the Tzedakah-Masters. In some cases they would also need to supply a supervisor to coordinate an apprenticeship program. And, of course, to provide funds for scholarships. Crassly put, as "human investment," there are few better places to spend the community's money.

A PROVISO

Many young people with problems go to Israel to find themselves — if they do not take the other routes (Eastern religions, TM, the many gurus). Since this apprenticeship program is not a panacea, then we should understand that every person is *not* suited for this work. This is not the place for deeply troubled individuals, and no one is offering the ultimate solutions to long-term, long-brewing problems. The disturbed and precariously balanced should not apply. The false hope alone would be disastrous.

But for the hundreds (perhaps thousands) of others, the door is open. For them, a day spent distributing Matzah, wine, eggs, and other Passover food is an invitation to richer experience, broader meaning. Three months with the Rabbanit Kapach, five afternoons a week working at a center with Uri Lupoliansky, once-a-week preparing Shabbat with retarded adults at Magen, a summer program with Micha's pre-school deaf children — what miracles and near-miracles can happen are yet to be seen.

I exaggerate, using the word "miracles" again.

But the reports from the past are encouraging. The activities this year, at this moment are also encouraging. It remains only for us to expand this effort, to integrate it into a full apprenticeship program.

Inevitably we will have to refine and redefine our understanding of the word "miracle."

So many have considered the thought, after a one-morning visit to Life Line for the Old. They slowly redirect themselves to larger Tzedakah endeavors; little patterns change. So much greater would be the moves, the thrusts of our activities if we can have a sustained contact with such greatness. Whether or not The World will change is a question beyond my capacity to answer. That many smaller worlds will change — of this there is no question. Eighteen hundred years ago the Mishna proclaimed that truth:

> Whoever preserves a single life —
> It is as though he had saved an entire world.
> (*Sanhedrin 4:5*)

THE DREAM BUYERS
or
WHY IT IS IMPORTANT
TO KEEP A MANILA TZEDAKAH FOLDER

The newspapers call them human interest stories. I prefer to label them (if labels are necessary) "Tales of Tzedakah." Every day or every other day, if we but take the time to examine carefully the newspapers and periodicals, there are tales of human grandeur.

Two examples:

1. A policeman who used to guard a pediatrics hospital was so saddened by the death of the children, he decided to buy the children their last dreams. From his own modest income, and with help from friends, he would offer dying children an opportunity for a trip somewhere, or a night at a concert they had always wanted to attend. The article was poorly written, expressed with oversentimentality, but the acts of this Sunshine Foundation, the deeds behind the words, were nothing less than the greatest expression of Nobility of the Soul.

2. A letter to the editor in the Baltimore Jewish Times recalled the warmth and high emotion in the Bat Mitzvah celebration of a young woman with Down's syndrome. (I have similar stories in my files from the Los Angeles Times and The Reader's Digest.)

We read articles of simple humanity now and again in the course of our attempts to keep up with world events. Perhaps it is time to begin clipping them, collecting them, maybe making a scrapbook. Certainly teachers in our network of Jewish education should be doing this — gathering, posting them on the bulletin board, speaking of them in the classroom. It may give the students — and the teachers — a new perspective on the nature of Life's events. Adults are impressed, even stunned, when a ten-year-old can speak with some sophistication of rising and falling interest rates and sluggish economies. They are precocious, demonstrating a refined aptitude for getting ahead. But we rarely (if ever) hear equal intelligence applied to the basic happenings in the lives of people, how they show courage and kindness and sensitivity in everyday circumstances.

Let us review the first example, The Dream-Buying Policeman. It is a relatively easy task to extract an important, basic principle: simple gut reactions and elementary insights can lead to projects that inspire. My own experience in Israel has shown that some of the most impressive works have developed from the most elementary reactions to particular human situations. One woman saw old people begging in the streets of Jerusalem, and others sitting in rooms, all alone, waiting for death. She abandoned her career as a teacher, sick at the thought of having her students conclude that this is the only way old people end their lives. Years later, hundreds of old people are at work, starting again, a new phase of life, as they had started new turnings at marriage, at childbearing, at the initiation of other jobs earlier in their lives. Thus was Life Line for the Old born. *One woman* screamed back at society that old people were a meaningful, dignified part of the work force. (Indeed, Myriam Mendilow, the founder, the one who screamed, first went to the Ministry of Labor and not, as to be expected, to the Ministry of Welfare.)

And again: Reb Osher Freund took note of the loneliness of mental patients. What followed were birthday parties in the institutions and work projects outside the hospital walls — Therapy Through Work. In many cases, and against all indications and psychiatric prognoses — a complete cure.

And another: The Lupoliansky family of Jerusalem saw many people waiting for vital medical supplies, something for this ailment, a pair of crutches for another. The bureaucracy grinds slowly, but wheelchairs and vaporizers and oxygen were needed immediately. The result — within five years, twenty-four centers manned by more than 400 volunteers began lending out a vast supply of equipment that seems to appear "out of nowhere." Yad Sarah succeeded, and continues to succeed overwhelmingly, built on an ever-so-simple vision.

Let us also review the second example: the bat mitzvah of a young woman with a handicap.

Note Camp Ramah's two Tikvah Programs — summer Jewish camping for the retarded.

And Note P'TACH — Parents for Torah for All Children, Jewish schools reaching learning-disabled and retarded Jews in many cities.

And The Reena Foundation in Toronto, doing the same, including a tour of Israel for retarded adults.

And Sh'ma V'Ezer in Washington, teaching Jews with similar disabilities, learning problems, retarded.

And Raphael House in the same city, apparently the only Kosher and Jewishly-oriented halfway house for mental patients in the country.

And JESPY in New Jersey, a kosher group home for retarded adults, founded by concerned members of the United Synagogue of America community.

And more places, people, projects, concerned with special needs. The list could go on for pages. I picture for myself the Bat Mitzvat in Baltimore, the warmth, the tears of joy. People are redefining who is entitled to active participation in the Jewish community. By simple extension we can understand the hundreds upon hundreds of adult men and women celebrating similar bar and bat mitzvahs, handicapped through poor Jewish education, now standing proud, triumphant, some weeping at the recitation of the blessings — making up for the lost, but not irretrievably lost, time.

And by extension, Rabbi Dan Grossman of Staten Island, New York, taking hundreds of deaf Jews from the clutches of secular deaf education and offering them, also, a chance to grasp the essences of Judaism. He is perplexed (as are so many others) as to why the Jewish blind have been provided for so extensively over the years, and why it is only now that the Jewish community is realizing that a new sign-vocabulary of Jewish values is critical for the deaf, for all of us. Why have we neglected the Jewish deaf, he asks.

Blind, deaf, crippled, retarded, lonely — or just plain old and not-feeling-so-well — all these seem to go hand-in-hand. ("Hand in Hand" or "Yad B'Yad" is, incidentally, the pre-teenage Tzedakah project of the Kadimah organization of the United Synagogue Youth Department. Through this program, the children raise funds for Ramah's Tikvah Program.)

And by one more extension of this one brief note about a special bat mitzvah — people with so-called normal, everyday lives can become more and more aware of the considerable devotion, energy, and time-effort needed to work with "special projects." Issues of great importance are brought to our attention: raising a retarded child within the family, caring for an elderly parent, whatever . . . the "Jew in the Street" can become more appreciative and supportive of those who give so much of themselves. Rather than isolate and insulate themselves and their children from such realities, by means of these clippings they can bring these issues into the purview of their families, friends, and acquaintances. It is hoped that, thereby, the Jewish people can redefine itself to include all Jews as fully as possible in the life of the community.

The following suggestions are therefore offered as a simple educational tool:

1. Individuals should begin gathering articles and pictures, cutting them from any and every source in our media-saturated society.

2. As these fragments increase in number, categories of stories should be created: Dignity, The Life-Sustainers, Miracle-Workers, Money-for-Mitzvot, etc.

3. Evenings should be spent with friends, and classes at synagogues and JCC's should be held, with the intent of seeking the extended meanings and implications of these articles. Friday nights, a family might want to review the week's clippings as part of their Shabbat meal.

4. Torah teachers of every shade and calling should involve themselves in the project, seeking out the articles for their students, and relating these current events and "human interest stories" to our millenia-old tradition. They should raise questions: Why did we not learn these Talmudic sources in Hebrew school or adult education classes? Why were we not informed that our Jewish books ponder the topics of handicaps, of life-saving, of beauty and ugliness? Why did no one teach us about the Biblical, Talmudic, and later personalities who lived lives devoted to others? Why have we not seen the Jewish legal literature on the deaf and the retarded? Curricula may change as a result, and bureaus of Jewish education may decide to reorient their programs accordingly. (With more than a tinge of cynicism I often express my extreme doubts about this change of direction — so much of Jewish education is tied into bar and bat mitzvah preparation and the teaching of contemporary Hebrew conversation which enables its students to ask for directions in Haifa, but does not afford them the opportunity to open a Talmud to learn how to treat a not-so-senile grandparent.) (Enough!)

Most important of all, through our manila folders filled with articles, we, as Jews, will begin to sense the meaning of living in broader, richer terms. Considering starvation in the Sahara or tidal waves in the Orient or the aftermath of the Mount St. Helens explosions should not be the major source of our insight. Earthshaking (and soulshaking) events are to be found everywhere, but, more often than not, we will find instruction and wisdom in our own households, neighborhoods, and communities, if we but redirect our vision. It does not take massive catastrophes and international conflagrations to show us a way. An underpaid policeman with three children of his own, and a young, retarded woman in Baltimore can do the same, if not more. They can teach us new dreams, showing us how to bring them to fruition, so that we, too, may attempt to dream again, refreshing, vigorous dreams for our own lives.

Dear Danny Siegel,

My name is Jenny.

My Brownie troop number is 238.

We made the stuffed animals to send to Israel because many children there don't have toys. They don't have toys because some of their mothers and fathers died in wars, and they didn't have enough money to buy toys.

Your Friend,
Jenny

From a wedding invitation of two of my friends:

A NOTE TO OUR RELATIVES AND FRIENDS

The custom of offering gifts to a betrothed couple stems from the time when people married at a very young age, while their families and to some extent the community as a whole still had responsibility for their maintenance and support.

We feel fortunate to live in a society of tremendous affluence, and in an era when we as adults choose our own marriage partner and lifestyle.

Our household is already overflowing with a sometimes overwhelming number of seldom-used items. We would like to request, therefore, that your good wishes that might otherwise take the form of presents to us be channeled instead to *Tzedakah*. Please consider a donation in honor of our wedding to any of the following:

(After this brief statement is a list of five Tzedakot: Action for Soviet Jewry, the American Association for Ethiopian Jews, Tay-Sachs Prevention Program, Oxfam-America, and my fund.)

Dear Ms. Wolinsky,*

My name is Shari Kirshblum. I go to a Hebrew Day School and am in grade six.

I have three used dolls, which are in good condition. I have used them for a long time and would like other children to enjoy them like I have.

Danny Siegel, who our family knows, suggested that they be sent to you.

Like I said before, the dolls are in good condition. They are clean, along with the clothes which have been washed also.

The dolls have been packaged, and you will hopefully receive them in a few weeks.

I hope the children enjoy them.

Yours Truly,
Shari Kirshblum

*Toby Wolinsky works for Micha, Jerusalem, a project for pre-school deaf children.

Dear Danny,

Joanna and I gratefully received your $5 for our Tz'daka box. Our theory is that we are so fortunate, she and I, that it behooves us to share our good fortune. So when we get a nice phone call, see a good friend, get invited out to dinner, have an especially good day, receive a compliment, or whatever, we put some money in our pushka. It's been going for 3 months now. We are far from rich, so the amounts are not large, but each month we decide where to send our contributions. Some places may not even be appropriate, in terms of the greatest need, but it's instilling in my daughter the right idea about life. The first month we sent it to Greenpeace, an environmental organization working against whale, seal, and dolphin slaughter. The second month we sent it to the nursing home where my grandmother (and Joanna's great-grandmother) is a resident. This month it is going to the Pine Street Inn, the Boston Shelter for homeless men and women, the street people of our city.

The experience of giving is a total joy to us.

Shalom,
V.U.

ᔕ

Anonymous notes:

Dear Danny,

I am aware of the Tzedakot you allocate funds to in Israel and would like this to go with you. I wish I had the time to do the work . . . but since I can't, please help me by putting this money to good use.

Thank you

Dear Danny,

I hope this will make the new year a little brighter for someone. Again, thank you.

L'Shana Tova

Dear Danny,

I hope your Chanukkah was a happy one. I hope this helps you help others in the coming year.

Thank you

Dear Danny,

The last donation I made was only from my Tzedaka cans here and at home. Here is a donation that I hope will help you in any endeavors you feel are worthy . . .

ᔕ

Dear Friend:

I read your 1980 Tzedakah Report in Moment Magazine last night, when I had just come home from the very joyous celebration of our grandson's B'rit Milah. I send the enclosed check for $25.00 to your 1981 fund in his honor — Hillel Aaron Kurlandsky, of Hoffman Estates, Illinois.

The occasion was an especially joyous one because Hillel was born at the end of 27 weeks of gestation, at 2 lb. 10 oz., and his life hung in the balance for quite a while. This past week, when he was due to be born, he was actually three months old, and achieved the normal birth weight of 6 lb. 11 oz., and appears to be normal in every respect.

It's hard for me to choose among the projects you list; I have no organizational affiliation through which I can further the work; I don't expect to visit Israel in the near future, but I entrust this small sum to you out of the fulness in the heart. I feel abundantly blessed, and have been taught always to share.

My thanks to you for showing me — and many of us — a way.

Sincerely,
Mrs. Joseph E. Gould
Skokie, Illinois

᧚

From Rabbi Jack Riemer, La Jolla, California:

I look forward to seeing you here at the USY convention soon, but meantime I want to share a couple of tsedakah stories with you that I think you will appreciate.

I have just come back from sitting shivah for my mother, z'l [may her memory be for a blessing]. Shivah is like shock therapy, in that it makes you confront so much. This shivah had many highs and lows in it, moments of laughter as we remembered funny stories, moments of pain as we realized that a world was no more, moments of sharing as people told us what our mother meant in their lives . . .

My son came to the funeral. What do you give a son as a yerusha [an inheritance]? There was a wall full of tsedakah boxes that she would fill each week before candle lighting. I gave him one. We opened it and found a note in my father's handwriting. He had written: I owe this tsedaka box 29 cents. I paid the debt. Isn't that a nice memento?

. . . .

The mishulochim [tsedakah collectors] loved to come to the house — not only for the tsedakah but for the warm welcome. Dad would take the receipt for the pushke from them so as not to embarrass them but never kept it; he would throw it away as soon as they left. And Mom would feed them. We remembered one who would get up refreshed and rested and say — this is the *besteh stantsia*, the best stop on his route. And this is perhaps what this world is — a *stantsia* — and if so, we can learn from her how to make it a good one.

I thought that I should share these stories with you since I know you collect tsedaka stories, and in sharing them there is a consolation.

With deep affection,
Jack

A letter to the editor of Moment Magazine *(December 1980), in response to an article I had written about physical handicaps and deformities:*

To the Editor:

With reference to "Beautiful People, Ugly People," I wish to commend the author, Danny Siegel, for dealing with this subject in such an honest manner. Too often we avoid giving this topic conscious consideration, and rather than comprehend and contemplate the implications involved, we avoid the issue. I speak from personal experience, for my own outward appearance has altered, due to years of ill health, from healthy, robust, attractive comeliness, to emaciation, gauntness and deformity. My only regret is that I cannot convey to those who regard me with sorrow, surprise, embarrassment or pity that my physical appearance does not bother me at all, and despite what I look like, I am thankful to God because the being that exists within the shell has remained unaffected. I thank Him for permitting me to retain my mental capacities and abilities, for the sensitivity that has always been a part of my psyche, for the ability to appreciate His wonders and creations. Mental stimulation, perception, the challenges that the academic world presents, the pleasure of exploring new ideas — I am far, far from crippled in this. I neither apologize nor do I resent whatever reactions others may exhibit when meeting me. I am only sorry that they feel uncomfortable, and don't know how to react, being more self-conscious about my appearance than I am.

Yet, were conditions reversed, I ask myself, would I behave in the same way? I have no answer — my only truth is my faith in God, stronger, perhaps, because of adversity, yet complete and fulfilling. That I am a Jew is enough for me, for I am proud that this is my heritage, and if, over centuries, Jews have survived devastating disaster, how can I complain about the minor discomfort that the term "ugly" implies? I am too busy living, while I am able, for one day my physical handicaps will become the hurdle that will destroy my present ability to remain above the confinement stage. Ugly or beautiful I am glad I do not have to make that choice, merely to live within its confines.

Shirley Harris,
Clearwater, Florida

From a letter from Rabbi Gary Greene, Longmeadow, MA, Congregation B'nai Jacob:

Our USY chapter is working with Beth El's chapter [Springfield] on a very beautiful Tzedakah project for Passover. The kids are preparing Seder plates with all of the appropriate symbols for Jewish patients in the hospital who can't go home for the Seder. A Haggadah will also be supplied. Many times a family will not have a Seder because they're all in the hospital visiting the loved one. This gives them the opportunity to celebrate as much or as little as they like.

I would love to take credit for this idea; however, all due credit must go to Barry Dov Lerner [the rabbi at Beth El]. It is his idea and my kids are jumping on the bandwagon.

March 17, 1981
Jerusalem

∽

Dear Seymour,*

Two days ago I received your check for $350 and Danny's letter. This morning I gave, 3,100 Shekels (62 bills of 50 Shekel denominations) to the Rabbanit Bracha Kapach. She has a "Purim list" of 65 needy families to whom she is giving Matanot LaEvyonim [Tzedakah money for Purim food.] She gave each of them a 50 Shekel note or the equivalent in wine, oil, sugar, and flour. With food prices so high, this extra 50 Shekels makes a real difference.

I must tell you that after leaving the bank, I saw an old, poor man lying on the street. He said he was "resting" but in the meantime, a sanitation truck was coming towards him! I pulled him up and asked him if he was alright. He then asked me for some money to buy wine for Purim. I gave him 20 Shekels of your money and 5 of my own. So you see, the minute I left the bank, your money mystically started falling into the hands of Evyonim for Purim!

It was my honor to be a partial Shaliach in your performance of this fine Mitzvah. Lastly, the Rabbanit expressed hope for additional monies for Pesach. Prices are very high and she has 1,300 families to help.

Best wishes,
David Morris

*For a number of years, Seymour Epstein of Toronto has gone to Israel for Purim, taking with him funds collected for this particular act of Purim Tzedakah. Unable to go this year, he channeled the funds through my project. I forwarded the money to my friend, David Morris, who has been coordinating a number of Tzedakah projects in Israel, asking him to deliver the funds in an appropriate fashion.

∽

Dear Danny,

I was somewhat mystified and pleasantly surprised when Harvey Fields [Rabbi of a prominent Reform Temple in Toronto] handed me $10.00 prior to our leaving for Israel, and saying that I was to spend the amount on some charity while in Israel. His subsequent explanation of what you intended clarified the mystery.

I want to report that, on November 17, as our interfaith group was heading for Shabbat service on the ruins of the old synagogue at Katzrin on the Golan Heights, our bus was forced to stop because of a table set up in the middle of the road with a group of beautiful teenagers around it. These were kids from the nearby kibbutz selling cakes and drinks, the funds raised from that sale to be used for Cambodian refugees. That is where your $10.00 went.

Thank you very much for the opportunity of doing Tzedakah with the money that came from you. I hope that our paths cross some day.

> Yours sincerely,
> The Reverend Stanford R. Lucyk
> Minister,
> Timothy Eaton Memorial Church, Toronto

&

From a woman who works with the Jewish blind to whom we sent some money to use at her discretion:

Dear Danny,

Just to report in on my "Tzedakah" fund. I am using $10.00 to cover membership fees for a blind woman, lovely and spirited, who is on a kidney machine 3 days per week. She likes our group because it gives her the chance to get out of her house. The expenses related to the machine — supplies, drugs, etc. — are very high and she doesn't have the money to join — so your contribution comes in very handy . . .

Thanks again for the "gelt" — your friends made one lady very happy.

&

Dear Danny,

. . . I told you over dinner about my work with the retarded children at Camp Ramah. (We call these Tikvah kids "Amitzim" – "The Strong Ones" because they are our source of strength throughout the summer.) They have taught me a valuable lesson. They have taught me to be more open and share my affection with others without restraint. A lot can be said in a hug, when you're up in the clouds and when you're low to the ground. They are a source of hope and inspiration to us all . . .

> Sincerely yours,
> S.J.R.

&

NB's husband was a physician who passed away a couple of years before this letter was written. During that period of time, she attempted to find a medical school or library that would accept his books as a gift — with no success. NB also wrote to me, but my contacts also failed. For a while we lost touch; then I wrote her a note asking if anything had finally happened with her husband's books. The following is her reply:

February 25, 1981

Dear Mr. Siegel:

I know you will be fascinated by the end of the story of my husband's books. They went to Israel, to the Kaplan Hospital. That is the bottom line, but the story is a little more complicated.

My husband worked with a resident years ago, here in Providence, who has recently made Aliyah to Israel. He is working with a Dr. David B. who met my husband the morning we left to go to Sloane-Kettering Hospital. This resident wrote me a letter saying that they were in need of books and he knew it would please my husband enormously to know his books had ended up in Israel. He offered to pay for the shipping, (which of course I wouldn't allow,) if I still had them, and would consider parting with them.

I was so thrilled, I packed up the books and sent them off on the next departing boat. I am looking forward to seeing the two doctors when I take the children and myself to Israel this summer.

NB

THE MAN ON THE STREET

The sun is very warm in San Francisco on this particular day. I have taken a long break from writing and flown cross-country to do some seminars for teachers and I feel very lighthearted. It has been a long two months stuck in front of my typewriter, and I am happy to be away from home. The few lectures I will have to do are a small price to pay for some freedom and peace of mind in one of my favorite cities.

On this morning my hosts are at work, so I am left to my own wanderings. I go downtown on the subway with my friend, Marv Goodman, and discuss the possibilities of the day with him. We agree that a cablecar to the wharf and a few hours at Ghirardelli Square will be a lovely way to pass the time. I can gaze out over the bay thinking of nothing in particular, waiting for ideas to arrange themselves into poems. I have taken my notebook, since I suspect from the feel of things that my relaxed frame of mind will lead to some creativity. The jet lag has worn off, and I am wide awake, soaking in the images and sounds of the city.

Before I go, Marv mentions to me that there is a gigantic secondhand bookstore nearby. He suggests that I browse in it for a while before heading down to the wharf. Unable to pass up such an opportunity, I walk around a little in the area just to get my legs accustomed to some leisurely strolling before going in.

It so happens that this part of San Francisco is near the center of the business district, though two or three blocks off Market Street a stroller easily encounters an array of flophouses and sleazy dives, a conglomeration of down-and-outers, winos and junkies. I begin to stroll, glancing at spontaneous intervals through the glass windows of the flophouse lobbies. Old, washed-out people are lounging around on the sofas and chairs. Some are reading newspapers, though others just stare. Their stare is empty, weary, and I begin to think of William Booth, founder of the Salvation Army — how he must have touched thousands and thousands of these people. And Roosevelt, putting the people back to work in the Great Depression, building dams and roads and public buildings with his WPA and CCC and other wondrous abbreviations. And then Emmanuel Ringelblum, chronicler of the days of the Warsaw Ghetto, recording in his diary how this group and that organization kept order, kept hope alive, even in the poverty and despair of the ghetto. Dorothea Lange's photographs. Roman Vishniac's. Faces and settings.

My day has not been ruined, but it has turned more somber, despite all the glorious warmth of the sun.

The bookstore is in the thick of the pornographic stores and saloons. I step inside but realize I will need more time, so I buy one book, then go back to Marv's office to rest for a moment. We chat for a minute, and then I set out again for a more thorough examination of the shelves. On the way back I stumble on another bookstore, almost as big, but better organized. I wander through the old, dust-gathering shelves, picking out paperbacks I need for my library. Stacks and stacks of old Life Magazines lie on a table, so I begin to explore. After a while I find a copy of an article celebrating Albert Schweitzer's 90th birthday. It was written in 1965, and I remember it from then, though many of the details are hazy. For fifty cents it is a wise investment, particularly since I am doing a lot of reading nowadays about people such as The Great White Doctor.

Emerging back into the sunshine, I begin to head back to Marv's office in order to leave those books before going to the other bookstore. On the way I see a young man, perhaps twenty or twenty-five, lying face down on the street. Because of the way he is lying, I cannot tell if he is resting, or injured, or drunk. Many people walk by, a few stopping to stare. Most of them have probably witnessed this scene before on any one of a number of occasions. I had seen something similar only once before: I was in high school and a painter on a high ladder lost his footing and fell to the sidewalk below. It was obvious that he was hurt — his head was bleeding — but I couldn't move. I stood at a distance and stared . . . I, a doctor's son, unable even to walk the ten feet to cover him up with my coat. This was for the hoods to do, the tough guys who didn't care much for things I cared about: studying, getting good grades, ranking well in my class standings. *They* took care of him, the guys with the hotrods, until the ambulance came.

Now I was faced with it again, twenty years later. And I walk right by. Halfway down the block I turn around to see if someone has helped, but the man is still lying there, face down on the concrete. (He wasn't bleeding. That much, at least, I could see.)

Still, I walk away, turning right at the next corner, back to the safety of Marv's office, making sure I don't have to see.

I CAN'T READ MUCH HEBREW, I CAN'T READ MUCH ARAMAIC, I NEVER WENT TO YESHIVA, BUT I STUDY TALMUD EVERY CHANCE I GET.

Brother, Can You Spare a Dime; The Treatment of Beggars According to Jewish Tradition: A Case in Point.

By Arthur Kurzweil*

In my neighborhood in Manhattan there is hardly a day when I am not approached by an individual who asks me for spare change, a quarter, a subway token, or some other request of a similar nature. These individuals (whom I will call "beggars" from this point on, though I am aware that this label is a narrow and therefore unfair one to use to describe a human being) come in various forms:

1. Some are bag ladies, dragging the sum-total of their worldly possessions with them in numerous shopping bags.

2. Some are "street people" who most probably live on the street, in the subway, or other public places.

3. Some are idle welfare recipients who would strike you as people who would probably be able to get some kind of job.

4. Some are alcoholics, constantly with bottle in hand or nearby.

5. Some are obvious drug addicts.

6. Some show no immediately-apparent reason to be asking for anything as they are well-dressed, groomed, etc.

7. They are of all ages (literally from 8 to 80).

8. They are both men and women.

9. They are usually Black or Hispanic (in my neighborhood, but in Greenwich Village however, where I often walk, they are mostly white and sometimes Jewish).

10. 99 times out of 100 they are nonthreatening (though I am a male and I imagine that if I were a woman I would have a significantly different perspective on this item.)

*Arthur Kurzweil, a resident of New York, is America's most important Jewish genealogist. He lectures in communities throughout the country, moving his audiences to greater understanding of, and commitment to, their Jewish roles in history through the search for their unique Jewish roots. Arthur and I studied Torah together for two years, *but because of a language-learning disability*, he was unable to master the original languages of the texts. He is convinced that others experiencing these same language problems can still benefit fully from exploring Jewish texts — even in translation, and has begun speaking on that topic, also. This article represents his first study-in-print of such an approach to Jewish learning. His chosen topic — Tzedakah.

Though the organized Jewish community has gotten the mitzvah of giving tzedakah down to a virtual science, and though I have also been a member of an alternative form of giving tzedakah for 4 years (a "tzedakah collective;" see *The Third Jewish Catalog*, p. 31, Jewish Publication Society, 1980), I was confused as to what I should do about the beggars I meet almost daily.

My habit regarding beggars was inconsistent:

1. Sometimes I gave nothing, both in one given day as well as for occasional blocks of time.

2. Sometimes I'd get into a giving mood and give to beggars in a flurry of giving over a period of time.

3. Sometimes I'd get into angry moods over the issue and never give a penny, thinking that they "ought to get a job" or "ought to go on welfare."

4. Sometimes I'd give consistently though selectively to people I decided were worthy recipients (the standards for *that* decision might be impossible for me to even document).

5. Sometimes I'd give enthusiastically to a familiar beggar, only to ignore the person the next day or week.

There were other inconsistencies as well, but those five listed above are enough to indicate that my thinking on the subject was, as I said, confused. But more than confused, I was troubled by it. A question loomed in my mind: What should my attitude towards beggars be? And secondly: Did Jewish tradition have anything to teach me on the subject?

The following are the results of my own exploration of those two questions. First, though, I would like to make a few things clear regarding my research:

1. I am not a Talmudic scholar.

2. I do not have a working knowledge of Hebrew or Aramaic, so all of the sources I have consulted are in English.

3. Every source quoted comes from my home library.

This third point is made for two reasons. First, I want to stress that the sources I have checked are limited. But secondly, I want to indicate that quite a bit of research of this kind can be productive by using readily available sources — again — in English. I will indicate more about my own research methodology later.

My approach to the question of "What should my attitude towards beggars be?" was to first sit down and list all of the questions I could possibly think of relating to my own personal dilemmas in regard to the subject. I came up with 15 questions:

1. Do Jews give to beggars? (Is there precedent for my giving to beggars — as a Jew who wants to fulfill the mitzvah of tzedakah).

2. What if they are fakes or frauds? (How many times I have wondered whether they are making more than me!)

3. What if they are nasty or otherwise offensive in looks, smell, etc.?

4. What if I feel I simply can't afford to give to beggars (having already given through other means)?

5. Aren't there better causes to give to than these people?

6. Shouldn't these beggars be supported by official or organized agencies?

7. Shouldn't I just ignore these people?

8. What if I am in a rush? (In my hectic life I barely have time to stop and negotiate a quarter for a "wino.")

9. What if they aren't Jewish? (Should my tzedakah priorities go to worthy Jewish causes exclusively?)

10. What if I have no money on me, or no spare change?

11. If I do give, how should I treat these people? What should I say to them?

12. What if I see the same people every day? (They'll get to know me as an easy sucker.)

13. What if I've given to a few beggars in one day? (Is there a limit to this?)

14. If they ask for money, perhaps I should go buy them a cup of coffee instead. After all, they will probably spend it on booze anyway!

15. Finally, if I do give to beggars, how much should I give?

The fifteen questions seemed to cover just about every possible question or issue I could possibly come up with regarding beggars. Interestingly, I noticed that the first 10 questions raised objections to giving to beggars while the last 5 seemed to admit defeat, wondering just how and what to give if I must. In all, my questions reflected a resistance to giving to beggars — while my eagerness to do research on the subject balanced that resistance.

While I was apparently born with an interest in research, I grew up in a home where my parents were constantly asking questions and forever referring to the family encyclopedia. Adding that to my training as a librarian, I find it rather easy to find simple answers to simple (and not so simple) questions. But I am also convinced that without any training — other than learning a few principles and doing a minimum of creative thinking — anyone can master the art of elementary research.

Joshua ben Perahyah says: Provide thyself with a teacher.

Pirke Avot, Chapter 1, Mishnah 6

No research skill, however creative, can endure without it being directed by a teacher, and as the Talmud urges in the quote offered above, I provided myself with the finest. Danny Siegel, teacher, poet, scholar and friend, guided me, on a weekly basis (a few hours each) for two years through the great works of our tradition. While we now live in different cities, hardly a week goes by when I am not on the phone to him, asking him for an explanation, a source, or simply a "talking out" of some Talmudic question.

So, principle number one for the kind of research that I am about to explain in detail, is, in the words of the Talmud: provide thyself with a teacher. You may not have the opportunity to sit with a teacher on a regular basis, but even to have a knowledgeable person who can get you out of some muddy water would be important.

At the end of this article I will provide a bibliography of the sources I consulted. Some, like the *Encyclopedia Judaica*, cost a few hundred dollars. Others, like some paperbacks, cost a dollar or two. I'd suggest you examine as many of the sources as you can to decide which would be of particular interest to you. (I have put an (*) next to the items which I highly recommend.)

The most critical items on the list — in my opinion — are also the most expensive. But for a basic Jewish home library they are essential. They also will last a lifetime and will be as valuable generations from now as they are to you. Invaluable in my research — and constant companions for me — are:

1. *Encyclopaedia Judaica*
2. *The Talmud* (Soncino Edition)
3. *The Midrash Rabbah* (Soncino Edition)
4. *The Minor Tractates* (Soncino Edition)
5. *The Legends of the Jews* by Louis Ginzberg

And perhaps the most valuable one volume item in my library is *A Book of Jewish Concepts* by Philip Birnbaum, Hebrew Publishing Company. Whenever I need a good explanation of a phrase, a topic, a notion, or a subject within Jewish studies, Birnbaum provides it. He gives the name of the item in Hebrew as well as English, so my limited knowledge of Hebrew is growing too. By the way, for those of you who do not know what items 2 through 4 are (above), Birnbaum's volume is the place to start — with definitions of "The Talmud," "The Midrash Rabbah," and "The Minor Tractates." (Consider that your first assignment!)

In my opinion, one of the great inventions of all times is the index. An index to a book or set of books is a magic doorway into the work. Some people begin a book with the first page; I start with the index. While the "Table of Contents" of a book is theoretically the place where you will find the "contents" of the work, it is actually the index where you will get a good picture of the inside workings. (In library school we used to play a game: can you guess the subject of a book by examining just the index? With a good index, it should be possible.)

Fortunately most of the books — including the Soncino edition of the Talmud (18 volumes) — have an index. So, my first question when looking for an insight into the Jewish view of beggars is to figure out what key words would help me to "dig out" the material. With some creativity and a lot of trial and error I found that beggars would appear under the following topics:

1. beggars
2. poor
3. charity

"Tzedakah" was never a category; it was always translated as "charity" in the indexes.

I spent a frantic and exciting few days running up and down my shelves, grabbing books which I thought might have items under these three headings. In a great number of cases I was quite successful. I read an enormous amount, copying lines, passages, quotes, and paragraphs. If a secondary source (such as a Jewish quotation dictionary) gave me a Talmudic passage, I was able to go to the Talmud itself — in English of course, and see it a little closer to the original — as well as the context in which it appeared. Often, by going to the "original" I was able to find more material on the subject which the secondary source left out. I was also able to compare translations (and when there were significant conflicts between translations I'd be on the phone to Danny Siegel once again for a glimpse — through his eyes — at the *original* original!)

After going through every book in my home library, I put each source on beggars which I had found on separate note cards. By the end I had about 60 cards! That is, 60 different times when some source added to my knowledge of how Jewish tradition views beggars. In the process, I read a great deal, learned more than I ever hoped to, and most remarkably I felt that I had a significant insight into the subject at hand.

Perhaps the most amazing result of my research on this subject (which might come as a surprise to some and none at all to others) is that each of my 15 questions about beggars was dealt with by one or more of the sources I discovered. Our tradition is amazing: what I would have thought was a quite contemporary question — such as what do you do if you think the beggar is a fake? — is dealt with in ancient texts. The following is the result of my exploration:

There was never any doubt in my mind that the giving of tzedakah was an essential part of being a Jew. One need only read "A Study Guide to Tzedakah" by Danny Siegel in his book *Angels* to see just how many sources urge the performance of this mitzvah in so many ways. But again, what about beggars? Here are my fifteen questions and the material I found which corresponds to each one:

1. DO JEWS GIVE TO BEGGARS?

> Our Rabbis taught: If an orphan boy and an orphan girl applied for maintenance, the girl orphan is to be maintained first and the boy orphan afterwards, because it is not unusual for a man to go begging, but it is unusual for a woman to do so.
>
> Ketubot 67a

(Already there are two things to note. One is that the passage is a bit sexist — reflecting the times in which it was written, of course. But I put it here, and put it first to indicate that it is sometimes difficult to "swallow" everything one comes across in the texts.

The second thing of note is: what does "Ketubot 67a" mean? "Ketubot" is the name of a section of the Talmud. "67a" is the page number. Every page of Talmud is numbered — but rather than each side getting a number, each leaf gets a number, with a side "a" and a side "b." So, this quote can be found in section Ketubot in the Talmud, on the second side of page 67.)

> R. Hiyya advised his wife, "When a poor man comes to the door, give him food so that the same may be done to your children." She exclaimed, "You

are cursing them (by suggesting that they may become beggars)! But R. Hiyya replied, "There is a wheel which revolves in this world."

Shabbat 151b

(The "R." before a person's name denotes "Rabbi.")

R. Abun said: The poor man stands at your door, and the Holy One, blessed be He, stands at his right hand. If you give unto him, He who stands at his right hand will bless you, but if not, He will exact punishment from you, as it is said, "Because He standeth at the right hand of the needy." (Psalm 109:31).

Midrash Ruth V:9

R. Isaac said, "He who gives a coin to a poor man is rewarded with six blessings. But he who encourages him with friendly words is rewarded with eleven."

Baba Bathra 9a

Question #1 is therefore answered. There is no question but that it is within the Jewish tradition to give to beggars. But we have 14 questions remaining, each of which tries to obtain a better understanding of the complexities of the whole issue.

2. WHAT IF THEY ARE FAKES OR FRAUDS?

Our Rabbis taught: If a man pretends to have a blind eye, a swollen belly or a shrunken leg, he will not pass out from this world before actually coming into such a condition. If a man accepts charity and is not in need of it, his end will be that he will not pass out of the world before he comes to such a condition.

Ketubot 68a

R. Avika said, He who takes even a penny from charity when he needs it not will not die before he requires the help of man. He said, He who binds rags on his eyes or on his loins and says, "Give to the blind man," or "Give to the man who is smitten with boils," will end by having good cause to utter this cry.

Avos d'R.Natan I,iii,8a

He who needs not and takes will not reach old age and die before he will really need help from others . . . He who is not lame or blind but pretends to be so, will not reach old age and die before he becomes really blind and lame.

Jerusalem Talmud, Pe'ah 8:9

If anyone is not in need of relief and yet receives it by deceiving the public, he will not die of old age before becoming a public charge. Such a person is included in the Biblical utterance: "A curse on him who relies on man." (Jer. 17:5)

Rambam, *Mishneh Torah*
"Gifts to the poor" 10:19

(These first 4 items agree and even seem to quote from each other. The message is clear, but it still doesn't help us. Should we give to the fakers? All we know so far is that they'll be punished for faking. Onward:)

R. Eleazar said: Come let us be grateful to the rogues for were it not for them we (who do not always respond to every appeal for charity) would have been sinning every day.

Ketubot 68a

R. Hanina was wont to send a poor man four zuzim every Friday. Once he sent them by his wife, who reported on her return that the man was not in need. "What did you see?" said the Rabbi. "I heard how he was asked, 'Would he use the silver outfit or the gold outfit.' " Then R. Hanina said, This is what R. Eleazar said: We must be grateful to the deceivers, for were it not for them, we might sin every day.

Ketubot 68a

(In other words, the fakers keep us in the habit of giving.)

A beggar once came to the city of Kovna and collected a large sum of money from the residents. The people of the town soon found out that he was an imposter; he really was a wealthy man. The city council wanted to make an ordinance prohibiting beggars from coming to Kovna to collect money. When R. Yitzchok Elchonon Specter, the Rabbi of Kovna, heard about the proposed ordinance, he came before the council and requested permission to speak. He told them that although he sympathized with them, he had an objection to raise. "Who deceived you, a needy person or a wealthy person? It was a wealthy person feigning poverty. If you want to make an ordinance, it should be to ban wealthy persons from collecting alms. But why make a ban against needy beggars?"

Ethics from Sinai,III,p.121

Rabbi Chayim of Sanz had this to say about fraudulent charity collectors: "The merit of charity is so great that I am happy to give to 100 beggars even if only one might actually be needy. Some people, however, act as if they are exempt from giving charity to 100 beggars in the event that one might be a fraud."

Darkai Chayim (1962), p. 137

(This last quote, from The Sanzer Rebbe Chayim Halberstam, who was the teacher of my great-great-great grandfather, Chayim Joseph Gottlieb, the Stropkover Rebbe, seems to sum up question #2 clearly: Don't let the frauds stop you from giving. And as the earlier sources quoted point out: the frauds will get theirs!)

3. WHAT IF THEY ARE NASTY OR OTHERWISE OFFENSIVE?

The Chofetz Chayim's son wrote that his father was particularly careful not to hurt the feelings of beggars, although sometimes these unfortunate people say things that could arouse one's anger.

Michtevai Chofetz Chayim (1953)
Dugmah Midarkai Avi,p.38

Rabbi Shmelke of Nicholsburg said, "When a poor man asks you for aid, do not use his faults as an excuse for not helping him. For then God will look for your offenses, and He is sure to find many of them. Keep in mind that the poor man's transgressions have been atoned for by his poverty while yours still remain with you.

Fun Unzer Alter Otzer, II, p.99

(This last quote, coupled with the first one, is somewhat helpful when dealing with the question of the alcoholic who asks for money. In some ways, the suffering he is undergoing is "punishment" enough. My denying him money "because he'd only use it for booze" is not helping anyone.)

4. WHAT IF I FEEL I SIMPLY CAN'T AFFORD TO GIVE TO BEGGARS?

To him who has the means and refuses the needy, the Holy One says: Bear in mind, fortune is a wheel!

Nahman, *Tanhuma*, Mishpatim #8

Even a poor man, a subject of charity, should give charity.

Gittin 7b

5. AREN'T THERE ANY BETTER CAUSES TO GIVE TO THAN TO THESE PEOPLE?

While it is commendable to aid students of the Torah more than commoners, the Jewish law knows no such distinction. The latter must also be aided.

Nachman of Bratzlav,
quoted in *Hasidic Anthology*

(This "excuse" noted above is a familiar one to me. How often I have passed by a beggar thinking: I gave to Oxfam International — The World Hunger Organization. The irony is too obvious to explain!)

6. SHOULDN'T THESE BEGGARS BE SUPPORTED BY OFFICIAL OR ORGANIZED AGENCIES?

In answer to an enquiry from a community, overburdened with beggars, Solomon b. Adret ruled that although, "the poor are everywhere supported from the communal chest, if they wish in addition to beg from door to door they may do so, and each should give according to his understanding and desire."

Responsa, pt.3,#380

7. SHOULDN'T I JUST IGNORE THESE PEOPLE?

R. Joshua b. Korha said, "Anyone who shuts his eye against charity is like one who worships idols."

Ketubot 68a
also Jerusalem Talmud, Peah 4:20

R. Joshua b. Korha said, "He who closes his eyes to a request for charity is considered as one who worships idols."

Baba Bathra 10a

(The same person with the same thought, in two different locations in the Talmud)

> A blind beggar accosted two men walking on the road. One of the travelers gave him a coin, but the other gave him nothing. The Angel of Death approached them and said: "He who gave to the beggar need have no fear of me for 50 years, but the other shall speedily die."
>
> "May I not return and give charity to the beggar?" asked the condemned man.
>
> "No," replied the Angel of Death. "A boat is examined for holes and cracks before departure, not when it is already at sea."
>
> Midrash in *Me'il Zedakah*

> If one noticed a poor man asking for something and ignored him, and failed to give tzedakah, he has broken a prohibitive command, as it is written: Do not harden your heart and shut your hand against your needy brother. (Deut.17:7)
>
> Rambam, *Mishneh Torah*
> "Gifts to the Poor" 7:2

> Rabbi Itzikel of Kalish was known for his kindness for everyone. Once a non-Jewish beggar asked the Rabbi's wife for some bread. At the moment she had only a full loaf, newly baked, and she disliked cutting it lest it become dry. But the Rabbi enjoined her to give the beggar a portion of this bread. A few years later, the Rabbi was travelling through the Carpathian Mountains toward Hungary. On the way brigands captured him and his companions, and brought them to their chieftain. The latter recognized the Rabbi as his benefactor when he came begging at his door. He freed Rabbi Itzikel and restored to him his possessions.
>
> *Or ha-Meir* (Lemberg, 1926), p.15

(The above is a strange story for a few reasons. First, the lesson is clearly not: give to beggars because they might become crooks and rob you. Second, like too many stories, the hero is the Rabbi, while the insensitive one is the wife. Thirdly, the beggar-thief is a non-Jew. Despite all this, the moral message still manages to sneak through: don't ignore beggars.)

> Rabbi Aharon Kotler once gave alms twice to the same beggar, upon entering and leaving a synagogue. He was afraid that someone noticing him pass the second time without giving might assume that he had reason not to give to this particular beggar.
>
> R.Shaul Kagan in *Jewish Observer*, 5/7

8. WHAT IF I AM IN A RUSH?

(The following story, from the Talmud, is one of the most vivid and powerful ones I've ever encountered. Every detail is radically unsettling.)

> It is related of Nahum of Gamzu that he was blind in both his eyes, his two hands and legs were amputated, and his whole body was covered with boils

and he was lying in a dilapidated house on a bed the feet of which were standing in bowls of water in order to prevent the ants from crawling on to him. On one occasion his disciples desired to remove the bed and then clear the things out of the house, but he said to them, "My children, first clear out the things from the house and then remove my bed for I am confident that so long as I am in the house it will not collapse." They first cleared out the things and then removed the bed and the house immediately collapsed. Thereupon his disciples said to him, Master, since you are wholly righteous, why has all this befallen you?" and he replied, "I have brought it all upon myself. Once I was journeying on the road and was making for the house of my father-in-law and I had with me three asses, one laden with food, one with drink, and one with all kinds of dainties, when a poor man met me and stopped me on the road and said to me, 'Master, give me something to eat.' I replied to him, 'Wait until I have unloaded something from the ass; I had hardly managed to unload something from the ass when the man died (from hunger). I then went and laid myself on him and exclaimed, May my eyes which had no pity upon your eyes become blind, may my hands which had no pity upon your hands be cut off, may my legs which had no pity upon your legs be amputated, and my mind was not at rest until I added, may my whole body be covered with boils." Thereupon his pupils exclaimed, "Alas that we see you in such a sore plight." To this he replied, "Woe would it be to me if you did not see me in such a sore plight."

Ta'anith 21a

9. WHAT IF THEY AREN'T JEWISH?

(The irony of this question is that when I was in Israel and when I met poor Jewish beggars in Eastern Europe, I never questioned the idea of giving to them. My own prejudices become crystal clear with this question!)

A Jew should give charity to poor non-Jews.

Rambam, *Mishneh Torah*
"Gifts to the Poor" 7:7

Poor Gentiles should be supported along with poor Jews; the Gentile sick should be visited along with the Jewish sick; and their dead should be buried along with the Jewish dead, in order to further peaceful relations.

Gittin 61a

(These last two items reflect a limitation on my part. In my reading I know that there are long discussions as to the true meaning and nature of the phrase "peaceful relations." On the surface it sounds as if we must do it not because it's right but for peace. The matter is much more complicated than that and is one that I do not have the ability to examine at this point. This is clearly one of the drawbacks of my own limited background.)

10. WHAT IF I HAVE NO MONEY ON ME OR NO SPARE CHANGE?

If a poor man requests money from you and you have nothing to give him, speak to him consolingly.

Rambam, *Mishneh Torah*
"Gifts to the Poor" 10:5

If the poor man stretches out his hand and he has nothing to give him, he should not scold and raise his voice to him, but he should speak gently to him and show him his goodness of heart; namely that he wishes to give him something but cannot.

Shulchan Aruch, Yoreh De'ah, 249:3 – 5

Walking one day in Jerusalem, Rabbi Aharon Kotler turned around, ran after a beggar, and gave him some coins. Rabbi Kotler later explained that several years previously, the same beggar had approached him for alms, but he was carrying no money. Spotting that beggar now, he hastened to make up for lost opportunity, and gave him a double amount.

R. Shaul Kagan, *Jewish Observer*, 5/73

11. IF I DO GIVE, HOW SHOULD I TREAT THESE PEOPLE? WHAT SHOULD I SAY? HOW SHOULD I APPROACH THEM?
    Rabbi Chana bar Chanila'i . . . would leave his hand in his pocket so that (by the immediacy and naturalness of handing him money) a poor person who came to ask would not feel humiliated.

Brachot 58b

R. Eleazar stated, The reward of charity depends entirely upon the extent of kindness in it.

Sukkah 49b

Anyone who gives tzedakah in a surly manner and with a gloomy face completely nullifies the merit of his own deed, even if he gives him a thousand gold pieces. He should rather give him cheerfully and gladly, while sympathizing with him who is in trouble, as it is written: "Did I not weep for him whose day was hard? Was not my soul grieved for the poor?" (Job 30:25)

Rambam, *Mishneh Torah*
"Gifts to the Poor" 10:4

12. WHAT IF I SEE THE SAME PEOPLE EVERY DAY? WON'T THEY GET TO KNOW ME AS A SUCKER?
    Though you may have given already, give yet again even a hundred times, for it says, "Give, yea, give thou shalt . . ." (Deut.15:10 – 11)

Sifre Deut., Re'eh, 116

13. WHAT IF I ALREADY GAVE TO A FEW BEGGARS IN ONE DAY?
    If you have given a 'perutah' to a man in the morning, and there comes to you in the evening another poor man asking for alms, give to him also . . ."

Avot d'R. Natan 19b

14. IF THEY ASK FOR MONEY, PERHAPS I SHOULD BUY THEM A CUP OF COFFEE INSTEAD?
    Nehemiah of Sihin met a man in Jerusalem who said to him, "Give me that chicken you are carrying." Nehemiah said, "Here is its value in money." The man went and bought some meat and ate it and died. Then Nehemiah said, "Come and bemoan the man whom Nehemiah has killed."

Jerusalem Talmud, Pe'ah, VIII:9,21b

(In this example, the case is reversed: the person wanted an item of food rather than money. But the point is the same: don't decide what is best for the beggar.)

15. HOW MUCH SHOULD I GIVE?

There was a poor man who begged from door to door, and R. Papa paid no attention to him. R. Samma, the son of R. Yiba, said to R. Papa, "If you pay no attention to him, then no one will, and he may starve to death." But is there not a baraita which tells us that if a man begs from door to door, the community has nothing to do with him? "The baraita is simply trying to tell us that he should not be given a large amount, but a small contribution should be made."

Baba Bathra 9a

A penny here and a penny there adds up to a great sum.

Nachman of Bratzlav, quoted in
Hasidic Anthology

A pauper who begs from house to house should be given only a small sum.

Shulchan Aruch, Yoreh De'ah, 250: 1 – 5

It is forbidden to turn away a poor man entirely empty-handed. Let him give something, if only a fig, for it is written, "Oh, let not the oppressed return ashamed." (Psalm 74:21)

R. Moshe Isserles,
note on *Shulchan Aruch*, Yoreh De'ah, 249:3 – 5

A poor man who goes begging should not be given a large donation but a small one. One must never turn a poor man away empty-handed, even if you give him a dry fig."

Rambam, *Mishneh Torah*
"Gifts to the Poor" 7:7

A penny for the poor will obtain a view of the Shekhinah.

Dosetai b. Yannai in
Baba Bathra 10a

R. Eleazar used to give a coin to a poor man and straightaway say a prayer because, he said, it is written, "I in righteousness shall behold thy face."

Baba Bathra 10a

As tiny scales join to form a strong coat of mail, so little donations combine to form a large total of good.

Baba Bathra 9b

Just as in a garment every thread unites with the rest to form a whole garment, so every penny given to charity unites with the rest to form a large sum.

Baba Bathra 9b

The message seems clear: don't ignore the beggar, don't treat him or her with anything but kindness, don't find excuses as to why not to give.

Rather give to everyone, regardless of who he or she is, but just give a little.

Each person's relationship to these texts is different. For me, the texts represent an ideal, and one which I confess I do not live up to regularly. Yet this research was not just an academic exercise for me. I certainly learned more than that the classical texts (and others) of our Tradition have a lot to say — in very contemporary terms — about the present issue. I certainly learned that I *am* able to explore the texts with a minimum of background and knowledge. But most importantly the exploration of the text moved me — literally — to avoid passing up the opportunity of observing the mitzvah of tzedakah each day in the neighborhood. I often fail at seizing each opportunity offered to me, but I struggle to come closer to the ideal — and that is, in my opinion, the purpose of the teachings.

Before offering a little more detail regarding methodology, it would be important to add a final note regarding the texts and the situations it discusses: As a male, I am much more secure on the streets of Manhattan than a woman is. This is not sexism but rather a sad reality. Because of this, and because a woman might be putting herself in a dangerous situation by stopping on the street for an encounter with any stranger, it must be noted that this is one contemporary condition which I did not find in any text.

But to conclude this section on a more positive note:

> R. Assi observed: Tzedakah is as important as all the other commandments put together.
>
> Baba Bathra 9a

BIBLIOGRAPHY

Only the sources listed here have been used for this article. Only the multi-volume sources in the "Classical Texts" section are expensive. The others are all either paperbacks or relatively inexpensive hardbacks. But even the expensive items should be seriously considered for purchase by any family interested in a lifetime investment in the basic texts of our Tradition. Actually, they would be more than a lifetime investment: they would surely stay in the family for generations.

There is one exception to something just mentioned: *The Encyclopaedia Judaica* (16 volumes) is also an expensive item. *But*, if there is any *one* item in the entire bibliography which would be a treasure to own it would be this! It is the most ambitious effort of this kind in our history, and is *the* source to have for just about any layman's questions on any Jewish subject.

If an item has an asterisk (*) in front of it, it means that it is of extraordinary quality. If you are using this bibliography to aid in your purchase of books for your home library, it would be these items which I would strongly recommend. If an item has an (o.p.) in front of it, it means that it is "out of print" and therefore no longer available from the publisher. Nevertheless I suggest you examine these books if your libraries have them — and keep an eye out for them in some good used bookstores. (Some of the Lower East Side bookstores may even have copies for sale.)

CLASSICAL TEXTS
(*) *The Torah; The Five Books of Moses.* Jewish Publication Society, Philadelphia, 1962.
(*) *The Babylonian Talmud.* The Soncino Press, London. (18 volumes)
(*) *The Midrash Rabbah.* The Soncino Press, London. (5 volumes)
(*) *The Minor Tractates of the Talmud.* The Soncino Press, London. (2 volumes)

BASIC REFERENCE SOURCES
(*) *Encyclopaedia Judaica.* Keter Publishing House, Jerusalem, 1972. (16 volumes)
(*) Birnbaum, Philip. *Encyclopedia of Jewish Concepts.* Hebrew Publishing Co., New York, 1980. (paperback)

QUOTATIONS, COMPILATIONS, SELECTIONS, ETC.
Alcalay, Reuben. *A Basic Encyclopedia of Jewish Proverbs, Quotations, and Folk Wisdom.* Hartmore House, Bridgeport, CT 1973.
(o.p.) Baron Joseph L. *A Treasury of Jewish Quotations.* Yoseloff, South Brunswick, NJ, 1965.
Cohen, Dr. A., *Everyman's Talmud.* E.P. Dutton, New York, 1949.
Feinsilver, Rabbi Alexander. *The Talmud For Today.* St. Martin's Press, New York, 1980.
(*) Klagsbrun, Francine. *Voices of Wisdom; Jewish Ideals and Ethics for Everyday Living.* Pantheon Books, New York, 1980.
Meiseles, Meir. *Judaism: Thought and Legend; an anthology on ethics and philosophy throughout the ages.* Feldheim Publishers, New York, 1964 (paperback)
(*) Montefiore, C.G. and Loewe, H. A *Rabbinic Anthology*, Schocken Books, New York, 1974. (paperback)
(*) Rosten, Leo. *Leo Rosten's Treasury of Jewish Quotations.* Bantam Books, New York, 1977. (paperback)

INTRODUCTIONS TO TALMUD
(o.p.) Bokser, Rabbi Ben Zion. *Wisdom of the Talmud.* The Citadel Press, New York, 1962.
(*) Steinsaltz, Adin. *The Essential Talmud.* Bantam Books, New York, 1976. (paperback)

MISCELLANEOUS SOURCES
(*) Newman, Louis I. *Hasidic Anthology; Tales and Teachings of the Hasidim.* Schocken Books, New York. 1963. (paperback)
Pliskin Zelig. *Love Your Neighbor; You and Your Fellow Man in Light of the Torah.* Aish HaTorah Publications, Brooklyn, 1977.
Twersky, Isadore. *A Maimonides Reader.* Behrman House, New York, 1972. (paperback)
(*) Steinberg, Milton. *As A Driven Leaf.* Behrman House, New York. (paperback). (Note: This is a *novel* which takes place in Talmudic times; no source material here, but a wonderful introduction to the Talmud and its major personalities. A wonderful book.)

METHODOLOGY: ONE EXAMPLE
When my teacher, Danny Siegel, and I study together, we find that by the end of an hour or so there are dozens of books all around us, opened to places we have referred to over the past short time. We are constantly jumping from book to book, trying to get a better insight into our subject and in particular the text we are studying.

Here is one brief example of this methodology: Since our subject is "beggars," I first go to the *Encyclopaedia Judaica*; it is the place to begin for any subject of Jewish interest. I am delighted to see that there is an entry titled "BEGGING AND BEGGARS." (this is not always so simple, in which case one needs to figure out what other words might be used for the subject in question.)

Reading the article on "Begging and beggars," I see that "Ket. 67b" and

"Ket. 68a" are frequently cited Talmudic sources. (I already know, through other reading as well as Danny Siegel that "Ket." is the common English abbreviation for the tractate Ketubot in the Babylonian Talmud — and that 67b as well as 68a indicates the pages in Ketubot. So, my next step is to go to the Soncino Talmud (English) and read Ket. 67b and 68a. I notice right away that the whole section is filled with material on tzedakah and beggars — more than the *Encyclopaedia Judaica* even indicated. It is also interesting to see that in a section of the Talmud labeled "Ketubot" — which is marriage contracts — you will find material on other subjects as well. Since the Rabbis of the Talmud often "free associated," they usually discuss other topics in the midst of their subject at hand.

I read the parts of the Talmud and at one point read a passage which intrigues me. It says:

> R. Abba used to bind money in his scarf, sling it on his back, and place himself at the disposal of the poor. He cast his eye, however, sideways as a precaution against rogues.
>
> Ket. 67b.

One of the strongest messages which I learned from Danny Siegel is that the Rabbis of the Talmud were human beings. They were not just names to be quoted. I was interested in the image of a man who would put money on his back in a scarf for poor people — apparently so as not to embarrass them. But he would also keep an eye out for fakers — in contradiction of what we have already learned was the general feelings towards frauds of this kind. In any event, I wanted to learn a little more about R. Abba.

I went back to the E.J. and looked up "Abba." There were dozens of them. But I knew that most of them could *not* be the R. Abba I was looking for since the E.J. listing said "Abba bar Aha," or "Abba bar Avina," or some other "Abba bar _____." The Talmud said "Abba." Still, there were a few Abba's listed. I'd have to check each one. Luckily, I found him on the first try. There were two Rabbis named Abba in the same time period, but I found mine since the Encyclopaedia Judaica (E.J.) article indicated which one was quoted in Ket. 67b.!

The E.J. then gives me a brief biography on R. Abba, constructed from the various facts throughout the Talmud and other sources. I learn, for example, that R. Abba was in the silk business and became quite wealthy. The E.J. said, "This enabled him to honor the Sabbath by buying 13 choice cuts from 13 butchers." (Shab.119a) This then leads me to that page of the Talmud in the tractate Shabbat, to read the context of the item about R. Abba and the 13 cuts of meat. I suddenly find myself in the middle of a fascinating description on how various of the Rabbis had unique ways of honoring the Sabbath.

And the process continues. The Talmud is called the "sea of Talmud," and as soon as one begins to study, one understands the metaphor. I have jumped into the study of Torah and Talmud, swimming down many paths. Some are simple, others difficult. Some I swim through like a breeze, in others I nearly drown (again, the need for a good teacher.) In all cases, I come out stimulated and refreshed, looking forward to my next "swim."

And I don't know very much Hebrew or Aramaic. But I know how to use my books, and I am learning some Hebrew in the process. Some day I hope to be comfortable in the original — but I need not wait until then to begin to study. Rabbi Akiva did not begin until he was 40 years old. And he was the foremost scholar of his time.

A STORY I ONCE HEARD
FROM A YOUNG MEDICAL RESIDENT

How much should one give to the poor?
Whatever it is that the person might need.
How is this to be understood?
If he is hungry, he should be fed.
If he needs clothes, he should be provided with clothes.
If he has no household furniture or utensils, furniture and utensils should
be provided . . .
If he needs to be spoonfed, then we must spoonfeed him.

(Shulchan Aruch, Yoreh De'ah, 250:1)

An eminent physician is taking his students on morning rounds. Here and there he explains to his entourage some fine point of the art of healing, adding to their store of insight and knowledge so that when they assume their positions as Healers, they, too, will demonstrate the requisite skill and wisdom needed to ease suffering and pain. The professor's expertise impresses the interns and residents.

As they go from room to room, the professor and students encounter an older woman recently arrived as a "social admission." She is not desperately ill, but her complex of ailments makes it impossible for her neighbors and friends to take care of her. The professor sees that she is depressed, withdrawn. She refuses to eat. There is nothing here to be revealed in the way of book-knowledge; no advanced scholarship is needed.

The professor stops, and for twenty minutes feeds the woman.

She is capable of feeding herself, but she refuses to do so. So, with deliberate and gentle care, the teacher teaches a lesson in kindness. He does not do it as a demonstration to the students. No . . . he spoonfeeds this old woman because that is what the demands of the hour are. If, as a result of this long delay, the students will have missed some detail of graduate training, some fact concerning prescriptions or diagnosis, it matters little to the professor.

Human beings must be served with a touch of humanity.

A STUDY GUIDE TO TZEDAKAH

Introduction

For a period of nearly five hundred years, the wise teachers of our people gathered in houses of study to discuss Life, how to live our lives fully as creatures made in the image of God. They realized that being a Mensch, living each day with an awareness of the Holiness of Life, required a conscious effort to actualize ourselves through specific Mitzvah-acts. Many of these Mitzvot were developed during that period — the Talmudic Period — through study of ancient texts such as the Bible and an examination of the way people acted in their daily lives. Their discussions, and sketches of their personal biographies, are recorded in the Babylonian and Jerusalem Talmuds and in various books of legal and non-legal texts known as Midrash, and it is primarily from these sources that this study material is drawn. Whether we look at their specific acts, their lyrical insights, or their careful collection of details, we cannot but be struck by the grandeur of their wisdom — a wisdom very much relevant to our individual lives today. As Jews, we are obliged to examine their words, to attempt to understand their insights into Tzedakah, and to apply them to today's immediate situation.[1]

Let us begin with a brief analysis of some essential vocabulary: the secular words charity and philanthropy, and the specifically Jewish terms Tzedakah and Tzedek —

"Charity" is derived from the Latin root *caritas*, meaning love, dearness, fondness.

"Philanthropy" comes from a combination of two Greek roots, *philia*, meaning love, and *anthropos*, meaning man.

"Tzedakah — צדקה is derived from the Hebrew root צדק TZ-D-K, meaning justice, that which is right, and is related to the word צדיק , Tzaddik, a person who lives according to Tzedakah and Tzedek — an upright, giving life.

Let us compare the implications of these terms. Charity and philanthropy, though they have been stripped to a bare meaning of the giving of money, originally indicated acts of love, actions motivated by an inner caring for others. Tzedakah includes this feeling, of course, but it goes further, superseding the immediate moods of the individual and demanding that — even if you are not in a particularly loving mood — the obligation, the Mitzvah, still requires us to give.

A prime example would be the Falafel Syndrome. Occasionally, a person enjoys the exotic foods of Eretz Yisrael too freely and, as a consequence of his overindulgence in the delicacy of falafel, suffers gastro-intestinal complications. Imagine someone stretched out on the bed, in the heat of a Jerusalem summer day, weak and miserable. A man or a woman comes to the door and says, "There is to be a bris, and there is a need for wine and cake for refreshments," or "We are going to visit Reuven in the hospital, and we are collecting money to bring him flowers and gifts to cheer him up. . . ." According to the connotations of the concept of charity and philanthropy, the ailing person need not give, since he does not feel in a particularly loving mood. By contrast, *Tzedakah* clearly demands a positive response, an overriding of the immediate blah-feelings, and a rising to the occasion to give freely for the benefit of those in need.

Tzedakah does not leave us to our individual moods. The pattern of giving suggested by this Mitzvah means we *must* respond — no matter how we feel at a particular moment. Furthermore, we are instructed to take the initiative in giving — not waiting for imminent disaster, such as the Yom Kippur War, to give. Were the Jews to wait for threats and emergencies, Israel and vital institutions, as well as individuals in great need of Tzedakah would not survive. Being a Mensch and integrating Tzedakah into our lives means aggressively seeking out situations and people and times and places where we may best apply our powers to provide a measure of תקון עולם, Tikun Olam — Fixing-Up the World. We must be on the lookout at all times.

There are two final terms that we must keep in mind when studying Tzedakah — Kavod and Bushah.

כבוד — Kavod is honor, dignity, respect. The Talmud says: — גדול כבוד הבריות-the kavod due to God's creatures is extremely great.[2] We are to treat every person with the sense of dignity he or she deserves.

בושה — Bushah is shame, humiliation, embarrassment, the opposite of Kavod. We are similarly expected to avoid causing a sense of Bushah in another person.

Many stories we read in the Talmud, and many tales passed on to us by others — as well as real-life encounters we may see — will be understood better with these two terms in mind.

Talmudic Material — Part I, Statements about Tzedakah:

The following are some selected statements the Talmud has made concerning Tzedakah, with a brief commentary.

"One who gives even a perutah — the smallest coin — to the poor, is privileged to sense God's Presence."[3] There is something unique about the act of giving Tzedakah — so unique that the amount given is often (but not always) secondary to the act of giving. Even the most insignificant sum of money, given properly, at the right time and place, allows a person to feel the deeper and higher meanings of Life.

"Even a poor person who receives Tzedakah must give from what he receives."[4] The Talmud is telling us that an individual's sense of Kavod — his self-dignity — is expressed through his giving. Freeing him from the responsibility of giving is really taking away a privilege. The Halachah — Jewish Law — allows two poor people to exchange with each other the same food for Purim.[5] Both remain with the identical items with which they began, but both have shared the Mitzvah of Tzedakah, thereby retaining their self-respect.

"The three most prominent characteristics of the Jews are that they are הרחמנים והביישנין וגומלי חסדים — filled with Rachmanut, non-arrogant, and do acts of extreme loving kindness.[6] Rachmanut is one of the many traditional Jewish terms for compassion. It is a kind of love that gives freely, openly, fully, and it is intimately connected with Tzedakah.

"Anyone who runs to do Tzedakah will find the necessary funds . . . and the proper recipients for his Tzedakah works."[7] As long as there is a strong desire to do Tzedakah, we are assured of success in our endeavors, both in financial and in human terms. Our Talmudic teachers felt certain that giving money away would not lead the giver to personal poverty. Here are two other thoughts on this matter:

"If a person sees that his resources are limited, let him use them for Tzedakah — and so much the more so if he has extensive resources."[8]

"Give away a tenth, so that you may become wealthy."[9] Returning to the idea of Kavod — one's sense of dignity and self-respect, we can readily understand that the enrichment of a person's life is expressed Jewishly in terms other than financial. Giving away a percentage of our income is the most certain sign of our being concerned for living as a Mensch . . . an upright, giving person. Maimonides states this very clearly and succinctly in his Law Code, the Mishnah Torah:

"A person never becomes poor from giving Tzedakah, nor does any harm come from it, as the verse states, 'And the result of Tzedakah will be Shalom — Peace.' "[10]

Finally, mention should be made of one institution — לשכת חשאים, Lishkat Chasha'im — The Secret Chamber. It will help give us a sense of how the Rabbis' statements became a part of their society:

"There was a Secret Chamber in the Temple where pious people would leave money in secret, and those who had become poor would come and take in secret."[11] Another text adds that there were similar Secret Chambers in all major settlements in Israel — wherever there was a Sanhedrin.[12]

This is just one example of how our Teachers rooted Tzedakah into the life-patterns of the Jewish People. They wished to avoid all chance of Bushah for the poor, so they provided this storehouse for Tzedakah funds, thereby allowing absolute anonymity for those in need of assistance.

Talmudic Material — Part II, Tales from the Lives of the Rabbis

As important as studying the statements of the Talmudic Masters, is an examination of the way they themselves put into practice their ideas and insights. Their biographies reflect a profound concern for Tzedakah, and there are many examples of individuals whose actions, retold centuries later, serve as souces of inspiration for us. The following are just a few selections:

"Rabbi Chana bar Chanila'i had sixty bakers in his house day and night, baking for anyone who needed bread. He would leave his hand in his pocket so that (by the immediacy and naturalness of handing him money) a poor person who came to ask would not feel humiliated. His doors were open to all four directions, and anyone who came in hungry would leave satisfied. Furthermore, in times when food was scarce, he would leave wheat and barley outside the door, so that anyone who was too embarrassed to come and take in the daytime could come unnoticed and take at night.''[13] We are reminded of the stories of Abraham and Job, both of whom had their tents open to the four directions. Both took the initiative to be on the lookout to make Tzedakah part of their lives, and Rabbi Chana bar Chanila'i did the same — as well as adding many insights into the prevention of Bushah. A split-second act — taking a hand and putting it into the pocket to take money out — might have caused shame to the person in need — and this Rabbi wished to avoid that at all costs.

"Rabbi Yannai once saw a man give Tzedakah to a poor man in public. He said to him, 'It would have been better not to give than giving as you did, causing him shame.' ''[14] Apparently the contributor had given too openly, and the financial benefit for the poor man was not worth the humiliation he suffered as a result of the public nature of the act.

"Rabbi Tanhum, though he needed only one portion of meat for himself, would buy two: one bunch of vegetables, he would buy two — one for the poor and one for himself.''[15] Rabbi Tanhum was establishing a regulating pattern in his life, a Tzedakah-habit.

"Rabbi Zecharia, the son-in-law of Rabbi Levi, used to take Tzedakah money. His colleagues would deride him, thinking he did not need it. When he died, they discovered that he had been giving it out to others.''[16] Rabbi Zecharia's forgivable deception allowed him to do more Tzedakah work. The fact that he was giving it to others allowed him to overcome the harsh feelings of his friends. There are many people like this in the world: people who take ostensibly for themselves, and who in a private, sometimes secret, fashion give it to those who are in need.

"Rabbi Chama bar Chanina and Rabbi Hoshaya were touring the synagogues of Lod. Rabbi Chama bar Chanina said to Rabbi Hoshaya, 'See how much money my fathers have invested here!' He replied, 'How many souls your ancestors have sunk here! Was there no one here who wanted to study Torah (and who would need the money for support)?' ''[17] There is a subtle play on the Hebrew words here, but the meaning is clear — Rabbi Hoshaya is saying that his friend's ancestors should have had a better sense of priorities, providing scholarship money and living expenses for students, rather than building big buildings.

"Abba bar Ba gave money to his son Shmuel to distribute to the poor. He went out and found a poor person eating meat and drinking wine. When he told his father what he had seen, his father said, 'Give him more, for his soul is bitter.' ''[18] This story indicates an important Tzedakah-principle: a person who was once well-to-do and who is now poor must be allowed to adjust gradually to his diminished economic status. The poor man Shmuel found was evidently used to finer foods and wine, and Abba bar Ba is telling his son that he is suffering the trauma of poverty and must be allowed to re-orient himself psychologically and physically at his own pace. The "bitterness of soul" is a factor always taken into account by the Rabbis, and it was of critical importance, particularly for recently impoverished people, to preserve their sense of Kavod. A story about Hillel further illustrates this principle:

"(A person must be provided) even a horse to ride upon and a servant to run in front of him. . . . They said of Hillel that he once personally ran before the horse of a man who had become recently impoverished, because they could not find another person to do it."[19] We know from the Megillat Esther that riding through the streets on a horse led by a servant was a sign of great honor in ancient times. Hillel, realizing the danger of Bushah for this poor man, took it upon himself to fulfill this part of the Mitzvah.

Two final tales:

"When Tzedakah collectors would see Elazar of Birata, they would hide from him, because he would give away all that he had with him. One day he was on the way to the market to purchase something for his daughter's wedding when the Tzedakah-collectors saw him. They hid from him, but he went running after them. . . ."[20] Elazar of Birata was an overly-generous person, and the Talmud and Codes of Law carefully warn Tzedakah collectors not to go to such an individual too frequently, as there are limits to how much a person should give away of his own possessions. Here, the person (and others like him), must have his particular Kavod protected by those involved in the collection of funds.

"A story is told of Binyamin HaTzaddik, who was the supervisor of the community's Tzedakah-funds. Once, when food was scarce, a woman came to him and said, 'Rabbi, feed me!' He replied, 'I swear that there is nothing in the Tzedakah-fund.' She said, 'If you do not feed me, a woman and her seven children will die.' So he fed her from his own money."[21] This story simply states the principle: When nothing can be done, something can still be done. Even though his official responsibilities ended when the communal funds were exhausted, Binyamin's obligations as a Jew demanded some deliberate action. Something had to be done and Binyamin rose to the occasion.

Talmudic (and Post-Talmudic) Material — Part III, Legal Texts:

The Talmud establishes extensive rules for the giving of Tzedakah, laws which are codified in Maimonides' Mishnah Torah, in the Shulchan Aruch, and in later legal collections such as the Aruch HaShulchan and modern Responsa literature — the questions addressed to rabbis of our day, and their decisions based on the development of the Halachah through the centuries. The most important law for our study is the statement that "One should give up to a fifth of one's possessions — that is the Mitzvah to an extraordinary degree. One tenth is an average percentage, and less is weak eyesight."[22] There are some exceptions to the 20% maximum limit, e.g., when money is needed for redeeming captives; when the contributor is extremely wealthy, and concerning provisions made in a last will-and-testament, but the Jewish mode of giving definitely prohibits the giving away of greater amounts — and certainly a person should not give everything away. Maimonides clearly states that giving everything away is not חסידות chassidut — saintliness, but rather שטות, shtut, — foolishness.[23] This study material therefore assumes that we are speaking of the 10-20% range of giving.

Some modern authorities explain that these Tzedakah funds are to be calculated after income taxes and business expenses are deducted.[24] (The details concerning other kinds of taxes and what are to be considered valid business expenses should be studied at greater length as the need arises.) Furthermore, it is clear that inheritance money, *and money received as gifts*, should have an appropriate 10%-20% deducted for Tzedakah.[25] Therefore, since a person becomes obligated to do Mitzvot from the time of Bar or Bat Mitzvah, we should educate our youth to begin their active Life of Tzedakah by giving away a portion of what they receive on the occasion of their coming-of-Jewish age. In many homes, Jewish children are trained in the ways of Tzedakah by putting money in a pushka (any Tzedakah box), by planting trees in Eretz Yisrael, and by other practices. The privilege of giving is taught to them at an early age, and certainly by Bar and Bat Mitzvah, it should become a regular pattern in each Jew's life. It is one of the many ways of assuming one's full responsibility of being a part of the Jewish People.

Some other specific laws:

"A person should give pleasantly, joyously, with a good heart, showing sympathy for the poor, sharing in his sense of pain and sorrow."[26] Jewish tradition tells us that, besides the giving itself, we will form attitudes about people and human nature through the act of giving. As a result of Menschlich acts, we will become more aware of the nature of being a Mensch. that is a basic Jewish idea — *the doing forms the theory* — and not the other way around.

"One should not be arrogant when giving."[27] If Tzedakah is understood as a זכות — a Zechut, a privilege, and an act to be done with Simcha — joy, then the dangers of overwhelming egotism will be avoided. Jewish Tradition does not advocate the position that the giver is the All Good Helper dispensing pennies here and there to the poor, unfortunate souls of the world. Recalling our root-word צדק, TZ-D-K, we understand that it is right and just to give, and this is a part of the meaning of being created in God's image.

"If a person convinces others to give, his reward is even greater than when simply giving by himself."[28] The Shulchan Aruch is saying that encouraging others to give is a primary obligation for Jews. The dividing line between "convincing," "encouraging," "arm-twisting," "nudging," "pressuring," and "forcing" is often blurred today, but it is perfectly proper for us to make this a part of our conversation with others. There is nothing inherently sleazy or greasy about encouraging others to give money away and raising funds for appropriate people and places. Everything depends on the Menschlich tone when the subject is raised.

"There are eight degrees of giving Tzedakah. The highest degree is to aid a Jew . . . to become self-supporting, so that he will not have to ask others for anything."[29] Maimonides' eight categories of Tzedakah are a classic study-text, critical points for anyone wishing to gain a deeper understanding of the sensitivities involved in Jewish giving. The one just stated is the highest. The following is a list, in descending order, of the other seven:

"He who gives Tzedakah to the poor and is unaware of the recipient, who in turn is unaware of the giver. This is indeed a religious act achieved for its own sake. Of a similar character is the one who contributes to a Tzedakah fund. One should not contribute to a Tzedakah fund unless he knows that the person in charge of the collections is trustworthy and intelligent and knows how to manage properly. . . .

"The third, lesser, degree is when the giver knows the recipient, but the recipient does not know the giver. The great sages used to go secretly and cast the money into the doorway of the poor. Something like this should be done, it being a noble virtue, if the Tzedakah administrators are behaving improperly.

"The fourth, still lower degree is when the recipient knows the giver, but the giver does not know the recipient. The great sages used to tie money in sheets which they threw behind their backs, and the poor would come and get it without being embarrassed.

"The fifth degree is when the giver puts the Tzedakah money into the hands of the poor without being solicited.

"The sixth degree is when he puts the money into the hands of the poor after being solicited.

"The seventh degree is when he gives him less than he should, but does so cheerfully.

"The eighth degree is when he gives him grudgingly."

These Eight Degrees, as well as other laws mentioned in Maimonides' Law Code and the Shulchan Aruch would make excellent source material for a more extensive study of Tzedakah — either as a course, or for individual study.

Talmudic Material — Part IV, Gemilut Chassadim, Specific Acts of Sympathetic Lovingkindness:

גמילות חסדים — Gemilut Chassadim is a special category of Mitzvot related to Tzedakah. In its most restricted sense, Tzedakah is concerned with money (and goods provided with money) for the poor, while Gemilut Chassadim goes beyond this in three ways: it applies to rich as well as poor recipients, to a person's time and energy as well as money, and it extends to the deceased as well as to the living.[30] Sometimes the definitions intermingle but it is important to mention the specific nature of Gemilut Chassadim, Acts of Sympathetic Lovingkindness, in order to broaden our awareness of Menschlich living. Some define a wide variety of acts within this category,[31] though usually there are six specific Mitzvot mentioned in the texts:

1. הלבשת ערומים (Halbashat Arumim) — providing clothes for those who need them.

2. ביקור חולים (Bikkur Cholim) — visiting the sick.

3. ניחום אבלים (Nichum Avaylim) — comforting the mourners.

4. לוית המת (Levayat HaMayt) — accompanying the dead to their final rest.

5. הכנסת כלה (Hachnassat Kallah) — providing for brides.

6. הכנסת אורחים (Hachnassat Orchim) — hospitality.[32]

We are told that God Himself clothed the naked (Adam and Eve), visited the sick (Abraham), comforted the mourners (Isaac), and buried the dead (Moses),[33] so that in Gemilut Chassadim, we are imitating God, living out our image of Him. There are many examples of the Talmudic Rabbis doing admirable acts of Gemilut Chassadim, as in the case of Rabbi Chana bar Chanila'i's providing bread for the poor. We are even told that in a certain period of Jewish history, it was a custom in Jerusalem that at mealtime, a cloth would be hung on the door, indicating that as long as the cloth was out, whoever was hungry could come in and eat.[34] Many members of our parents' and grandparents' generations remember strangers being brought to their table, people found in the synagogue who had no provisions for a Shabbat or Yomtov meal. Hospitality committees have now become a part of many synagogue organizations, and it would be most worthwhile to extend this to other communities.

Other examples:

We know from the Talmud that Rabbi Akiva was not only concerned for the poor, but that he set a prominent example for visiting the sick. Once, a student of his fell sick, and no one went to visit him. When Rabbi Akiva went to visit, people cleaned and swept the house in his honor, and because the man no longer needed to worry about his day-to-day cares, he recovered more quickly.[35] And Rabbi Yochanan, leader of the Jews in Israel in the 3rd Century, did wonders for his sick student-and-friend, Rabbi Elazar. The recovery was brought about as much by his affection and friendship for the sick man as by any medicines he might have carried with him.[36]

Stories such as these should be studied carefully, and stories from life around us should be exchanged, so that we may gain more insight into the powers of these particular mitzvot to provide not only the bare necessities for fellow Jews, but also comfort, sympathy, and a greater Will to Live.

Conclusion — Thoughts, Suggestions

The Zohar, a classic text of Jewish mysticism, refers to Tzedakah as אילנא דחיי — a Tree of life.[37] What is now necessary is a further study of Living-through-Tzedakah-and-Gemilut-Chassadim. More important, perhaps, than the study, is the necessity of gathering experience through the actual giving away of money and performing the all-important Mitzvot of visiting the sick, comforting mourners, providing hospitality, and doing the other Mitzvot in this category.

We should examine how Jewish communities of the past provided — and how our communities today provide — for the poor, the sick, the elderly, the retarded, the deceased, learning about Free Loan Societies, Bikkur Cholim Societies, Societies for Poor Brides, Chevra Kadishas (Burial Societies). We should spend time with people who are involved in this work, learning from their experience. Some of these people are Tzaddikim, truly Righteous Ones, and it is of supreme importance that we seek them out.[38] Some do their work so quietly and secretly, they are difficult to find. Nevertheless, it should be our priority to search for them and to watch them work. Whether it is money-turned-Mitzvot they speak of, or time-and-energy-made Mitzvot, their insights will be invaluable to our own work and our individual search for Menschlich living.

Through these various means, now and again making mistakes as we grope for our sense of what is wisest in Tzedakah, we will learn priorities — where and when and how to give best of our time, our money, ourselves. We will more and more assume the decision-making processes of our communities, and we will have to, with the help of our fellow Jews, choose how to apportion our financial and personal resources for the sake of Tikun Olam — Repairing the World.

It is best to close with the words of one of the Righteous Ones of Jerusalem, the Rabbanit Bracha Kapach: "נזכה למצוות" — Nizkeh LeMitzvot, may we be privileged to do these Mitzvot together, building a chevra based on the actualization of our potential-to-Menschlichkeit. That is, perhaps, the ultimate privilege of being a Jew.

Footnotes:

[1] Yerushalmi Shekalim 5:4.
[2] Berachot 19b, Shabbat 81b, et al.
[3] Bava Batra 10a.
[4] Gittin 7b.
[5] Mishna Berura to Shulchan Aruch, Orach Chayim 694:1.
[6] Yevamot 79a.
[7] Bava Batra 9b.
[8] Gittin 7a.
[9] Shabbat 119a.
[10] Mishna Torah, Hilchot Matnot Ani'im, 10:2.
[11] Mishna Shekalim 5:6.
[12] Tosefta Shekalim 2:16.
[13] Berachot 58b.
[14] Chagiga 5a.
[15] Kohelet Rabba 7:30.
[16] Yerushalmi Shekalim 5:4.
[17] Ibid.
[18] Yerushalmi Peah 8:8; a similar story is told of Mar Ukbah and his son in Ketubot 67b.
[19] Ketubot 67b.
[20] Ta'anit 24a.
[21] Bava Batra 11a.
[22] Shulchan Aruch, Yoreh De'ah, 249:1.
[23] Mishna Torah, Hilchot Arachin V'Charamin 8:13.
[24] Aruch HaShulchan, Yoreh De'ah, 249:7, Igrot Moshe, Yoreh De'ah, 143.
[25] Aruch HaShulchan, Yoreh De'ah, 249:6, and conversation with Rabbi Shlomo Riskin.
[26] Shulchan Aruch, Yoreh De'ah, 249:3.
[27] Ibid., 249:13, note by Isserles.
[28] Ibid., 249:5.
[29] Mishna Torah, Hilchot Matnot Ani'im 10:7-14, Shulchan Aruch, Yoreh De'ah, 249:6-13.
[30] Sukkah 49b.
[31] Entziklopedia Talmudit 6:149-153.
[32] Sotah 14a, Eruvin 18a, Shabbat 127a-b.
[33] Sotah 14a.
[34] Bava Batra 93b.
[35] Nedarim 40a.
[36] Berachot 5b.
[37] Zohar, Leviticus 111.
[38] Cf. Moment Magazine, July/August, 1975, "Gym Shoes and Irises."

THEOLOGY AND TZEDAKAH:
TWO POINTS

#1 — ORIGINS

It has been years since I have taken a course in philosophy or theology. Even when I was in college, I took only the minimum requirements, perhaps one or two semesters of each. I felt uncomfortable in the rigorous framework of building systems from premises, piecing many building blocks into distinct shimmering palaces of thought, wonders for the mind. I was never much good at that, making things. In junior high school we had to take a class in industrial arts, and now looking back, I see that the ashtray and bookends I made were embarrassingly crude. Somehow this lack of manual skill must have carried over into the college courses — intellectual structural skills — and even years later I lose patience when trying to follow an argument that builds from too many logical axioms. My lectures lack coherence; free association carries me from one point to another, and the audiences often struggle to find the connections. I concentrate on single points, pausing to examine from many angles a specific idea that excites my imagination: what does it mean, a curved universe? How much of an uncertainty factor is there in physics, in life? What is the Nothingness out in space, in between atoms and molecules stationed at incomprehensible distances from each other? One at a time, at different times, I would put haphazard energies to wandering through these problems, unsystematically, and as to be expected, often without any productive results. Still, the few rewarding breakthroughs encouraged me, and continue to encourage me, and I continue to work with this flexible method from time to time. For the present, I am concentrating on aspects of origins and birth: the Creation story of Genesis, Adam and Eve, the birth of children, whole and healthy, and also defective infants.

Birth — the amazement a parent must feel as the baby breathes through lungs for the first time, no longer dependent on nourishment through the umbilicus. Birth, a passage from slavery inside another body to freedom in the outside. A paradigm for Passover, a birth of our people, forever having to struggle with the new constraints of freedom. Birth and death — their proximity, the utter contradiction of their realities, the multiplicity of Talmudic and Midrashic tales linking the two. I even discovered an ancient custom of burying the placenta shortly after birth . . . a guarantee to the earth (from which we were taken), that some day we shall return to it.

Even now, in the midst of considering the broader meanings of Tzedakah, I see connections. I call to mind a critical passage in Pirke Avot, The Sayings of the Fathers:

Against your will you were created;
Against your will you were born. (*4:22*)

It is such an obvious fact: we were not consulted as to whether or not we wished to be conceived or born. Our most basic existence as human beings began before — long before — we were capable of evaluating the implications of such an event. We were conceived and born encompassed by an aura of surprise, and as the late Professor Abraham Joshua Heschel warned us again and again, we must retain this sense of surprise throughout our lifetimes. It is essential to our humanity.

As the first light strikes our eyes as a seconds-old infant, we are filled with wonder. Were we able to express this feeling at that time, I am certain our parents would join us in reaffirming that emotion. We are, in those moments, a gift. Two become three, as later on (so the Talmud tells us), two becomes three — when we are old, and weak, and our two legs can no longer carry us, and we are left to walk with a cane. It is all so mysterious. One moment we do not exist, and another we are alive, shielded for years from that other mystery, the presence of the Angel of Death. For days and weeks, months and years, we move along, unaware.

We did not ask to have eyes to delight in the Springtime, nor vocal cords to allow us to pronounce blessings at seeing the trees' first blooming. We were given, unsolicited, tongues to taste Shabbas wine, hands to make *fraylach* music on the clarinet, to make even the most discouraged creature's heart beat to enlivened rhythms. Hands even to burst chains, feet with which to dance. Everything about us is a gift, given freely, openly. That is, perhaps, more poetry than theology, but in the world of Tzedakah, it leads to a logical conclusion:

If we, as people, all share that common origin, that first dazzle of light in our eyes, that first warmth of body touching body, mother and child, if we are grateful for waking each morning and seeing our fingers move, the machine of our body restored to new vigor . . . then the least we can do is give to others some portion of these gifts, to share, in some way the joy of this surprise. Jewish tradition offers us two ways to do this: giving away ten to twenty per cent of our incomes, and a portion of our time and energies, for the benefit of others. It seems like a simple, positive gesture of gratitude, to a certain extent — modest. It is not such a great demand when the larger context of life is considered: God does not demand back from us *all* of our possessions. He does not ask that we give to others *all* of our time, *all* of our energies. Just a specified portion.

I am well aware of the fact that we do not usually think in these terms. On most days we cannot be bothered with such high-sounding thoughts, for there are much more mundane struggles with which to wrestle each day. Perhaps the theologians and philosophers (and the poets) can treat themselves to the luxury of basking in this lyricism — perhaps the obstetricians and midwives, too. But for the mythical Person in the Street, it is not a prime force in the activities of the moment. And yet, at some point, the element of birth must be considered: on Rosh HaShana we consider the world's birthday; on Passover we take note of freedom and slavery, rebirth; on Shabbat or on a vacation, when our mind is free to roam the horizon or admire the sunset, we ought to say to ourselves, "I am indeed alive. Therefore, . . ." It is a logical "therefore," though we may be embarrassed that we have risen to such heights. From that single insight, the many acts of Tzedakah may flow more easily. Even if we but consider

it from time to time, once or twice a year. In a way, perhaps not an absolutely systematic way — still, in a way, it makes sense.

#2—JEWISH HISTORY AND TZEDAKAH, FROM A BROAD,
THEOLOGICAL VIEWPOINT

If my grandparents did not actually see pogroms, then their parents
or grandparents certainly did. They may have been awakened at dawn,
shaken, terrified to think that their town, too, was being struck by the
hordes. My not-so-distant cousins never left Europe, and when the War
came, though my father's mother's mother died before the rise of Hitler,
other members of her extended family lived to die at the hands of the
Nazis. I am confused.

"Tzedakah saves from death," the Book of Proverbs proclaims. It is
not enough that King Solomon records it once (in Chapter 10) . . . he
repeats it again in the following chapter. How many sermons have been
delivered based on this statement! How many eulogies!

One rabbi says, "Tzedakah-money saves the despairing from their
ultimate despair — suicide."

Another announces, "Your money prevents starvation in so many
places. It helps others escape oppression and death at the hands of war-
ring enemies. It buys freedom."

And another, "Tzedakah saves the living from a living death. There
are many who plod through life, reamed clean of their enthusiasm, their
joy . . . they can be revived through Tzedakah."

And yet another declares, "The good acts of Tzedakah live on after
you. They are a memorial to your upright manner; they shall be remembered long after you have passed away."

And, to some extent, all these sermons are true. And they are comforting. But they do not explain why so many were not saved from the
storm of the Holocaust, or from the other catastrophes of Jewish history.
They do not tell me why, during the Inquisition, so many good people
were burned at the stake, as the Holy Church sat in judgment, gloating
over their victories over the unbelievers. They do not tell me why Cos-
sacks could pillage and murder and then go home to their families and
drink their vodka with roaring gusto, and no hint of regret.

I wonder why life is so cheap. I wonder — perhaps too often for my
own good — about the senseless killings in the streets of New York, Los
Angeles, Atlanta, Miami, the bystanders chosen for no apparent reason to
become victims of wild maniacs or cool-headed killers.

How dare I say, "Tzedakah solves all of that. It makes Life not a Hell,
but an opportunity to rediscover the wonders of Eden"?

How — with a million Armenians dead at the sword of the Turks, and
millions more in Stalin's purges, and the Devil Ayatollah's firing squads
cracking at dawn, snuffing out life after life — how dare I say, "Nevertheless, let us proceed with the Tzedakah-work at hand"?

There are so many larger unknowables, so many factors that smash
into our comfortable systems of thinking. Dark moments dim our vision,

and groping in frustration we say, "It doesn't work. It just doesn't work."

I see it in the life of the poet — the singing on one day, the depression on another. I ask a friend, a psychiatrist, "What is the nature of the manic-depressive patient?" — wondering if I, too, am a textbook case of mania and depression. I sing — I exalt in the onset of Fall in Virginia, gazing at the reds and browns and rust colors that will charge my senses. And then I grumble to myself, "The car crash in Dayton, the deaths, the nice kids." It sounds all-too-confused, even with the Great Surprise of being born. A tension, a very great warping bends the poet's mind too far in both directions, with no logical compromise.

"I don't know" or "Maybe" or "In some cases" seem like the necessary compromises. It would appear that, to proceed with Tzedakah, we must have blinders or be naive or bullheaded to an incredible degree. Tzedakah must demand a faith, an affirmation that rides high over bodies strewn everywhere and at every time. But what a bizzare kind of faith!

It is all so confusing, so disheartening. Are we, then, placed on this earth to be shortsighted? Must we refine our ignorance, consciously forgetting a world of senselessness, so that we may at least, somehow, go our way as people, alive and functioning?

Even Woody Allen addresses one aspect of this problem, writing in his Chassidic tales of a certain Rabbi Zwi Chaim Yisroel. He says, "Once, while on his way to synagogue to celebrate the sacred Jewish holiday commemorating God's reneging on every promise . . ." It is funny, it is sad, it is present in the midst of all our celebrations.

I am not so simple-minded as to say, "Yes, despite it all, we must." I have no pat answers, nor am I pleased that I have no answer. I am enraged that I have discovered so important a question, only to be taught by my teachers that the questions are more important than answers. I find no comfort in that.

I must leave the matter rest with a story, a story of some illumination in the midst of my dark moments: I am speaking to Rabbi Jack Riemer in a synagogue parking lot on the way to an afternoon service. He is one of my teachers, a Rabbi in the greatest sense of the word. I confess to him that I do not understand "Tzedakah saves from death." I say, "And what if, God forbid, we are set upon by the Enemy?"

The Rabbi, quoting in turn from his Rabbi, Abraham Joshua Heschel, says, "It may be that we will not be saved, but, at least we will be worthy of being saved."

Not enough! Profound as it is, something is still wrong. It is comforting, but troubling, answering and yet not answering completely. It soothes, but is insufficient to soften the blows.

Let us suspend the matter for now. This is, after all, only one essay among many. It is not meant to be all-pervading, casting a pall on the other affirmations I speak of.

For now, let us choose ignorance and blindness.

After a talk:

An elderly woman approaches and explains, "I didn't realize what kind of a woman my grandmother was until the family sat Shiva for her. It was years ago, but I remember. People kept coming up to us to tell us stories of what a Righteous Woman she was. They kept telling and re-telling tales of this act of kindness, that gesture of generosity. It was overwhelming."

The Name:

A woman passes away in America. She and her husband have no children, so he searches for someone to take her name. The man writes to a friend in Israel who discovers a family that is willing to name their next-born child after his wife.

Every year, from across the ocean, he will remember the child's birthday. And the holidays, and other events.

He does not pay a grand Finder's Fee to the middleman. He is not *buying* immortality for his wife. He is just doing what any Jew would do in such a situation — a Mitzvah.

The Tree Lady:

A few years ago I was a guest in one of the southern Jewish communities. After the talk, an eighty-year-old woman introduces herself to me. For sixteen years she has handled the sale of trees for JNF. It is *her* Mitzvah, and everyone knows to go to her to plant a tree in honor of someone, in memory of someone, for any occasion, or for no occasion in particular.

The Survivor:

A survivor solicits funds for UJA and other Tzedakot. We spend the afternoon together at his house, and he tells me stories. He says that when the War ended, he and some friends found a group of Nazis hiding in a basement. One of the group shot all of them.

Other stories are as stark, incredibly painful to listen to.

It is not difficult to understand why he pressures others for contributions to Tzedakah. He is impatient with those who hesitate or give excuses. The survivor understands the needs of the Jewish people and has no time for excuses.

On the way back to Newark Airport after a talk. My driver is a young rabbi:

My grandmother is taken care of by a group of yeshiva girls. She is old and frail and can't get around. They come by frequently to see what she needs, what has to be bought, what straightening up is necessary around the house.

These girls keep her alive.

During one of my talks:

One of the local rabbis tells me that when he was a poor yeshiva student in Jerusalem he was plagued by the rains. He couldn't afford a raincoat. Seeking out a distribution center for second-hand clothes, he approaches a building where a stranger greets him. The man leads the student into a room filled with clothes. "Take a raincoat. Any one," he says.

The student does just that. There is no charge, and for years afterwards the student, now a rabbi, remembers the Mitzvah. He tells the story, and it is obvious that he has contributed to Tzedakah sums worth many times the value of one raincoat. He lives warm and dry in New England winters, but never forgets his younger days in the drizzle of Jerusalem.

He often wonders what the man's name was, the one who led him into the Palace of Tzedakah.

From the New York Times, a summary of an article:

Jerzy Kosinski, winner of the 1969 National Book Award for his novel, *Steps*, describes a curious custom of his—

On occasion he will go to a nursing home or hospital late at night — to the wards for the incurable — and offers to read stories to anyone who wishes to listen.

As he describes the passions of those moments, I realize the complexity of his images, the stretching of language to its very limit. It seems that words themselves are being tortured to yield some comfort.

Beyond the agonies of the patients, and beyond the agonies of the language, the simplicity of the Mitzvah remains—another variation on *Bikkur Cholim*, Visiting the Sick.

In the midst of insult and degradation to the human body, dignity is preserved.

Alumim is a school for retarded children in Jerusalem:

The summer program has begun. I visit with my friend and watch the teenagers with their teacher out on the playing field. The teacher is teaching them how to hit back. He punches one of them lightly and says, "Hit me back." They shy away, they try to hide, but the field is wide open. No one is *slugging* anyone else, but they are slowly learning to hit back. One tall teenager moves up slowly towards the teacher, moving carefully, still afraid. Then he hits him on the arm.

"*Tov* — Good!" the teacher shouts. He is pleased.

I do not know whether or not this is sound pedagogy, but I am deeply struck by the novelty of the idea. All the abuse these children must take — at least they should know that sometimes it is human and dignified to strike back in self defense.

Who would have ever thought to teach the retarded how to hit back?

After a talk:

"My mother's Mitzvah was to sew shrouds for the Burial Society."
The woman tells me this without a shred of horror or embarrassment.
Pride shines through her eyes, warmth, happiness that her mother chose
such a Mitzvah.

A NEW FLOOR
OR THE STORY OF THE ROCKING CRIBS

Many is the sleepless night a father recalls, the stillness of 3:00 a.m. broken by the sounds of a rocking crib. The parent awakens once a week, perhaps twice or three times, through two years times three children. The toll is heavy. Later on a mother or father can laugh about it . . ."Dear, would you see what is bothering the baby?" Later on, perhaps before a wedding, the mother can recall for the bride how much drudge went into child-raising.

They may laugh about it now, but there is no doubt that it is a test of endurance. The midnight callings — "Water!" Or just crying for no discernible reason, even for parents who have begun to interpret baby-sounds. I suppose that is why the Jews have coined a term "Tza'ar Giddul Banim — The Discomforts of Raising Children."

Now, with that background of memories, I must tell you a story about a new floor. It is not a terribly exciting topic, I admit. Better to tell dazzling tales of swashbucklers, of bravery and rescue and the swish of flying capes.

But this story of a new floor must be told.

It takes place in Israel, in Ramat Gan, outside of Tel Aviv. On a side street stands a large house with a pleasant front lawn; toys and children's climbing places dot the concrete pathway to the front door. The place; Ma'on LaTinok, a noninstitution for infants with Down's Syndrome, presided over by Ramat Gan's own miracle-worker, Hadassah Levi.

Some forty children live there, most of them because their parents left them behind in the hospital.

I myself have not raised a retarded child, so I offer no judgments of this new-found trait of the Jews. I want only to tell the story of the new floor.

The forty children are raised well: clean, lively, well-fed, with hope in their eyes, and the strong, clinging arms of children who love being loved.

By now, Americans have realized that Down's men and women, if given the opportunities, integrate well into society, working in sheltered workshops, going their own individual ways with personalities considerably more pleasant than the norm. They are good people, only limited in certain ways. I have met Americans and Israelis with Down's in their forties and fifties, and I believe my statement about their nature stands undeniably firm.

But here we are working only with babies, up to age four. Babies are supposed to be adorable. Try to tell a mother of a brain-normal child who happens to be ugly that the child is ugly (. . . before or after she exclaims, "Isn't she just the most darling child you have ever seen?") Just try to think of an appropriate phrase.

It is different here, though, in Ramat Gan. When she was about to move in, Hadassah Levi had to obtain a court order to allow the home to stay. The neighbors objected. Now, we know this happens everywhere with group homes for the retarded. The neighbors are worried about dangers, property values, harassment of their children by the retarded . . . all expressed behind the veil of "zoning laws." One such place in the United States was torched, shortly after "60 Minutes" did a story on it. Others are openly and unashamedly fought tooth and nail. Indeed, in Jerusalem, the Irene Gaster Hostel for Retarded Adults will have to move for much the same reason — noise being one of the complaints. I am told (on good authority) that the building used to be a whorehouse — but at that time there were no complaints of the noise.

Oh, well.

Back to the floor.

Hadassah Levi has made things move nicely there, at Ma'on LaTinok. Doctors are learning to treat her and her babies with respect. She shouts, loud, obstinately, with the bullheadedness of visionaries.

So things were settling in . . . until the babies began rocking their cribs. "See! We told you! They make too much noise!" (The stern voice of the neighbors.)

But they are babies — they are supposed to be adorable, lovable, cuddly. They aren't dangerous, harassing passers in the night.

It is truly a black-and-white situation: Not wanted. Move them somewhere else, like freight delivered to the wrong freightyard.

That's where the new floor comes in. People got together and bought the babies a new floor, a softer, quieter one, so no one would complain about the noise of the cribs.

Now Hadassah Levi directs her energies once again to the babies themselves. A new disaster has been averted, though I imagine she waits for some other foolish objection, some pretext, and all hell will once again break loose.

A POSTSCRIPT

It's funny. I am sitting here in a comfortable apartment, typing long past midnight. I wonder if the neighbors will complain of the noise. I, at least, can fight for myself. I am neither particularly adorable nor essentially charming — especially in an argument — so I suppose a face-to-face confrontation would assure a victory for the neighbors. Still, it would be a fair fight among equals.

We are fortunate that some people are on the look-out for the welfare of the babies. I would imagine that, under Hadassah Levi's care, they will become good, kind neighbors when they grow up. Yes, I am sure of that. Perhaps, upon their reaching maturity we should go to seminars conducted by these unique individuals — "Good Neighborliness and Judaism." It would be good for the Jews. Without a doubt, it would be good for us.

13 THINGS JEWISH KIDS DO AND DON'T KNOW ABOUT THINGS JEWISH

The following is the second article of this kind that I have written. A while ago I wrote an essay called "13 Things Kids Don't Know About Tzedakah." Now the list has grown, with additions, variations, new emphases. As I continue to listen to the "kids," I have taken note of other areas including — and beyond — the realm of Tzedakah which do and do not trouble them. Thus, the new list is things the kids *do and do not* know.

As I begin to piece this together, I see that there will be more articles similar to this one.

The items are listed in a haphazard manner in an attempt to give a limited sense of how these ideas are presented. There is never any true order, and, following our intuitive, associative sense, the audiences and I go from theme to theme, with different connections in each discussion. Usually we cover only a few items of the New Thirteen, so this is a composite summary.

There will be limited commentary, even at the conclusion of the article. Most of the topics speak for themselves, and they are obvious starting points — both the positives and the negatives — for rebuilding our systems of Jewish education.

Finally, the "kids" I speak of are generally thirteen years old and older — into their twenties ("post-kids" as it were). Apparently, the older ones are still suffering the hangovers of missed and missing opportunities in their own Jewish educational experiences. Sometimes the hangover extends into the thirties.

A SPECIAL CASE

1. *They do know about suicides:* Some young man or woman inevitably freezes up when I mention suicide during a talk. Along the way, even in their brief lives, a friend or a friend of a friend has chosen to cut his or her own life short. In high school, in college, or shortly thereafter. Trying to ease the tension, I redirect the conversation to one specific problem — suicide among the elderly. I explain some facts I have heard:

A. I tell them I heard on a newscast that the suicide rate for the elderly in New York is six times that of the general population.

B. I tell them the Miami Herald-(January 9, 1981) reported that the suicide capital of the country is the South Beach of Miami, an area densely populated with older Jews, many living on bare-minimum incomes. These are the comparative statistics — The national average is 11.7/100,000 population. Nevada, with its Las Vegas syndrome, stands at 30.5/100,000. Florida: 16.2/100,000. Now for the critical numbers. According to the study by the American Jewish Committee, in 1977-78 "the city of Miami Beach and its contiguous areas had the nation's highest suicide rate — 50 per 100,000 population . . . The South Beach area alone accounted for 53 percent of the region's total." The South Beach is not all old Jews, but it is still predominantly so, and 25.7 of the elderly in that area live alone. Even though some authorities have disputed these figures, somewhere in that mass of data is a message the kids understand.

C. I mention a fact they already suspect: suicides at holiday periods are always higher. People with nowhere to go, living in sadness, cannot tolerate the heightened joy of the season's celebrations. Conversely, I ask how many of them have relatives (or have heard stories of relatives) who were supposed to have died by a certain time, but lived through one more Passover or Rosh HaShana. Many kids respond. They know that for those destined to die, if they have friends and relatives and a sense of belonging, the will to live may carry them through to one more holiday, one more family gathering.

I do not always raise the topic. It is too potent, and unless there is appropriate follow-up discussion after I leave, it would be irresponsible of me to leave the wounds opened, untended.

If they have been with me to Life Line for the Old in Jerusalem, (many of these discussions take place right there, after our tour), if they have seen Life Line, they wonder about the many steps up to some of the workshops. They begin to realize how strong the human will can be: if the old people *want* to work, they will make a deliberate, mighty, and often incredibly heroic effort to get to that work, even if it entails a slow, laborious climb up steep steps.

TWO ITEMS SPECIFICALLY RELATED TO THE ELDERLY

2. *They know there is a Jewish old-age home in their communities.* Other than the synagogue and the JCC, the home for the aged is the most well-known community agency, better known than the Federations, certainly better known than the local Free-Loan Society or Chevra Kaddisha, the Jewish Burial Society.

Some of them have estimated that 70 – 80% of old Jews live in old-age homes. The official statistics I have heard are 5 – 10%. Somewhere, somehow, their perceptions are being starkly warped.

3. *They do know about books brought over from the Old Country.* Many have these books in their own homes: Peretz, Sholom Aleichem, a Chumash, sometimes a Talmud, brought over by some patriarch or matriarch on a long-ago boatride. Some have seen them only in synagogue libraries. But the books are in Yiddish and Hebrew, and therefore of little use to them or their parents. They are treated with respect, though, and if they were to fall to the ground, the owners would kiss them. And, I suppose, if they decay much longer, they will be buried, unopened.

JEWISH EDUCATION

4. *They do know they received a lousy Jewish education.* Some teachers and rabbis will be indignant at the word "lousy." But I am a teacher, too, and I understand the frustration behind the kids' harsh words. Most people in Jewish education would agree with the kids, and would fight to change the situation. It is obvious that more and more kids are going to dayschools now, but the percentages are still devastatingly

small. Some kids say, "I'll send my own kids to a dayschool," but others are uncertain, though most know they will consider the option.

Then they begin the long list of complaints — it all comes pouring out: boredom, bad teachers, subjects that did not hold their attention nearly as much as the movies or TV, little or no support from home. They pull out all the stops, and I encourage them. *They* exaggerate. *I* exaggerate, performing satires on Hebrew language courses, hideous retellings of Jewish history, pantomimes of "The Day The Substitute Came." We make jokes, to release the tension.

But the fact remains: they are entering adulthood grossly ignorant of almost anything relating to Judaism and the Skill of Living. If they are lucky, they can follow a Shabbat service or recite some form of blessing after a meal. Beyond that, they are in trouble, and they know it.

A corollary: *By now they are aware that many of their Hebrew-language teachers were bad.* They know that just knowing how to speak a language (whether the teacher is American, Canadian, or Israeli) does not necessarily mean you can teach it. They feel shortchanged.

Another corollary: *They do not know why their teachers, rabbis, families and friends did not prepare them better.* They do not believe it was only a matter of budget and finance. I provide the following fantasies for them to consider:

(1) Let us say the best-paid teachers in the community get a $45,000-a-year salary.

(2) Better, let us say the highest-paid Jewish professional in the Whole Town is the Torah-teacher, more than the director of the JCC and the Federation professionals.

(3) Let us say the communities began to pay adult education teachers $45,000 and up.

(4) And let us say that teachers will get paid (by definition) more than principals.

I ask, "While it will not solve all the problems, don't you think this would help?" Usually there are cheers. In a way, it is like the way they feel after a ride at Disneyland — unreal, but fun.

One more corollary: *They do not know how to follow-up on their intense Jewish feelings after a high-powered experience.* After they return from a summer at Camp Ramah or Massad or the UAHC camps, or a first-class summer tour of Israel, they are left hanging. The community will not (and often *cannot*) provide a satisfactory support-structure. They are left with the forbidding and thankless task of creating their own Jewish educations. Some will sign up for courses at colleges of Jewish studies — with mixed results. Some will go to seminaries — with the same mixed results. Some will also take Jewish courses at their universities, but, again, with the same mixed results. They are overwhelmed with obstructions of every shape and size, and the foul smell of defeat permeates the air. Many give up.

And yet one final corollary: *They know that knowledge always takes precedence over wisdom.* That is how they are trained: Wisdom is something to be worried about later on. They do not even think about the difference between knowledge and wisdom until some delayed stage of life, when wisdom is desperately called for, and found lacking. In the meantime, they have been learning and amassing facts and ideas and formulae . . . and winning awards. Somewhere along the way, though — a suicide in the dormitory, a high-pressure argument between Mom and Dad, a job proposal or proposition — sometimes they begin to ask the truly significant questions: why do people tear at each other? How do some get along so well, and others destroy and destroy themselves? Why was the Shiva for Grandfather such a circus? Why did we not stay until the coffin was completely covered with dirt? Who, if not we, ourselves, will demonstrate and raise hell on behalf of Iranian and Soviet and Syrian and Ethiopian Jews? How do I balance my time for Them and for Me?

All those glorious, crashing questions they should have been asking all along.

THE DISAPPEARING JEW

5. *They do know how non-Jewish their families are becoming.* I ask them, "How many of you have relatives who have married non-Jews?" (I am afraid to ask how many have relatives who have converted out of Judaism.) The hands go up, at least a third, sometimes half, and what is particularly surprising is how quickly the hands are raised. Even with the youngest group, the hands fly up, unhesitatingly. That is the telltale sign. They are aware that, even though two generations ago some fringe member of their extended families might have married a non-Jew, they now see how quickly the situation has degenerated into a mass of ominous figures and charts, zooming percentages. They even have a healthy fear of the implications for the next generation, and for the one after that. Many see themselves right in the very focus of the problem.

(One child, not sure if his answer fit my question adds, "My brother is living with a non-Jew." He doesn't know if "living with" counts.)

MENSCHLICHKEIT

6. *They know "goody-goodies" and dislike them, but they do not know why they should seek out the Good People.* From earliest schooldays they have made pariahs of the goody-goodies (unless they themselves were a goody-goody). This is continued on into the teenage years, and it is tied up with the idea of "coolness," being "in," being "with it," or whatever the contemporary phrase might be. Cool means being laid back, downplaying enthusiasm, even if the person they admire is doing admirable, Menschlich things. Some goody-goodies give off an obnoxious aura of self-righteousness. I explain that I am not speaking of them, but rather of the plain, straightforward Good People, people of integrity, kind. I encourage them to rethink their relationships to the goody-goodies, though I sense it will be a long time before they are at ease with the admirable people.

I pick up the thread of "coolness," for a moment, recalling for them an article I read about shoplifting . . . The author of the article has a visit from an old friend. They reminisce about many things, including how their buddies used to snitch candybars and other little items from the store. It was an accepted thing to do. The author remembers having done so himself, once, and is dismayed at having given in to the peer pressure. The visitor tells him he still does it now and again, putting a steak from the grocery store inside his coat. His expression changing, the author looks back at the visitor after this revelation, and the old friend realizes he has gone too far, spoiled the moment. He says, "I bet you think I'm a schmuck." I remember the ugly word, obscene, very much appropriate. The author thought that was exactly what he was . . . End of article.

THE TIME-GAP

7. *They know Elie Wiesel. They do not know* Night *or* The Jews of Silence. *They know who Simon Wiesenthal is. They know much more about the Shoah and about Soviet Jews than I did at their age.* But they are backlogged. The two basic books that moved my generation of friends (*Night* and *The Jews of Silence*), came to us right off the presses. For them, they are books from way-back-when. Books still to be read, yes, but not "contemporary" books.

Another time-gap: They haven't the vaguest idea how Jerusalem, United Jerusalem, became part of Israel. The Six-Day War is "history" to them, and they are certainly unaware (except perhaps from some course) of the status of Jerusalem previous to 1948. They know nothing of the corridor up to Mt. Scopus, the ambush of Dr. Haim Yassky and the Hadassah medical staff on the way to the hospital. Some may eventually come to suspect that, for all they know, it would be a good idea to internationalize the city, have all religions share the holiness. The unique Jewish agonies of Jerusalem — except for the most contemporary ones — are foreign to them, through no fault of their own. They're just young.

They also don't know where all those Palestinians came from.

THE TIME-GAP: II

8. *They do not know that their grandparents and parents had a childhood of their own.* They have heard some bare, stray stories, but they have no sense of how important it is to hear the stories, and to encourage the others to tell them. What they will learn is immeasurable, far-reaching. It is time for them to see that those who were responsible for bringing them into this world were also, once upon a time, Jewish children. Let them explore a mother's or father's or grandmother's or grandfather's childhood Jewish experiences, to compare and contrast with their own. What did they laugh about as children? Were they scared of God or the Boogeyman? Did they love to ice-skate, and did they skip out of shul to do it? Did the female ancestors miss out completely on Jewish education because — well, because it wasn't important? Were they ever called Kike or Sheeny? Did they hate Cheder or Hebrew School as much as their offspring do?

Gutsy, wonderfully intimate stories to be passed on.

TESTAMENTS

9. *They do not know what an ethical will is.* They have heard of wills — money, candlesticks, stocks and bonds, paintings, the house and car. But the Jewish idea that people should write ethical wills . . . they have never heard of it. I encourage them to ask their parents to sit down and compose a document that expresses their feelings about what exactly has been important to them in their lives, and what they wish their children to carry on after them: the meaning of a chevra, friends, the qualities of decency and fairness, the power of kind words. Let them use all those unfamiliar phrases: Torah, Rachmoniss, Tzedakah. The candlesticks and silverware will take care of themselves.

A SPECIAL CASE: II

10. *They know about hospitals, and they know they do not like them.* Perhaps a grandparent has died in an intensive care unit. I pose the question, "Was the visiting time over, and your grandmother forced to leave the room when your grandfather died?" Sometimes yes, sometimes no. They are surprised to see that Judaism and Jewish texts deal with this issue: under what conditions do you leave a sick, elderly, senile, or mentally disturbed relative in the care of others, and when do you keep them under your own supervision? I tell them that "Dying At Home" is a Jewish issue that they should study. It is a good starting point, particularly with older teenagers. It is a real problem, it hits home, and it is a pardigm for a *Jewish* study of contemporary issues. They could invite a two-person panel to speak: a hospital physician discussing the medical world's ideas of Death with Dignity, and a rabbi or teacher offering the Jewish view of the same topic. (The latter will not focus on pulling the plug. He or she will begin with *Kavod*, dignity, the very essence of the grand stature of the human being, even when wracked by cancer.)

MORE ABOUT THE JEWISH RETARDED (PREVIOUSLY MENTIONED IN "13 THINGS, ARTICLE I")

11. *They know about special education for the retarded (because of mainstreaming in the schools), but they do not know about* special *special education for the Jewish retarded.* I ask, "Out of a thousand families in a large synagogue, how many Jewish retarded people should there be, just taking into account the law of averages?" I don't have the figures, nor do they, but we all assume there must be *some*. Where are they? Why aren't they in shul? Where are the deaf, blind, crippled, and other handicapped Jews? I was happy to learn that three deaf Jewish children will be bar and bat mitzvahed this year in Northern Virginia synagogues.

I am impressed by how many know that Moses had a speech impediment. Quite a few even know the story of how he tried to eat a hot coal when he was a child. (Parents can well understand that!) But none — well, maybe 1% — has ever analogized from that kiddies' story about Moses-with-a-defect to the lives of all Jewish handicapped. It is a rich tale, this biography of Moses, a life to consider with great care. Here, the greatest leader of the Jewish People, mumbling, stuttering, sounding like an idiot in Pharaoh's presence, an object of ridicule in the Palaces of Egypt. The story they learned in Hebrew school — that is knowledge; deriving life-sustaining and life-giving principles from it — that is wisdom. But, they were shortchanged on wisdom.

I offer the kids two suggestions. First — since I know that many of them saw "Like Normal People" on TV (the story of a retarded couple that wanted to get married) — I tell them to read the book. They will discover that the husband was Jewish by birth, but that the wedding took place in a church, under a cross that looks about forty feet high in the picture. I hope they will be curious enough to explore the abyss between the groom's birth and his wedding. I hope they will ask soul-searching questions when they find out why.

And second, I ask them to review with me a story in the Talmud:

> Two people were walking in the desert. One of them had a flask of water. If both of them drink, they will both die, but if one drinks, he will reach the town.
> Ben Petura explained, "It is better that both drink and die, so that one will not have to witness the death of the other."
> Then Rabbi Akiva came and said, ". . . In this case, your life takes precedence [and whoever owns the water should drink]."
>
> Bava Metzia 62a

We discuss Rabbi Akiva's opinion: whoever owns the water is entitled to drink. I ask, "What if the one without the water is 17 years old, and the other, holding the flask, is 85?" Many react by saying that the younger one deserves the water. "He still has his life to live." I say what the Talmud says, "No. Two *people* walking in the desert." It doesn't say young or old.

I ask, "Physicist vs. car mechanic?" The same answer from Rabbi Akiva — whoever has the water is entitled to drink.

And finally I ask, "And if the one with the water is retarded, and the one without it has an IQ of 140?" The same answer from Rabbi Akiva. It is, after all, two *people.* They are equal (at least in this situation), with no discriminatory factors of age, usefulness to society, or intelligence.

I ask the kids to think about that. I ask myself, again and again, to think about that, too.

They often move from here to other life-and-death situations: a fetus endangers the life of the mother, hostages and terrorists. I refer them to Rabbi Louis Jacobs' book *Jewish Law*, pages 79 – 84. They are happy to see that these, too, are Jewish subjects. They want to know whose life is more valuable, when are we all absolutely equal, what values make up a life.

But they are still uncomfortable with the answers about the water in the desert. I think that is good. Let them — let me, re-think the value of life.

TZEDAKAH, IN A STRICT SENSE

12. *They know they do not want to be forced to give money to Tzedakah.* Many are willing to give, many have been involved in fund-raising

projects and many give freely and openly. But they object to being pushed. Often they are unaware of the immense needs for Tzedakah, but once they have been appraised of these needs, a number are willing to give. But they do not want to be strong-armed. I can understand that. I shuffle small amounts of friends' money from place to place, and sometimes I feel inundated with demands for this Tzedakah or that project, some worthy, some not so much in need. This is in addition to the normal round of mail-order solicitations I get (and everybody else gets).

The kids know what schnorring is, even though they may not know the Yiddish word, and they are very sensitive about the fine line between coaxing and forcing. And yet, they are disturbed by another, clashing fact. During the summers in Israel with United Synagogue Youth, I ask them, "How many of you know someone who would have wanted to go on this trip, and who would have benefited considerably from it, but couldn't go because there wasn't enough scholarship money available?" At least one out of three hands goes up. That means that there would have been 900 USY'ers in Israel during the summer of 1980, instead of the 600 who did go. At least 900. Then they understand more readily how and why some Tzedakah-collectors get so fired up. They see the needs so clearly, they burn with a desire to help, and will, themselves, come down strong on the ones they ask to contribute.

When the kids get back to their home communities, they talk to those who would have liked to go: some spent the summer at home, some took a summer school course, some went to a day camp with moderate Jewish content. Then the kids begin to speak with a greater urgency. They begin to sympathize with those who make demands for more and more Tzedakah money.

I remind the USY'ers what their own Tzedakah money has done in different places. I read them the list of USY's Tzedakah allocations. They are impressed, and once again re-evaluate their own views on giving and encouraging others to give. They still do not want to be *told* to give, but they are more sensitive to the overall picture.

THE SAD JEST

13. *Some of the kids know they have been "dumped" for the summer.* While we are in Israel together, I sometimes ask the teenagers, "How many of you feel you've been dumped here for the summer?" A few hands go up, and then there is some laughter, and a slight feeling of discomfort for a few. I joke and add, "How many of you were sent away to summer camp starting at age 2?" They laugh, and I tell them one more joke, "I knew my parents didn't love me when they began sending me to school with my lunch wrapped in a road map." We all laugh, but the tinge of loneliness for some of them still remains. There is a faint feeling that, for those few, something is catastrophically wrong in their families. I am not speaking only of broken homes.

But I go on to other things, breaking the tension, perhaps calling Mrs. Mendilow, Our Heroine of the Day, out for one last round of thank-you's, another picture. She has built Life Line for the Old, and we are grateful.

Let the day end on heroics — admiration for one woman giving life to hundreds of old people.

Still, afterwards, I walk back to my apartment and wonder how many of them feel the deep hurt?

THOUGHTS ABOUT THE OLD CITY

The examples generally speak for themselves. The sum total of the essay is: it is a long road for the kids from their shoddy Jewish educations to a full and fulfilling life as an active, concerned Jew.

I repeat my standard rejoinder: I am not a sociologist, nor a statistician, demographer, nor an ethno-anthropologist. I am a Jewish poet who takes very much to heart the words of the Talmud:

> Rabbi Chanina said:
> Much have I learned from my teachers,
> more from my friends than from my teachers,
> and from my students, more than from all the others.

(Ta'anit 7a)

The implications of what these students say are very great, for a broad range of fields of Jewish endeavor, and particularly in my field of interest, Tzedakah. Knowing the frustrations and gaps they feel in their Jewish consciousness, we can attempt to rebuild the ruins. The Talmud states it succinctly:

> You learn Torah best when the specific material you study touches your heart.

(Avoda Zara 19a)

By listening carefully to what the students are saying, we know what troubles them, what has deadened their minds, dulled their sensibilities. Starting at that point, there may yet be some hope.

I keep thinking of the Old City of Jerusalem, the Jewish Quarter. When we recaptured it in 1967, we found a colossal ruin. Every year now that changes. Something is added, something replaced, something is more beautifully finished than the year before. It is a breathtaking experience. The wreck has been reconstructed with wisdom and a sense of holiness. I think that this is the best symbol of the task of the Jewish educator: taking shattered stones, broken walls, sludge and refuse in the byways — and (with the help of miracles), reworking it into a vision of holiness.

THE BROWN ENVELOPE:
USING CASH IN THE JEWISH SCHOOL

Usually it's a brown envelope.

At the beginning of Hebrew school or Sunday school classes, a teacher passes around a brown envelope, and the children dutifully put in their nickels, dimes, and quarters. Hopefully, the process begins with the very first day of Hebrew school. Unfortunately, it usually ends when the child makes his last visit to the synagogue for his formal Jewish education. Through those years, the brown envelope becomes deeply embedded in the memories of millions of Jews; it becomes one of the most basic physical objects they recall, the most common experience of our children as they begin their lives with Tzedakah. Sometimes the teacher uses a pushka, but I think that a simple poll would reveal that the brown envelope is the visual key.

So much for the collecting. The other end of the process — the allocations — produces much more hazy remembrances. I am startled at the number of teenagers and adults who admit that they do not really know where the money went at the end of the semester or year, after all the money from their class and other classes was tallied. For all too many of them, that part of the Tzedakah work was left to the teachers or principal. Worse, after raising this question of "Just where did the money go?" — they are not even disturbed that they had not actually done anything to help decide. They were confident that it was used wisely, and, I am sure, in most cases that is certainly true: Israel, JNF's forests, poor Jews in America, Canada, wherever, were no doubt, the beneficiaries. In some cases the money was sent to the local UJA or Federations or to Soviet Jewry projects, but, more often than not, the children did not really know for sure.

I assume that even first graders can cultivate a sense of how beneficial their money can be, if given the appropriate opportunity. The specific mechanics of distribution varies from school to school: (a) each grade may decide for itself, (b) a committee composed of representatives of each class may decide, (c) the entire school decides in a mass meeting. Entire study units may be devoted to educating the group, examining the many possibilities under the guidance of a teacher. The important point is that the distribution must be brought home to them forcefully and honestly. They must feel that *their* money was used wisely and as efficiently as possible. (It is shocking to note how many pass through their Jewish educations — through age 13 or 15 or 18 — never once having been exposed to the questions of overhead. They never think to ask, "Of the $356.49, we distributed, how much was used for secretaries and mailing?")

They have been, as it were, shortchanged on Tzedakah. From the coins they placed in the brown envelope, to the food or clothes or hope their money bought, there are great gaps. I would like to offer one technique which, I believe, can close part of that gap. It is simple, direct, straightforward.

THE PROPOSAL

At the end of the school year, when decision-making time has arrived, either the class or the committee should meet with the teacher or supervisor. In front of them should be a long table with the sum total of contributions laid out — *in cash*. Most of the money should be in one-dollar bills, with some fives, tens, and twenties, and a few dollars in coins.

Using cash opens their minds to many possibilities, wide-ranging, important thoughts. First, and most important, the students will see that it is, indeed, *money* that they are working with. There is nothing theoretical about this thing called "Tzedakah," but rather real, negotiable sums that have tremendous power to buy things and to change things. No matter what the amount is on the table, the session should begin with the question, "If you had this much money for yourself, what would you buy?" The answers will inevitably be a revelation to the teachers, and to the students themselves. By their answers they will reveal some of their own personal values. Even if they joke around and say, "A vacation in the Bahamas," or "boots and jeans," they will be laying bare some part of themselves. (The Talmud informs us that a personality is revealed even through the things a person jokes about.) Of course there is the danger that the students will give answers "the teacher wants to hear." They will recite all manner of sophisticated lines, dignified suggestions, way above and beyond their real thoughts. These are easily noticeable, though, and, at that point, the students should be encouraged to reveal their own, real thoughts.

The next step: a student should hold up $4.00 and say, "This will buy one adult ticket to a movie," or $35.00 and say, "This will buy a reasonable pair of shoes for your brother in college." They can add others: $60.00 for a tire, $450.00 for monthly rent for their apartment, $685.00 for interest payments on a mortgage of a house. Small figures should also be used — $1.00 for such-and-such number of candy bars, $.75 for a slice of pizza at a stand, $1.50 for a pair of sox. That will sharpen the sense of buying-power in their own lives and the lives of their families.

At this point, the teacher can say, "Now, what can we do with all this money for Tzedakah?" It is hoped that prior to this session they will have considered where the money would go, but, in any event, the time has come for them to decide exactly what to do with these dollars. Additional suggestions may be presented, perhaps in the form of a xeroxed sheet describing various projects, including ones that have not received money in the past. I am absolutely opposed to the One-Hundred-Percent-Renewal syndrome. If, every year, the money always goes to the same place, the students will gain the false sense that one brief session, a five-minute decision, is all that the Mitzvah of Tzedakah entails. They will learn that there is no real need to search and question in order to make the *best* and most careful use of whatever money is available.

In some situations, there is good reason to give to the same place — there may be a scholarship fund in memory of a fellow student who passed away, or there may be a particular desire to help the elderly of the community, or the deaf. But that should never be the total and exclusive result of the committee's decisions. Each year they should reach for a broadened sense of the variety of needs of the community, and often it is the teacher's responsibility to assist in additional research in this area. If we ourselves are tired of seeing foundations granting large sums to the same limited number of recipients — universities, heart and kidney funds, Jerry Lewis's Telethon — then we should pass on that same frustration to the students. Let them realize that there are other avenues to be explored.

This is certainly reinforced by the everpresence of the money itself. If you say, "If we give all $389.40 to JNF, how will we have provided for the Matzah Fund in our own town?" or "If we give only to the Jewish Institute for the Blind, what part have we personally taken in the rebuilding of Israel?" — if you ask these questions, it is certain that thought-provoking discussions will follow.

To return to the importance of the cash itself . . . whoever is chairing the session should periodically pick up the money and hold it high, reminding them again and again that it is very real, it offers opportunities, possibilities for them to move and change things. If it is a very large sum of money, the impression will be very great, and, if it is a small sum, the question should be raised, "How can it be that, with a Hebrew school of 326 kids, we have raised only $929.10? That's only $2.85 per student." (Count out the $2.85, to show them. It might be wise to break it down per capita, per class, allowing for smaller amounts for the younger grades, making small piles of bills and coins to represent each class's contributions, total, and per child.) I believe that is a powerful moment in a child's education, one which each child should long remember. *Let them be troubled by the unfortunately small amount available for Mitzvah-doing.*

Then they should proceed with the allocations. No time limit should be set on this process. The principal should schedule a special open-ended session for this purpose. If the committee or class is limited to one class-hour, the end result may well be a sense of distress that they did not have enough time to consider all the possibilities, to weigh how much, for which recipient, with the appropriate care. With such critical experience at their fingertips, they should not be crippled by the pressures of time, and, indeed, if it turns out that sandwiches have to be brought in because one hour has led to three or four, so much the better. They will acquire a sense of just exactly how careful everyone must be with his or her Tzedakah money.

I once observed such a session with teenagers at a convention. No more than $78 or $79 was involved. We began at about 10:30 at night, and I tried to set a time limit — till 1:00 a.m. At 2:30 in the morning they were still tying together their thoughts, making the final decisions of how to balance this sum equitably among all the places they wished to help. I was impressed by their passion and high emotions, and though the meeting occasionally produced some giddiness (the hour was late), the end result was encouraging: over forty teenagers had successfully and meaningfully allocated the funds to a variety of places which satisfied their communal sense of what is right and fair. That is the ultimate meaning of Tzedakah — *Right*eousness.

I observed a similar event at another convention, this time with about $275 available. In both cases I served only as a resource person, leaving the proceedings and decisions to the teenagers themselves, though I offered a number of suggestions for places to send the money.

When these sessions were over, the money itself — the hard, cold cash, was given to individuals in the group to deliver or send to the recipients. This, too, should be the case in the Hebrew schools. Individuals from the committee should take the $25 or $36 or $50 home with them, and send it to wherever the committee has decided. They are responsible (a) to prepare an appropriate letter explaining the source of the contribution, and why it was decided to send to this particular place, and (b) they have to get a check or money order to exchange it for mailable funds (if it is being sent to a distant place). In many cases this will involve the assistance of a parent, which is a positive step towards getting Tzedakah reintroduced into the home. (The vacuum in the home is a much-noted sore point. It is impossible to discuss that crisis at this juncture.)

Afterwards, after the children have done the letter-writing and the distribution, they can come back and report to the committee, bringing copies of the letters they have sent, and the replies and receipts. These may be posted on the school bulletin boards. In brief, the entire mechanism of giving is theirs to work with — it is not to be left to the teachers and principal alone. It is *their* money, and therefore *theirs* to distribute as they see fit. I am sure they will be impressed by the outcome, and it should carry over well into subsequent years, to the time when they will have to make the same careful, thoughtful decisions on their own.

A CONCLUDING COMMENT: ON THE NATURE OF "PROCESS"

It has become fashionable in pedagogic circles to stress the importance of "process." The advocates of this position explain how emphasizing "the process" sharpens the critical talents of the growing child. Yes, that is true, and it is certainly evident from the above discussion that this method is valid, useful, and successful if supervised carefully. The Hebrew school children will have taken an active part in the process of deciding where this money is to go. Nevertheless, Tzedakah work allows for more than just process. In fact, it is the end results of the process that are the most important aspects of the Mitzvah. It is critical that the students understand that what has actually taken place is that *real money* has been distributed to *real people*, to relieve despair, to alleviate hunger, or cold, or pain, bringing a sense of well-being, joy, and physical comfort to many. They themselves know pain, so it is possible that they will recall their own moments when they were hurt. They may then sense how they have eased someone's similar or greater pain, whether it be the pain of disease, or starvation, or loneliness, or hopelessness. If, for example, some of their money has gone to an association working with Soviet Jews, they should invite one of the local immigrants to speak on "The Life of the

Refusenik." They should hear, first hand, the struggles for freedom of one individual Jew, and how their money from far-away helped bring that person to freedom. If they have provided a scholarship for a Jewish camp or for the Jewish day school in their community, a staff member or camper or student from that camp or school should come to them and speak of how that money has offered someone richer possibilities of Jewish experience. They should know, graphically and in detail, how Tzedakah money has sustained the Jewish People, and will continue to do so, as long as they continue to give.

Hopefully, they will then want to continue giving — and then give more than in the past. They will come to realize that $258.61 can only do $258.61 work of Tzedakah-Mitzvot, and that $875.32 can do $875.32 worth. They will know, plain and simple, that more can do more. And they will also come to realize that pooling their small individual contributions can produce larger sums, an important feeling for all of them. At the same time, they should not be discouraged from considering what their own $1, $2, or $5 contributions can do when they also carry out their own individual Tzedakah projects outside of school.

Most of all, they will see that Tzedakah is not just theory and thought, but practical action. It simply cannot be done without taking their own money and giving it away. "It's the thought that counts" does not apply to Tzedakah work, and while it is important that they give openly, caringly, and with great care, the essence of the work is in the *doing* of the Mitzvah to a greater and greater extent, and more and more frequently.

The Prophet Isaiah eloquently expresses our hopes:

And the work of Tzedakah shall be peace,
And the effect of Tzedakah,
Calm and confidence forever.

(32:17)

The beneficiaries — both the givers and the recipients — shall be afforded moments of peace and peace of mind, calm and confidence. For the recipients: hope, a chance at another beginning in life, a reappraisal of their fortunes and misfortunes. And for the givers: with a *Meshuggeneh Velt* — a crazy world — all around them, crashing into pieces in so many places — for the givers, a sense that the sharing of their possessions can, indeed, make repairs. Even the $1, the $2, and the $5 gifts constitute the foundations of a magnificent structure, perhaps a cornerstone of some new Jerusalem in the making.

UNRELATED TOPICS (IN NO ORDER)
ONE OR TWO PARAGRAPHS EACH

I. Fear of Bad or Wrong Decisions

No amount of research will yield an absolutely clear set of guidelines as to exactly how much Tzedakah money should go where. As our experience grows, though we feel we may have made bad or wrong decisions along the way, this should not paralyze our desires to give. In "normal life" we also make bad decisions and mistakes, but continue, having taken those shortcomings and failures into account. Since Tzedakah giving is a combination of carefully prepared contributions *and* an element of spontaneity, we should be prepared to continue to give enthusiastically, even knowing that mistakes will happen. The only danger to guard against is sloppy or haphazard giving.

II. Finding Worthy Recipients in Your Local Community

Most usually the local rabbi will be able to direct you to worthy recipients for your Tzedakah donations. Local Jewish agencies can also point you to individual situations where you may wish to give. If, for example, you wish to provide furniture for a recently-arrived immigrant family, any one of a number of Jewish organizations will assist you.

Beyond that, though, it is important simply to begin asking anyone you trust. The question to pose is very plain, "Who do you know who is doing good things?" More often than not you will acquire a sizable list to satisfy your Tzedakah desires.

III. Resource People and Materials

There is a network of "experts" in specific areas of Tzedakah work. In some cases your search may entail a long-distance phone call or letter. Among my friends, for example, I could count the following:

1. The Jewish Deaf — Rabbi Dan Grossman, 451 Windham Loop, Staten Island, NY, 10314, 212-494-2493, or (synagogue) 212-948-6782).

2. Jewish Learning Disabled — Joel Dickstein, 3225 Johnson Ave., Bronx, NY 10463, 212-796-6107.

3. Jewish Retarded — Rabbi Joseph Kelman, 100 Elder St., Downsview, Ontario, M3H 5G7, 416-633-3838, or Dr. Morton Siegel, 155 5th Ave., New York, NY, 10010, 212-533-7800.

4. Ethiopian Jews — Allan Gould, 31 Glen Rush Blvd., Toronto, Ontario, M5N 2T4, 416-486-7425.

5. Teaching Tzedakah in the Schools — Abraham J. Gittelson, c/o CAJE, 4200 Biscayne Blvd., Miami, FL 33137, 305-576-4030, or Susan Shevitz, 30a Inman St., Cambridge, MA 02139, 617-354-3005, or Barbara Summers Steinberg, 213 Astoria Place, Union, NJ 07083, 201-686-8839.

6. The Jewish Blind — Linda Millison, 320 Wellesley, Philadelphia, PA, 19119, 215-Ch 2-2294.

7. The American Jewish Tzedakah Scene — Rabbi Yitzchak Greenberg, 4620 Independence Ave., Bronx, NY 10471, 212-548-4211.

In one way or another, each of these people is involved in his or her own

field of expertise. They are not sociologists or statisticians, but rather individuals involved with people working in these particular fields, people
with a human insight into each area I have described. There are, of course,
many more . . . I have just listed a very small number as an example.

Concerning resources of materials — study guides, films, tapes,
videotapes and the like — the local Jewish or public library can be of great
assistance. To obtain films such as "The Miracle Worker" or "Queen of
the Stardust Ballroom" or the filmed biography of Wilma Rudolf — very
worthwhile materials — may be a relatively simple matter. Two people
who can help on more difficult problems of films, books, records, and
tapes are:

1. Allan Gould (address above).
2. Arthur Kurzweil (a trained librarian), 623 Cortelyou Rd., Brooklyn,
NY, 11218, 212-693-7540 or 282-8647.

For example *the single most important documentary on retardation*,
"Best Boy," is available through Documentary Films, Inc., 159 W. 53rd
St., New York, NY, 10019, 212-582-4318. There are hundreds of other
resources available to anyone seeking them out.

IV. Finding Yourself, a Personal Opinion

There are two schools of thought: first you "get your head together"
and then you go out and become involved in life, and — getting involved
in life is one of the best ways to "get your head together." I do not deny
the importance of soul-searching and self-examination, but I believe the
thrust of these essays lends substantial support to the second approach to
living. No single person will have all of his or her problems solved by
becoming involved in Tzedakah, but there is reason to believe that the
very involvement itself opens up new realizations to the committed individual. A prime example is the extraordinary therapeutic benefits afforded
students in Reb Osher Freund's special Yeshiva for disturbed young people. Reb Osher — and his Yad Ezra staff — have worked for years with
emotionally and mentally troubled people, and it is apparent that they
have succeeded in a reasonable percentage of instances. The essay on
"Tzedakah Apprentices" develops this thought more extensively.

V. Giving to Non-Jewish Recipients

There is no question that giving to non-Jewish causes is well within
the realm of the Jewish mode of Tzedakah. One need only note Elie
Wiesel's trip to Cambodia, and the many synagogues and Jewish groups
that sponsored Boat People, to understand how much this is a part of the
Mitzvah.

My one uncomfortable feeling is this — and I have noticed it on occasion during my talks — when Jews give to non-Jewish causes, they should
do it from a Jewish sense of Tzedakah. All too many Jews contributing to
these causes do it exclusively — with nothing left over for the Jewish recipients. There seems to be an element of self-denial and self-hate in this and
it is an old story. Still, it is worth mentioning.

Many non-Jews contribute to Jewish causes, and it would be difficult to imagine that they are doing it out of a sense of denial of their own heritage of Christian Charity. It is a strange phenomenon of Jewish life.

VI. Pledges and Payments

The Wayne State University student UJA campaign gathered in approximately ½–⅔ of the money pledged. The Washington, DC, adult UJA-Federation campaign receives approximately 97% on all its pledges.

The latter figure is encouraging, but we should wonder about the college students. More research should be done, more analysis. It is a tricky phenomenon, and difficult to grasp. College is an ambivalent time for Tzedakah giving, and it should be studied as a class-by-itself. Perhaps Wayne State was not typical, though I suspect it was (within a few percentage points one way or the other). It is troubling, very disturbing.

VII. Toys and Clothes

On a tour of Israel, if at all possible, travellers should leave a little room in the suitcase for toys or good, used clothes. By taking one or two hours in an afternoon, the so-called "tourist" can switch over to Tzedakah-messenger, delivering the clothes at the Rabbanit Kapach's storeroom (or if they are baby clothes to Hadassah Levi's home for retarded infants). If they are toys — there are many places to take them. Since toys are so expensive in Israel, whatever minimum sum you might spend on them over here can be multiplied two or three times to give a sense of how much they are worth over there. They are appreciated *very much* at Micha (for deaf children), Hadassah Levi's, Alumim (for the retarded), Akim (for the retarded), any one of many places.

You will then get to meet some of these heroes, and will see them at work. As is always the case with Tzedakah, both the recipient and the donor will benefit immensely.

VIII. Volunteer Projects with the Elderly: Personal Contact

Though there are many worthwhile personal-contact projects connected to services with the elderly, I would mention three with which I have had substantial and satisfying contact. They are all located in New York, but the principles upon which they base their Tzedakah-work are adaptable to other locations as well:

1. Project Ezra — contact Misha Avramoff, Educational Alliance Building, Room U-3, 197 E. Broadway, New York, NY, 10002, 212-982-3700 or 982-4124. This project works with the elderly Jews of the Lower East Side. Project Ezra also offers tours to individuals and groups.

2. Hatzilu — 1770 Pitkin Ave., Brooklyn, NY 11212, or Al Cohen, 38 Gainsville Dr., Plainview, NY 11570, 516-349-7063 or 536-0290. Hatzilu works with the Jews of Bedford-Stuyvesant, older neighborhoods in the Bronx, and other areas within the environs of New York.

3. Dorot — Temple Ansche Chesed, West End Ave. and 100th St., New York, NY, 10025, 212-362-3353. Dorot's work covers the area of the Upper West Side of Manhattan.

IX. *An Important Article Concerning Personalized Tzedakah*

"Nonconventional Philanthropy" by Dr. Eliezer Jaffe (mentioned a number of times in this volume) is an excellent, brief summary of the principles of personalized, careful Tzedakah-giving. The article was printed in *Moment Magazine*, May, 1979 (Volume IV:5). It's conciseness and clear articulation of the issues make it a basic text for all concerned about human contact in the giving process.

X. *The Tzedakah Slide Show*

A fifteen-minute slide show, "Tzedakah: The Road to Dignity," produced by Beth Huppin, may be purchased through Torah Aura Productions, 4423 Fruitland Ave., Los Angeles, CA 90058, 213-908-1436.

FOUR MISCELLANEOUS TZEDAKAH PHENOMENA (PEF, NIF, THE COLLECTIVES, AND A NEW DIRECTORY)

Many of my personal friends manage extensive Tzedakah projects within their own specific circles. For example, Rabbi Martin Edelman of the North Shore Jewish Center on Long Island is always generating new ideas, writing columns in the synagogue paper, delivering sermons, talking to individuals, offering his congregants opportunities for action. Whenever we speak, he is always informing me of another activity — additional funds he is raising for Passover food, boxes upon boxes of clothes for Israel and local Soviet Jewish immigrants . . . so many projects. And Rabbi David Nelson in Oak Park, Michigan, sends me the synagogue bulletin with his column listing suggestions for Tzedakah projects. He, too, delivers sermons about this Mitzvah. And Jonathan Wolf on the Upper West Side of New York, holding meetings and cultural events with thirty to fifty people in attendance. There are always pushkas prominently displayed on a table for different Tzedakah programs.

And Beth Huppin in Los Angeles is everywhere showing her slides of Life Line for the Old, Ma'on LaTinok, other places, encouraging people to visit, exciting students in Jewish schools to become involved in this great work.

And Peretz Rodman and Miriam Laufer in Boston, sharing their Tzedakah experiences in Israel for the Jewish student paper in that region. Sitting at their dinner table, guests often hear of the Rabbanit Kapach, Reb Osher Freund, and the others they have met who do so much for many people.

Rabbi Jonathan and Deena Porath do the same, speaking the highest praises for Hadassah Levi's work with Down's Syndrome infants in Ramat Gan. Even on their last trip to Israel — not even three weeks — they made sure to visit again, to gather new impressions and stories.

Each one of these in his or her own way has a bit of an evangelical look. Raising the subject of Tzedakah, their enthusiasm is sparked, their speech heightened, they become more energetic. They have settled upon one of the topics that is closest to their souls.

That is just the beginning of a list of resource people. Besides, there are foundations scattered everywhere doing great works of generosity: The Samuel Rosenthal Foundation, the Gimprich Family Foundation, the Levinson Foundation — legal structures established for the sake of different kinds of Tzedakah work. Each has its own aims and objectives, and each goes about carrying out those objectives in its own unique way. This list, too, is long.

I could never provide an exhaustive accounting of the available resources in this field. That kind of research is not my forte, and the sheer numbers of listings is much too great. However, I would like to mention four specific phenomena which are important for interested individuals to know about. Each serves a specific function, each assists in carrying out this Mitzvah in its own fashion. They are listed here, and *very* briefly described, for those who wish to pursue this matter more fully. They are listed in no particular order of importance.

I. P.E.F. ISRAEL ENDOWMENT FUNDS, INC.

The PEF was founded in 1922 by such prominent personalities as Justice Louis D. Brandeis, Stephen S. Wise, Nathan Straus, Jr., and Robert Szold. Over the years it has disbursed millions of dollars to many projects in Israel — in some cases $500,000, in others $1,000. Schools, the Weizmann Institute, Yad VaShem, the Israel Museum, projects for the handicapped, Life Line for the Old, and Yad Sara are among the many beneficiaries.

Their purpose is to channel individual contributions to Israel; they also administer trust funds. They are fully registered within the American tax-law structure and manage the disbursement of funds with the highest integrity. They do not employ a professional fund-raising staff, but rather accept contributions willingly from a variety of sources that come to them. They serve essentially as a funnel for funds from America to Israel, and I must repeat, their supervision of the funds demonstrates extraordinary insight and wisdom. Their 1979 Annual Report records the following astounding statistic: grants totalled $2,099,853 for that year, while administrative costs amounted to only $35,124. That constitutes an extraordinarily low figure of 1.67% for expenses.

The board of directors receives no salary whatsoever.

I have been impressed by the sincerity and devotion of the people involved in this organization, and I find that when I lecture on Tzedakah, people in the audience occasionally will raise their hands to repeat what I have just said: honest, careful, devoted.

The PEF is an excellent way to channel funds to Israel. They, themselves, can explain to you the details you need to know about doing your specific shade of Tzedakah-Mitzvah.

Contact: Mr. Sidney Musher, c/o, PEF, 342 Madison Ave., Suite 1010, New York, NY, 10173, 212-599-1260.

II. GIVING WISELY, THE PHILANTHROPISTS' GUIDE TO NONPROFIT SOCIAL AND VOLUNTEER SERVICES IN ISRAEL (Koren Publishers, Jerusalem)

Dr. Eliezer Jaffe (see "The 1980 Tzedakah Report," VIII:F) is compiling a directory of registered Tzedakah organizations in Israel. He is a member of the faculty of the Paul Baerwald School of Social Work at the Hebrew University, and one of the founding and moving forces of "Zahavi" — the grass-roots organization concerned with families in Israel that have four or more children. He is eminently qualified to manage this task: the amassing of a list of over 400 nonprofit social service organizations in Israel, the vast majority of which are unknown to the serious Tzedakah contributor. The directory will describe the function, historical background, organization-structure, and financial status of each project.

In addition, *Giving Wisely* will review the Israeli laws regulating nonprofit tax-deductible organizations, and will also include suggestions as to how to evaluate where a potential donor might wish to give his or her donation. Changes and current needs in the various welfare fields will also be analyzed . . . and an overview of the general social welfare situation throughout Israel will be presented.

There is no question that *Giving Wisely* will be an invaluable tool for all serious Tzedakah contributors. It will open up to them a wide range of possibilities they had never considered before. The reason we have been unaware of these places is relatively simple: either they are too small, or because they do not spend vast sums of their money on printed publicity. Dr. Jaffe has done superb research in preparing this volume. It is available through The Jerusalem Post, 120 E. 56th St., NY, NY 10022, 212-355-4440.

For further information, contact Dr. Eliezar Jaffe, 37 Azza St., Jerusalem, Phone 637-450 or 661-908.

III. THE NEW ISRAEL FUND (NIF)

In October, 1979, a group of eighty-two individuals from the San Francisco Bay area established the New Israel Fund, a tax-exempt foundation serving various needs in Israel. They particularly wish to provide for lesser-known creative and innovative projects, giving seed money and support in the areas of community action, civil rights (including an organization called "Next of Kin Widows" — not war-widows, just widows, a neglected area of social protection in Israel), women's rights (including a battered women's shelter in Jerusalem), innovative services (including "Ohel Shmuel," allowing for a neighborhood group to organize services for the homebound elderly), and Arab-Jewish relations. In addition, they seek out other individual projects that do not fall into any of these categories. (For example, they have underwritten $10,000 in expenses for the printing of Dr. Jaffe's *Giving Wisely*, contributed to Life Line for the Old, etc.) Some of the projects would have faded out of existence without their assistance; some would have never begun their work.

Their Interim Report of February 1981 records the encouraging figure of nearly $120,000 in allocations, with the amount continuing to grow — quickly. The list of contributors has grown to hundreds, with contributions now ranging from $5.00 to $35,000.00 I have met the executive director, Jonathan Cohen, on two occasions and have been very much impressed by the absolute integrity of the NIF's endeavors. The people involved are straightforward, energetic, and extremely devoted to their work. Most impressive is their extensive and careful selection and review procedure for grants in Israel.

As I listen to Jonathan Cohen explain the activities of the NIF, I pause to remark, "It sounds too naive, too simple." He speaks of ideals, of self-help projects, of immediate and direct assistance, of supporting places on the verge of disappearing. But it is apparently all true — and it is hoped that the NIF will continue to grow and provide more funds for many worthwhile projects. His enthusiasm is contagious.

For copies of their reports and further inquiries, contact Jonathan Cohen, c/o NIF, 22 Miller Ave., Mill Valley CA, 94941, 415-383-4866.

In Israel: NIF, POB 7029, Jerusalem, 02-631-316.

IV. TZEDAKAH COLLECTIVES

Over the past number of years, groups of individuals have appeared in various cities whose desire it has been to learn more about Tzedakah — and to *perform* the Mitzvah. They have formalized their work into Tzedakah collectives, and their procedure is relatively simple:

1. They educate themselves and each other about traditional texts dealing with Tzedakah. They review legal and Midrashic material describing the age-old methods and ideas involved in this Mitzvah.

2. They gather materials concerning specific places and projects which might be in need of their funds.

3. They commit a certain percentage of their incomes to a communal fund, and by means of differing rules for allocations, give these monies to the projects.

Each group sets different percentages for contributions, different priorities for disbursements, different by-laws concerning what constitutes an appropriate voting percentage for an allocation. The size of each collective varies from city to city — some have ten, some fifteen, others more. Meetings are set more or less frequently, depending on the specific composition of the collective. Some groups are more politically oriented than others, some allocate higher percentages to Israel. In general, a very broad spectrum of interests is represented.

What all these groups have in common is the desire to commit themselves to this Mitzvah through informed, thoughtful giving. The discussions at these meetings are conducted on a very high level. The collectives have, indeed, served many Jews well — offering them a vehicle for performing Tzedakah work in an appropriately sophisticated manner.

I have spoken at some of these collectives and have been in touch with a number of others by phone and through the mail. They are extremely serious endeavors. I am particularly impressed by the time and effort invested in seeking out appropriate recipients. There are groups in St. Louis, Boston, Philadelphia, Washington, Los Angeles, and other cities. New collectives begin each year as the need is felt among circles of friends.

For further information, contact: Arthur Kurzweil, 623 Cortelyou Rd., Brooklyn, NY 11218, 212-693-7540 or 282-8647.

FORGETTING, A MITZVAH

OUR TREE OF LIFE

I wonder just how many mathematicians the Czar of Russia really needed. I am forever travelling to lectures where people recite for me their family histories. Even now, long after "Roots"-fever has died down, Jews everywhere are looking back into their personal heritage, telling of this and that revelation, opening musty boxes of pictures, listening to old, old aunts and uncles they had neglected for years. Much of this can be attributed to the work of Arthur Kurzweil, the most prominent family tree expert in the country. His book, *From Generation to Generation*, and even more, his lectures, have stimulated a very deep and sincere concern for recapturing a Jew's vital connection to his ancestors — and to the Jewish People as a whole. I am certain he has heard thousands of stories from his audiences, and received hundreds of letters. Some are profoundly moving, some humorous, some describing events so incredible that even those attuned to the irrational in Jewish history are still astounded. Many of these tales are of little importance in the grand scheme of things. He and I hear them again and again: interesting, but not cosmic; they miss the guts of the matter. Usually it is something like, "My great-grandfather was the Mathematician to the Czar." The word "Mathematician" is pronounced (of course) with a Capital "M" and requisite awe. I swear I have met at least eight offspring of these Mathematicians to Nikolai I & II and Alexander I, II, and III. Why they should need so many calculators and geometers and algebraists is beyond me. And why they needed so many *Jewish* calculators, geometers, and algebraists, I shall certainly never know.

In this web of family history, naturally enough, most Jews are unable to work themselves back beyond some eighteenth or seventeenth century patriarch or matriarch. From that point back further into time, it becomes a matter of imagination. Fact is superceded by creative visualization, leaps of thought that bring us to Abraham and Sarah, our own personal Exodus from Egypt, the Stand at Sinai, and the entering of the Land of Israel for the first time in centuries — under Joshua the General. This factless *tour de force* is no less a form of truth than is the well-documented recollection of names from 1891, the gathering of marriage certificates and death certificates from the years on the Lower East Side, the citizenship papers.

Indeed, there are times when the search for earlier origins takes precedence: it is those early years with Abraham, Isaac, and Jacob, Sarah, Rivkah, Rachel and Leah that make us Jews in the first place. We know for a fact that we are descendants of these First Jews. But in between, from the twelve sons and one daughter of Jacob onward, we begin to lose the thread. Between that time and the pogroms in Russia is a centuries-wide gap which only the imagination can fill in, with a reasoning power of its own.

Let us examine one of these imagined periods of our personal histories.

MY FATHER WAS A WHEAT FARMER IN ISRAEL

It is the time of King David, Slayer of Giants, Psalm-writer, red-haired genius. My ancestor, Chanania, and his wife, Devora, own a wheat field in Israel. The Lord is kind to them, and the harvests are spared the tragedies of blight, storm, and locusts. Their crops are plentiful. Besides, they have some olive trees, some fruit trees, a small herd of livestock. They eat well, and the family is grateful for God's blessings.

Following the prescriptions of the Torah, these ancestors of mine perform various acts of Tzedakah at different intervals during the year: they journey to Jerusalem with the first fruits, they set aside the corners of the field — unreaped — for the benefit of the poor, and the gleanings, too, some few sheaves of wheat that fall by the rows as the reapers bring in the grain. The lame, unable to till the soil, and the blind, unable to sustain themselves, and the deaf-mutes, unable to be self-sufficient merchants — they come by and take their rightful share. It is a wonderful system, a sharing, a kindness . . . and it works. For centuries and centuries this principle holds good: let us share God's bounty with others in society.

We owe much to this Mitzvah of Tzedakah, even the life of King David himself. It was the King's own ancestor, Ruth, who scanned the fields of a certain Boaz, seeking food for herself and her mother-in-law, Naomi. She was dependent on the goodwill of others, and one day this Boaz took note of her among the gleaners. Things led to other things, and their great-grandson was David, King of Israel. Jewish History would continue because of the beneficence of God — and His messengers on earth.

We modern Jews, stuck in cities choking with traffic and fumes, we Jews find these scenes appealing. The pastoral feeling, the rustic landscape, the bulging and gleaming muscles of the reapers excite our imaginations. The sheaves are raised high and stacked, and the poor and downtrodden take their share. My ancestor, though no Mathematician to the Czar, must have played his part in this process. All our ancestors must have at one time or another. Before all the complexities of today's style of living came crashing in — there was this Mitzvah of Tzedakah in a pure form — moneyless, direct, immediate.

A FORGOTTEN MITZVAH

There was at least one more Tzedakah-Mitzvah our ancestors performed, but only on occasion. It is a difficult one to actualize, a curious one in the long list of provisions for the poor, the hungry. This is how the Torah describes it:

> When you reap the harvest of your field and overlook a sheaf in the field, do not turn back to get it; it shall go to the stranger, the fatherless, and the widow — in order that the lord your God may bless you in all your undertakings.
>
> (Deuteronomy 24:19)

This is the Mitzvah of *Shichecha*, Forgetting. One may not perform this Mitzvah with any premeditation. Our ancestors could not "plan" to forget fifty or a hundred sheaves per harvest, to provide that much more for the needy of their communities. It just had to happen. They forgot. Good! It shall remain in the field for those who need it.

What a peculiar Mitzvah! Making the human act of forgetting into a Mitzvah! It is such an unusual rule, it stands out clearly in the series of 613 Mitzvot. How can it be explained? One medieval text, the *Sefer HaChinuch*, offers the following commentary:

> Among the purposes of the Mitzvah:
> Since the poor and destitute . . . look longingly at the harvests (seeing the landowners making piles of produce in their fields, according to God's blessings which He has given them) — they think to themselves, "O, if only such were my situation, gathering such sheaves for my own household. Even if I could have only one sheaf, how happy I would be!" . . . Therefore, it was one of the Holy One, blessed be He's, kindnesses to His creatures to fulfill this yearning. When it might happen that the landowner would forget some sheaves, [the poor could come and take them.]
> The landowner also derives benefit thereby, acquiring a generous spirit, because, in truth, a generous character and magnanimous nature derive from *not* setting his mind on the forgotten sheaf, but rather by leaving it for the poor.
> God's blessing shall forever rest on such a generous person.
>
> Mitzvah #592

The benefit to the poor is obvious: this is one more way of sharing our resources. The benefit to the donor — even the unwitting donor — is particularly striking: once more he has become aware of the importance of generosity. His very nature may be changed thereby, becoming a more giving person . . . even when he did not *intend* to be generous.

An extraordinary Mitzvah. In other ancient texts we are taught that we must certainly be *consciously* and *intentionally* generous, actively providing percentages of our livelihood for others. But now it is evident that, even beyond those rules, we are instructed to try to understand the nature and essence of forgetting, of sensing the meaning of unintentional Mitzvot that produce the same results as our conscious actions. No, we cannot plan to forget, but, having forgotten, we must appreciate that this, too, is an opportunity for giving.

EXTENDED IMPLICATIONS OF THE MITZVAH

If anything, we Jews are obsessed with remembering. We make Kiddush on Shabbat, and the words of that prayer bid us to remember both the Creation of the World and the Exodus from Egypt. The Ten Commandments instruct us to remember the Sabbath day, to preserve its holiness. Purimtime we recall how the Amalekites cut down the weak and straggling elements among the Jews. We must remember, never forgetting what they did to us. And Haman, a descendent of Amalek — each year we read the story of his undoing. And in our own day, in our long history of remembering, never to forget the horror of the Shoah. Holocaust Remembrance Day grows in importance each year: memorial services are held everywhere, survivors speak, names of those who were destroyed are read, posters are everywhere saying *Remember-Zachor-Gedenk* in English, Hebrew, and Yiddish. Remember!

This very fantasy-tour into our ancestors' lives is, itself, a Great Remembering, a latching on to ourselves by calling to mind Jews who preceded us, but are, at the same time, a living part of us.

We Jews are good rememberers. We fight forgetfulness, and justifiably so: we are angry at the people who forget our history, our interplay with the world. Even in the smaller things in life, forgetting the car keys, the mail, something on the grocery list, we shout, "Damn!" If anything, we have made this act of forgetting into an absolute negative, and most certainly we have never considered Forgetting a Jewish issue, worthy of examination through Jewish texts.

But it *is* a Jewish issue, as much as the size of a Tallis or the shape of a Menorah or the sequence of prayers in the prayerbook. This Tzedakah-Mitzvah of forgetting — how it is a blessing — is just one aspect of the question. The list is long, but I would give only two examples.

The Shulchan Aruch states:

> One should not mourn too much for the deceased . . . Rather, there should be three days for tears, seven days for lamenting, and thirty for refraining from cutting the hair and wearing pressed clothes.
>
> (Yoreh De'ah 394:1)

And beyond that, of course, a *Yohrtzeit*, the annual commemoration of the passing of a relative. But to mourn eternally for a husband, wife, son, brother, or sister is the stuff of medieval tales of romance or the movies. Jewish tradition sets graduated time limits for mourning. Beyond that, harsh as it may seem to some, life must continue.

A quote from the Talmud extends this idea:

> Our rabbis taught:
> By His will, God established three phenomena in Life, and even if He had not willed them to be, it would have been only right for Him to do so.
> These are they: that corpses should decay, that the dead should be forgotten from the heart, and . . .
>
> (Pesachim 54b)

Rashi comments on the first phenomenon:

> That corpses should decay:
> Otherwise the relatives would keep the bodies, and, as a result, they would see their pain and sorrow in front of them all the time.

Both ideas proclaim the same principle: life must continue. Pain, sorrow, and mourning have their place, but at a certain point we are required to forget. One more text offers exquisite symbolism:

> We are taught:
> If a funeral procession and a wedding procession meet at a crossroads, the funeral must make way for the wedding.   (Ketubot 17a)

THE CLASSIC EXAMPLE: THE TENSION

The prophet Isaiah mentions a particularly powerful exchange between God and the Jews:

> Zion says,
> "The Lord has forsaken me,
> My Lord has forgotten me."
> Can a woman forget her baby,
> Or disown the child of her womb?
> Though these are forgotten,
> I shall not forget you . . .
>
> > declares the Lord.
>
> > > (49:14 – 15, 18)

Resh Lakish, a Third-century Talmudic personality fills in the details of this conversation:

> The Assembly of Jews said to the Holy One, blessed be He,
> "Master of the universe, even when a man marries a second
> wife, he still remembers the deeds of the first one. But
> You have both forsaken me and forgotten me!"

> The Holy One, blessed be He, replied,
> "My beloved one — I have created in the skies
> 12 constellations with
> 30 hosts of stars in each with
> 30 legions in each host and
> 30 clusters in each legion and
> 30 groups in each cluster and
> 30 sub-groups in each group,
> and in every single one of those sub-groups is
> 3,650,000,000 stars —
> and all of them I have created just for you.
> How can you say, 'You have forsaken me and forgotten me'?
> Can a woman forget her baby? . . ."*

> The Assembly of Jews replied,
> "Master of the universe, since You never forget, perhaps You
> will not forget the events of the Golden Calf?"

> He replied,
> "These shall be forgotten."

> The Jews said,
> "Master of the universe, since You *do* forget certain things,
> perhaps You will forget how we responded at Mount Sinai?"

> He replied,
> "I shall not forget you."

> > Berachot 32b

*The Midrash continues with a play on words, not germane to the flow of this article.

Even God remembers selectively . . . and forgets with the same sensitive selectivity. What began as an act of Tzedakah in an ancient wheatfield has become a broad, general rule of living: neither remembering nor forgetting are inherently good or evil. Both are instruments, means to serve us in life, and both must be used with the utmost care. Just as the farmer was instructed to remember to leave the gleanings and the corners of the field for the poor, so, too, upon forgetting some sheaves, he was to appreciate that very forgetting, prizing it as one more aspect of the pattern of Mitzvot. What appeared to be an inadvertent act became, in the larger realm of meaning, an opportunity for Tzedakah. This strange, forgetting act of giving, carried the same force of the Mitzvah as any active, positive deed the farmer might perform.

AFTERTHOUGHT: ANOTHER FORGETTING

I have often wondered why some old people recede inextricably into their childhood memories. Is it the breakdown of cells in the brain? Is it psychological escape from the fear of death? What causes them to blot out an interim of seventy years, the fragile elderly? Is there some accumulation of pain, of anger, a frustration that they had not accomplished what they had set out to do when they were young?

It may be that this forgetting is one more form of blessing, a Mitzvah of sorts. While these elders may rave about their childhood Warsaw — before the storm troopers reigned supreme — or while they review the simplicity of life in Plonsk or Dobromil before the turn of the century, at least they are free of other agonies. They are soothed, comforted. Even in this case, then, in the tragedy of senility, is a last gracious gift, an act of Tzedakah.

TZEDAKAH AS ANTIDOTE –
A NOTE OF HOPE FOR THE ABD'S
AND OTHER INTERIM GIVERS

WHO ARE THE ABD'S?

They are a select crowd, pockets of individuals locatable near universities, bright and torn. They are the ones who have done all their graduate course work, passed their examinations, and now have one last duty to perform: the writing of a dissertation. They are the ABD's — All But Dissertations.

On a visit to Chicago or Detroit or Philadelphia I might see two or three of them. Our conversations usually range from the weather to the workings of the local Jewish community to inflation to some recent event in Israel. Any reference to the work-in-progress (if any mention is made at all), is as brief as possible.

I am an outsider, so it could be that this analysis is a study in sour grapes. I was supposed to get a PhD in math, then literature, then Bible. All were dropped, at different times, by the wayside, and now, more than ten years out of college, I have lost the quantity of time and the tenacity to sit and study ten or twelve hours a day, like I used to in the "good old days."

So consider my analysis with the appropriate skepticism. And be careful to remember that the ABD's are my personal friends.

They are the ones who, because of various circumstances, have approached the marathon finish line, but have not managed to crash through the ribbon. They have families to raise, or they have hit a long dry spell, or they are depressed because of the shrinking job market. They turn cynical and ask, "So why get it anyway?" I sense no anger in their words — they are not jealous of their friends who have received their diploma. If there is anger, it is turned inward, tying them in knots, forcing them to silent oaths, "This year I will do it!" Few of them have turned against learning and the search for truth *per se*, though, over the years of grinding away at the books and manuscripts, some have become suspicious of the world of Pure Ideas as a meaningful home for themselves. Sometimes it is their burning concern for the life of the Jewish community that frustrates them — there they are sitting in ivory-towered libraries, inking away at hundreds of note cards, writing drafts and rewriting drafts, and all they can think is "Intermarriage is up; Jewish education still has many shortcomings; Israel is in serious trouble; Ethiopian Jews must be saved, soon." The knots grow tighter, more complex; weaving new, frustrating webs upon webs.

They're good people, all of them, yearning to be free — even if the end of the long journey leads to no jobs. At least they aren't quitters. That's how they console themselves. "At least there is some hope," they say.

SOME JEWISH THOUGHTS ON THE MATTER

Jewish tradition stands behind them: the respect for learning is so great, they know they are standing in a mighty stream of generations of rabbis and scholars. They need only open the Talmud to see geniuses in many fields, experts not only in Torah, but also astronomy, agriculture, medicine, language, literary criticism . . . vast minds conquering masses of material, digesting, organizing, reorganizing, breaking through to new ideas. Line after line of our ancient text supports them, and they have been told again and again that *Torah Lishma*, Torah for its own sake, is a sacred value in Jewish life.

They know that, in the realm of thought, of ideas located and shuffled, they know that a basic faith operates at all times: the human intellect can bring us to positive, substantial achievements in the human realm. Even my friends in the most abstract fields of mathematics and physics know that the Upper Worlds and Lower Worlds emerge, whether by logic or by mysterious interplays grasped only by a select few.

But there is a creeping frustration that burns away at their hearts: they see fellow ABD's making the classic move: they mark off a period of time wherein they will cut themselves off from the rest of the community, to allow themselves the opportunity to get down to the real work at hand. In the end, they will emerge victorious in the struggle to complete the dissertation. During that ascetic era, though, some become uncommunicative, rubbing spouses and children to the frazzled ends of tension, dropping contacts with longtime friends, showing crestfallen faces during their few public encounters with society.

It is a heavy price to pay, and the toll often takes great stretches of time to repair. They know this, because they have seen other ABD's do the same, scars healing slowly on their psyches. On the one hand, their minds remain sharp, incisive, stimulated by the work, but other aspects of their personalities become dulled and frayed, and they are not happy with what they see. It is a cutthroat world out there for many PhD's, and the interim waiting period only serves to heighten the frustration: while writing, they are contemplating the battleground of the job-search, the thought of being stuck in some Godforsaken college in the middle of nowhere, with no Jewish friends for sharing Jewish insights, a reawakening craving for Jewish community. Athens, Georgia, Denton, Texas, and Wichita, Kansas, are hardly the places to invigorate a renewed sense of Jewish life, and they are concerned, deeply troubled by the ominous probability of isolation.

AN ARRANGEMENT OF TEXTS

The Shulchan Aruch, the most well-known of Jewish legal texts, places the laws of Torah study immediately before the laws of Tzedakah giving. Torah study is in the section Yoreh De'ah 246, with 26 subsections. The laws of Tzedakah begin at 247 and extend to 259, with 111 subsections. Torah study covers approximately 5½ pages, and Tzedakah about 22½, in the large, full edition with commentaries.

The sequence is interesting, and the comparison of quantity is awesome. On both counts, the message is abundantly clear: Torah study — whether it be physical or chemical phenomena or Talmud and Midrash — Torah study must lead into acts of Tzedakah. Furthermore, for all the complexity of the rules of study, the rules of human interactions are that much more complex and must, as a result, be studied with even greater care.

So many statements we have heard reflect this attitude. Study is not the essence, but action; applying texts to the world of joy and suffering is a basic axiom of the Jewish way of learning. A pure scholar who remains entrenched exclusively in his ivory tower, or worse, one who is a bastard or animal in relation to the world around him — such a scholar represents a radical contradiction in Jewish terminology. By definition, this is not the meaning of "Jewish scholar."

The sheer comparison of quantitative rules in these two realms — study and Tzedakah — also indicates that the rules and methods of caring for others is more difficult to master than the regulations governing the rigors of study. The. Shulchan Aruch is reminding us that there are so many human relationships, so many kinds of human relationships, so many problems and situations to be considered, that we must take particular care to prepare ourselves for all eventualities. To operate a just and concerned world demands great insight and a strong foundation of interlocking ideas. Hopefully, the methods of study outlined in the Laws of Torah Study will be a useful tool for the fulfillment of the ideas in the latter section, the laws of Tzedakah.

There is, I believe, one other insight to be culled from the arrangement of the two sections: while the first part — Torah study at its highest level — may be open only to those with specific talents (and who by circumstance have been afforded the opportunity to study), the latter section is open to everyone. The strange, the less-than-average, the poor and the crippled all have opportunities to perform the Mitzvah of Tzedakah . . . even those slipping into senility, whose minds no longer make amazing leaps into abstruse reaches of insight — even those have the chance to do Tzedakah Mitzvahs. The depressed, the shoemakers, presidents, and the deaf, tinkers, submarine sailors, shirt distributors, waiters and stewardesses and stewards — every range and type of person can do the same. For the PhD's and particularly the ABD's, this should be a refreshing thought. It is an antidote to ivory tower tendencies. It keeps them from intellectual arrogance, and they can broaden their own education by acquiring new instructors and professors from the people of the People. the rarified atmospheres of the bibliophile and the scholar become clear as the learned ones intensify their contact with all of us who constitute The Jews, from the watercarrier of the *shtetl* and the woodchopers of 11th Century France, to today's Simple Jews scattered throughout the world. It is, in the original sense of the word, a *Mechaya*, a revivifying experience.

A TROUBLING REFERENCE

Rav Huna said, "Whoever occupies himself only with Torah is like one who has no God." (Avoda Zara 17b)

Reviewing this Talmudic passage, I often wonder about Rav Huna's surroundings. Were all his friends great scholars, so wrapped warm in the mantle of learning that they did not have enough time or desire to bury their dead properly, to visit their sick, to provide for their hungry and lonely? Why is he so harsh, declaring pure Torah-learning insufficient, even accusing the Torah-students of Godlessness? Was there, in his day, a warping of the meaning of *Torah Lishma*, Torah for its own sake?

Rav Huna lived hundreds and hundreds of year ago. His words are faithfully recorded on pages replete with the names of great Torah students and Torah teachers. I believe his words are intended as a warning — in the midst of this twenty-volume weight of words we know as Talmud, a warning in the thick of the *magnum opus* of Torah — Beware! Do not forget the people. Do not forget the People, their aches, their exhilarations, their individual trials and fears.

Worship of the human mind is paganism. It is a forgetting of the basic responsibility we have to respond to the needs of the community. For all the glory of studying God's word in its seventy languages and infinite manifestations, the word itself is arid, without life, without the contact we need with the individuals who make us Us, the Jewish People. At all costs we must avoid that danger; otherwise, Rav Huna is saying, we are nothing more than bright, learned, Godless people.

Rav Huna's words are a welcome shock to us. We are the children and grandchildren and great-grandchildren of ancestors who dreamed of college educations for their descendants, who sacrificed and pushed and wheedled to insure this learning. Rav Huna reminds us that these dreams and hopes must be expanded, that theory and theoreticals are fine, good things, but not enough. There are those 111 subsections of Tzedakah work that await our talents, ways to make life decent, warm, a celebration. If we are frightened by the power of the Rabbi's statement, that was surely his intention. It is good to be reminded, daily, of his words. It may even be that they should be inscribed on institutions of higher learning, secular or Jewish, to give us a perspective. A much-needed perspective. Let us indeed have Torah, Rav Huna would say, but with the human touch.

A TRIBUTE TO MY FRIENDS
IN THE RABBINATE

All too often I am criticized for writing about people who are larger than life. The people I describe are visionaries, strong-willed, energetic individuals who move mountains and bureaucrats and slow-to-shift societal currents into some prophetical program more grand than the status quo would believe possible. The names of Mendilow, Lupoliansky, Freund, and Gaster appear again and again in my articles and poems, colossal souls achieving and surpassing and carving out human triumphs on a grand scale. Still, it often seems that, because I am so impressed by their accomplishments, I am advocating similar lifestyles for all Jews. The Romantic Poet, as it were, wishes to bring people with ostensibly limited capacities into more expansive, breathtaking realms.

It is true that I believe that there are more of these "unbelievable" people in our communities, more than most people believe. And I believe they can be "discovered," much as one young woman, a certain Rachel, "discovered" the great Rabbi Akiva in the clothing of a crudely clad shepherd one day in the Fall sometime in the First Century. Underneath the coarse appearance, she knew that here was a Jewish Leader personified, someone at once noble and humble, and that he would reveal himself to himself and his people, if only he were offered certain opportunities . . . he must be exposed to the Great Teachers. Indeed, though he was forty years old, their combined wills produced the classic metamorphosis: a Jewish peasant assumed his place in the course of Jewish history as the greatest teacher of the Talmud. Thinker, Mensch, embodiment of the best of Jewish values, molder of a new vision of Jewish life.

But he, too, appears larger than life. So it is unfair to analogize from his biography, just as it is unfair to expect a randomly-selected woman from Dallas or a man from New Orleans to suddenly throw away his former lifestyle and turn to other, greater things. A new life — with new-found energy, new spiritual resources, less sleep and less time for shopping, business, and the full array of errands needed for survival. No, that is not a realistic expectation, and I believe (as I often mention) that is why the Talmud tells us there are only thirty-six Righteous Ones in the world. That figure might not be absolutely accurate — there are other opinions in the Talmud — but clearly the number is limited.

On the other hand, if I did not believe that the so-called "average Jew" could not broaden his or her vistas — accommodating to the larger considerations of Life-through-Tzedakah — I would not spend as much time as I do thinking, writing, and teaching about that Mitzvah. Now and again I hear stories of local Tzaddikim, quiet people wholeheartedly giving to others, beyond the expectations of the "norm." But more frequently I am told of individual acts, small patterns of giving which are truly impressive. Generous gestures abound, kindnesses are freely offered, devotion is ingrained in personalities I hear about in scattered sectors of the Jewish world. That is the model I seek — rather than the lives of the Thirty Six.

AN OVERVIEW OF SOME FRIENDS

Because of the direction my thinking has taken, I have recently taken to considering my many friends in the rabbinate. They occupy pulpits in Massachusetts, Florida, New Jersey, New York, Minnesota, Louisiana — in most of the States in the union, and in various locales throughout Canada. Some are great teachers or preachers, some have organized and packaged programs in their synagogues that would be the envy of any impresario on Broadway — powerful events in honor of Soviet Jews, affairs for the sake of Torah-study which are truly moving, strong, memorable moments in the lives of their congregations that bring the message of Judaism deeply into the minds and hearts of their people, our people. Others are by no means as talented. Their sermons are — just sermons, lacking sweeping imagery or charismatic delivery. Their adult education classes are not dazzling, though their sincerity and personal integrity come through to the students.

Each one, however, has his weak points. I have visited some three hundred synagogues in the last two decades, and though I have been very much impressed with many great personalities in the pulpit, each has his faults — as we all have faults in our own lives. Some are great figures, some minor. But the basic humanity of all of them is obvious, both in the strengths and the failings of the person.

It is a thankless job. Meetings, contract hagglings, and the rampant ignorance, apathy, and insensitivity of select congregants are only a few of the tensions that plague my friends. Many is the time I have heard congregants complain that their rabbi is paid too much, though the same congregant does not apply the same criterion to his stockbroker or accountant or dry cleaner. "The rabbi is never around when you need him" is ritually recited over and over again, as if it were wrong for a rabbi to take off one day a week. He is working and sometimes overworking on Shabbat and holidays, and they begrudge him a Tuesday or Wednesday with his family, and some time for reading and Torah-study. Of all my friends in the rabbinate, I cannot think of a single one who could be labelled "lazy." If anything, they are sadly overburdened in their official duties, and even more exhausted in subtle ways, through hidden responsibilities that they have undertaken by assuming the title of rabbi. While their devotion may be praised on occasion, more often than not, it is trampled in the dust by unappreciative individuals who spread distasteful gossip about this or that shortcoming the rabbi may have. It is bad enough that too many American Jews have collectively defined the rabbi as "their Jew" — the one who has to do all the Mitzvot, for themselves, *and for their congregations*. This, of course, frees the congregants from the need for personal commitment. Their three-day-a-year visit to the synagogue has apparently fulfilled their Jewish obligations, and the rest of the year can be taken care of by "their rabbi."

By this I do not mean to malign congregational Jews *per se* (who, as is well known, constitute only a small portion of all Jews in North America). Nevertheless, any pollster who spends two days in a synagogue can easily note all the phenomena I have mentioned. It is indeed a thankless job, and, in some cases it has led to my friends' abandoning the rabbinate for other fields of endeavor: counselling, business, professorships of Judaica and secular subjects at different universities. As I see them leave, I realize I am neither angry nor frustrated nor disappointed. I generally feel a sense of relief for my friends who are now home with their families more often, and free of the immense pressures they once knew every day, throughout the year. For the younger ex-rabbis, this sometimes means the end of job insecurity, that underlying fear of no-contract, a shift of neighborhoods, of cities, of friends every two or three years. Leaving the rabbinate often means a new stability and a chance to begin life again, hopefully without an insurmountable measure of despair and cynicism. They will remain good Jews, as they always were, but now it will be on their own terms.

I believe it is time for the Jewish community here to take note of this crisis. It is time for a warning: Jews — be gentle with your rabbis.

THE RABBI AS PASTOR

After that overlong introduction, I wish to address the unsung heroics of the rabbinate — the deeds of the rabbi as pastor. For centuries a rabbi was essentially a teacher. That is no longer true. The pastoral demands — the duties of a shepherd tending his flock — have taken precedence. They are time-consuming and emotionally draining duties; so much so, that, whenever I am with a friend who is a rabbi, I ask, "How many funerals and shivas do you do a year? How many weddings, conversions, and how many visits to the hospitals and homes of congregants who are sick?" The sheer numbers are staggering, and each experience is an emotionally charged event that would turn many nonprofessionals into manic-depressives.

How many people can one person bury in a year without a great strain on his emotional energies? How many breaking marriages can he counsel, how many fragmenting children can he see — five days a week with one parent, weekends with the other? How many times can he enter the wards of a medical center to see a sixteen-year-old with leukemia, balding in a laminar-flow room? And even with weddings — the ostensible joy is often darkened by inter-family and intra-family strains, stresses of every shade and pitch, bride's father and groom's mother tearing away at the soon-to-be-married couple. The seating arrangements alone present disturbing problems: for a wedding or bar or bat mitzvah, who sits where? Are the natural mother and father together, or is the father with his second wife and the mother with her second husband? I have listened to this specific tale of woe on many occasions, and it is a very real, frustrating issue.

I listen to the conversation of my friends The Rabbis, the talk of how thick-skinned you have to be to be in the rabbinate, how often and how many people do *not* say "Thank-you, Rabbi," just once in a while, how they wish people would treat them at least as fairly as they do their law clients, their customers in the store.

It is indeed a thankless job.

I do not envy them.

But I do admire them . . . not their tenacity in the face of utter lack of cooperation and support, but I admire the accumulated human-sensitive Mitzvot they have performed: holding the hand of the patient in the ICU, speaking words of Torah wisdom at a Shiva-Minyan, delivering eulogies that do honor to the dead and to the living. Again and again and again, and yet once again. I recall a rabbi's daughter telling me how rarely she and her father would go to the movies or circus or ballgame or county fair — there was always a call for a funeral, a last minute phone conversation in low tones. And father-rabbi would disappear into some congregant's house to console and comfort a Jew overwhelmed by a great sadness.

Parties — we all have parties; we all count on friends being there. The rabbis, too, are entitled to the same — a bash, a blowout, or a small dinner get-together with friends. But the phone rings.

Vacations — we are all entitled to vacations, and yet, even then, sometimes, a week in Florida or the Great Smokeys is broken up because the phone rings.

It is true that the rabbis do not carry beepers as many doctors do, but the word gets to them anyway. "Mr. Steinberg had a stroke." "Max Wasserman's daughter was in a car accident. You'll have to tell him." "Anne Levy's mother broke her hip." Make any combination of names, pick any combination of circumstances . . . my rabbi-friends have heard all of them.

For all their personality differences, this one factor — being a pastor to their congregants — ties them together. They have in common a mass of shared pain, a complex of human frustrations, a combination of deep apprehensions and moments of despair (even in the midst of some Simchas). Throughout any week you choose, an occasion that triggers these phenomena is bound to stand square in front of them and stare them directly in the face.

They are not superstars. However, if I were to write a book about them, I would change James Agee's title *Let Us Now Praise Famous Men* slightly, to *Let Us Now Praise Famous Jews*. Famous in small ways, in gentleness, in comfort, caring, masters of the wise words in moments of high and low emotion. I have often jokingly said, "I have too many friends who are rabbis." Now that offends me, for they are worthy of nothing less than our admiration and our praise whenever we have (or create) the opportunity to sit with them in their homes and their studies. They are heroes in the true Jewish sense of the word.

AN ADDENDUM: THE DISCRETIONARY FUND

Nearly every rabbi I know has a discretionary fund. It is a bank account with money from various sources used for Tzedakah purposes: Matzah for poor Jews for Pesach, free-loans, scholarships for Jewish educational programs, books for Jews who very much want to read Jewish books. It is money for down-and-out Jews whom we rarely see, vagabonds and ne'er-do-wells in the Twentieth Century who travel from town to town, often making ends meet only through the kindness of the local rabbi.

Some discretionary funds contain a few hundred dollars a year; others run into the thousands, depending on the sources. The money comes in through individual contributions for a variety of occasions, and frequently the rabbis deposit in it all the fees they receive from weddings, funerals, bar mitzvahs, and other similar occasions. If a grateful family wishes to thank the rabbi for having performed a Menschlich, sensitive funeral, or if they have helped a convert enter the fold of the Jewish people with warmth and care, the rabbi often insists, "Make a contribution to the Discretionary Fund." There are a couple of thousand of these funds in North America, each in its own way helping to sustain elements of the Jewish community that might be ignored.

Let us assume that from funerals and weddings and bar mitzvahs a rabbi could gain three thousand to five thousand dollars in additional income. Does it not strike us, the congregants, that most rabbis could make good personal use of the money? They have families to support, day-school tuitions to pay, book bills higher than most of us — perhaps even a need to support an older relative trapped in the confines of a fixed income. Would this money not be most welcome in their personal budgets? And yet, they have set their standards: these dollars are for the Discretionary Fund. To them, it is Mitzvah-money, and it is to be used only for Tzedakah . . . this besides their own personal contributions to Tzedakah. (After all, they, as all Jews, are required to give of their own incomes.)

Not every rabbi has the same policy, but I have been deeply impressed over the years by just how many of my friends do this.

I, as one Jew, wish them a Yashir Koach — more strength, more wisdom, more powers of insight in this work. Though the cynics and iconoclasts damn the organized Jewish community, screaming of crudeness and ugliness, I stand at the side of my friends, the rabbis, who are carrying on Jewish life in the highest sense, with dignity, with devotion, with love.

Indeed, Yashir Koach to them — may their strength grow over the years, moving people, changing lives, bringing warmth and hope to all Jews who come to know them.

THE FINAL LETTERS

Project Hope, a B'nai B'rith Passover package project in Washington, DC — bringing food and dignity:

Dear Gentlemen:

A B'nai B'rith member just brought to my house a supply of Passover food. I wish I could express how excited my daughter and I were (as soon as he left).

Despite working a full-time job, inflation has hit me hard. This is the first year that I knew I would not be able to buy Passover food. It's not terribly spiritual of me, but I knew what I would miss most was the gefilte fish. For my daughter, I regretted the lack of some special Passover candy.

Now — we have two jars of gefilte fish, candy, egg kichel, *and fruit,* and two little bottles of wine. I shall join all the Jews in the world in 4 glasses of wine on Passover night.

Everything you brought was what I needed. With the chicken I already have, we are all set. The social worker who put my name on your list said she was told your baskets weren't anything special this year. She was wrong. Everything in them is special.

Because other Jews cared enough, my daughter (who, by the way, became Bat Mitzvah this year) and I will observe Passover. You have made us feel a part of a wonderful extended family. I'm sure this feeling will remain with us throughout the holiday and afterward.

Thank you very much.

From Myriam Mendilow, Director of Life Line for the Old, a final note, expressing the ultimate meaning of this Mitzvah of Tzedakah:

I regret to inform you that we lost Rachel, from Ceramics. She was 100 years old when she died — she just lay down and fell asleep forever. For me, she represented the story of Life-Line. I shall always remember her. From a beggar in the streets, we made of her an honourable and beautiful citizen.

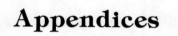

Appendices

SELECTED SOURCES

(A Personal, Nonexhaustive List)

I. *Traditional Legal Material*

1. *Maimonides*, Hilchot Matnot Ani'im (The Laws of Gifts to the Poor), *Mishna Torah*, (English selections, Mishna Torah, Philip Birnbaum, editor, pp. 153 – 159).
2. *Shulchan Aruch*, Yoreh De'ah, Hilchot Tzedakah (The Laws of Tzedakah, sections 247 – 259 (no English translation).

II. *General Jewish Source Material*

1. *Tzorchei Tzibbur: Community and Responsibility in the Jewish Tradition* (with teacher's guide), printed by United Synagogue of America, Department of Youth Activities. (Excellent, essential material.) Barbara Fortgang Summers. (155 Fifth Avenue, New York, NY 10010.)
2. *The Third Jewish Catalogue*, Strassfeld and Strassfeld, pp. 12 – 91.
3. *The Second Jewish Catalogue*, Strassfeld and Strassfeld, pp. 422 – 423 (Federations), 424 – 425 (free loans, free shelter).
4. *Encyclopaedia Judaica*, "Charity," Vol. 5, pp. 338 – 353.
5. *The Jewish Almanac*, eds. Richard Siegel and Carl Rheins, pp. 558 – 564 (Deeds of Righteousness and Lovingkindness), pp. 564 – 567 (Tzedakah).
6. *Tzedakah: Not Charity But Justice*, The Central Agency for Jewish Education, Miami, FL (4200 Biscayne Blvd., Miami, FL 33137). (Curriculum for the schools.)
7. *Moray Tzedakah*, pamphlet series from the Bureau of Jewish Education, New York, Dr. Abraham B. Eckstein.
8. *Love Your Neighbor*, Zelig Pliskin, Aish HaTorah Publications.
9. *Maaser Kesafim: Giving a Tenth to Charity*, ed. Cyril Domb, Feldheim Publishers.
10. *Ahavath Chesed*, the Chafetz Chaim, Feldheim Publishers (Also in the original Hebrew, Torah VeDa'at Publishers).
11. *The Talmudic Anthology*, ed. Louis I. Newman, Berhman House Publishers.
12. *The Rabbinic Anthology*, ed. Montefiore and Loewe, Meridian Books.
13. *Angels*, Siegel, Town House Press.
14. *A Tzaddik in Our Time*, Simcha Raz, Feldheim Publishers. (Biography of Rabbi Aryeh Levin, one of the Righteous Ones.)
15. *Balm In Gilead: The Story of Hadassah*, Marlin Levin, Schocken Books.
16. *Why They Give: American Jews and Their Philanthropies*, Milton Goldin, McMillan.
17. *Gadol Kvod HaBriot: Jewish Perspectives on Beauty and Ugliness*, Siegel and Katz, pamphlet for Leaders Training Fellowship, 3080 Broadway, New York, NY.
18. *UJA Shabbat Study Guide*, Rabbi Bernard Raskas, based on Tz'dakah: Privilege, Joy, Dignity (Siegel).

III. *General Literature: Biographies, Research Studies, etc.*

1. *Charity USA*, Carl Bakal, New York Times Books (extensive study of the

mechanics and nature of philanthropy in America. A critical source for all Tzedakah work.)
2. Helen Keller
   A. *The Miracle Worker*, play by William Gibson.
   B. *Helen Keller: The Story of My Life.*
   C. *Helen and Teacher*, Joseph P. Lash.
3. Albert Schweitzer
   A. *Out Of My Life and Thought.*
   B. *The Light Within Us.*
   C. *The White Wizard's 90th*, Hugh Moffett, Life Magazine article, February 19, 1965.
4. Tom Dooley
   A. *Doctor Tom Dooley, My Story.*
   B. *Deliver Us From Evil*, Tom Dooley.
   C. *The Edge of Tomorrow*, Tom Dooley.
   D. *The Night They Burned The Mountain*, Tom Dooley.
5. *Saints Among Us*, article in Time Magazine, December 29, 1975 (including the story of Mother Teresa).
6. *God Bless You, Mr. Rosewater*, Kurt Vonnegut (the story of a man attempting to live the life of a Tzaddik).
7. *Miss Lonelyhearts*, Nathanael West.
8. *Report To Greco*, Nikos Kazantzakis (Kazantzakis' spiritual quest).
9. *Like Normal People*, Robert Meyers (the marriage of a retarded couple).
10. *Death Be Not Proud*, John Gunther (the courageous life of Gunther's son, dying of a brain tumor).
11. *Stay of Execution*, Stewart Alsop (Alsop's struggle with leukemia).

IV. *Films*
   1. "Best Boy" — the story of a retarded man as documented by his cousin. Academy Award winner for Best Documentary.
   2. "Titticut Follies" — documentary of the horrors of a mental hospital.
   3. "A Plain Pine. Box" — documentary about the Adath Jeshurun Burial Society (the Chevra Kvod HaMet). For information, write Adath Jeshurun, 3400 Dupont Avenue S., Minneapolis, MN 55408.
   4. "I Never Sang For My Father" — about the elderly.
   5. "Harry and Tonto" — the dignity of old age.
   6. "Welfare" — Frederick H. Wiseman. (Same director as "Titticut Follies")
   7. "Hospital" — Wiseman.
   8. "Tell Me A Riddle" — story of an elderly couple.
   9. "The Street" — 10-minute cartoon, story of the death of a grandmother.

V. *Additional Jewish Sources in Hebrew*
   1. *Vayikra Rabba*, Chapter 34. (Translation in English: *Leviticus Rabba*, Soncino Publishers).
   2. *Babylonian Talmud, Bava Batra*, pages 9 – 11 (also available in English translation, Soncino Publishers).
   3. *Tzedakah U'Gemilut Chassidim*, Yariv Ben Aharon, School of Education, Haifa University (collection of xeroxes of primary sources. Superb.)

4. *Sugyot Shel Tzedakah*, compiled by Rabbi Yacov Simha, Providence Hebrew Day School (pamphlet, collection of primary sources).

5. *Entziklopedia Talmudit*, "Gemillut Chassadim," Vol. 6, pp. 149 – 153.

6. *BeDerech Tovim*, Yehuda Moriel, HaHistadrut HaTzionit HaOlamit, Department of Torah Education and Culture for the Diaspora. (Excellent sources on Menschlichkeit and character education.)

7. *Yesoday HaMiddot*, Yisrael Shimon Feldhorn, Hadar Press (superb collection of sources on visiting the sick, comforting mourners, Tzedakah, Rachmoniss, etc. Difficult to locate copies.)

8. *Ma'aser Kesafim*, Avraham Mordechai Albert, Me'or Press (covering specific Tzedakah issues based on Maimonides and the Shulchan Aruch.)

9. *Likkutei Halachot Al Hilchot Tzedakah*, Shabbetai Shlomo Vigedor, Balshon Printing (excellent commentary, line-by-line, on the Laws of Tzedakah from the Shulchan Aruch).

10. *Sefer HaAggadah*, section V, pp. 501 – 534, Chaim Nachman Bialik.

11. *Otzar HaAggadah*, "Tzedakah," vol. III, pp. 1047 – 1055 (258 sources from Jewish literature, from the Talmud to the Zohar). Mossad HaRav Kook Press.

GLOSSARY

(H = Hebrew, Y = Yiddish)

Aliyah (H): moving to Israel. Literally, "going up" to Israel.

Alta-kocker (Y): pejorative term for an old person, comparable to, and sometimes harsher than, "old dog."

Amitzim (H): The Strong Ones.

Aretz (H): *The* Land; Israel.

Avot (H): Fathers, The Fathers, as in Pirke Avot, "The Sayings of the Fathers," a section of the Mishna containing ethical aphorisms.

Bar Mitzvah (H) (Fem.: Bat Mitzvah): young Jew's ritual ceremony for entering Jewish adulthood.

Baraita (Aramaic): A Talmudic statement from Mishnaic times (1st – 2nd Century), from external sources other than the Mishna itself.

Baruch Atta Adonai Elohaynu (H): "Blessed are you, O Lord, our God, . . ." traditional opening words of a Jewish blessing formula.

Besteh (Y): the best.

Bikkur Cholim (H): the Mitzvah of visiting the sick.

Bris (Y): (H = Brit Milah): circumcision.

B'Shalom (H): with peace, peacefully.

Bushah (H): embarrassment, humiliation, shame.

CEJWIN: the oldest Jewish camp in the United States.

Chagiga (H): a section of the Talmud dealing with sacrifices, but containing mystical material and important texts on the lives of the Rabbis.

Chassid (H, adj.: Chassidic): follower of the Chassidic movement, founded in the 18th Century by the Baal Shem Tov. Chassidism is known for its sense of joy and ecstasy, particularly manifested in prayer, song, and dance.

Chassidut (H): Chassidism.

Chevra(h) (H): a group, specifically a group of friends.

    Chevra Kaddisha (H): The Holy Society, whose purpose is to bury the the dead.

    Mitzvah-Chevra (H): a group of people joined for the sake of doing Mitzvot, upright deeds commanded by God.

Chometz (H): leavening, leavened bread, forbidden on Passover.

Days of Awe: The High Holidays, Rosh HaShana and Yom Kippur.

Edel (Y): refined, genteel.

Ehrlich (Y): honest, upright.

Eretz Yisrael (H): The Land of Israel.

Federation: local and national organization of combined Jewish philanthropies. Similar to the United Way in the general community.

Gemillut Chessed (H, pl.: Gemillut Chassadim): acts of sympathetic loving-kindness. Sometimes used to mean specifically the giving of interest-free loans.

Grayser (Y): great, as in Grayser Mensch, a great human being.

Hachanassat Kallah (H): the Mitzvah of providing the necessities for a poor bride and newly-married couples.

Hachnassat Orchim (H): the Mitzvah of hospitality.

Haggadah (H): the book containing the liturgy for Passover-night rituals (Seder).

Halachah (H): Jewish law, also a specific Jewish law.

Halbashat Arumim (H): the Mitzvah of providing clothes for those in need.

Haray Zeh Meshubach (H): "It is praiseworthy;" so much the better.

Hatzilu (H): save!

Hilchot Matnot Ani'im (H): the Laws of gifts to the poor, a section of Maimonides Law Code.

JNF: The Jewish National Fund, the major project in Israel for reclaiming the land, and for the planting of trees.

Kavod (H): dignity, respect, self-respect.

Kedusha (H): holiness.

Keren Ami (H): Jewish Tzedakah, specifically familiar to Hebrew-school children as their class project.

Ketubot (H): a section of the Talmud dealing with marriage.

Kibbutz (H): collective settlement in Israel, largely agricultural.

Levayat HaMet (H): the Mitzvah of burying the dead.

Lishkat Chasha'im (H): "The Secret Chamber." A room where people could anonymously leave money for the poor, and where the poor could come and take the money, also anonymously.

Magen David Adom (H): the Red Star of David, first aid organization in Israel.

Ma'on LaTinok (H): "Infant's Residence." Hadassah Levi's project for infants with Down's Syndrome in Israel.

Ma'ot Chittim (H): the Passover Tzedakah project in local communities, collecting funds to insure that the poor will have provisions for the holidays.

Matanot La'Evyonim (H): the Purim-holiday Tzedakah project, local communities collecting funds to insure that the poor will have provisions for the holiday.

Mensch (Y): an upright, responsible person living fully a life as one created in the image of God.
(adj.: Menschlich)
(abs.: Menschlichkeit)

Mezuzah (H): a small container holding an inscription from the Torah that is hung on the doorposts of Jewish houses, according to the instructions in Deuteronomy 6.

Micah (H): one of the Hebrew prophets.

Mishnah (H): the earlier portion of the Talmud, edited around the year 200 C.E.

Mishulochim (Y, Var: Meshulochim): Tzedakah collectors who go from door to door, usually representing Yeshivot, academies of Jewish learning.

Mitzvah (H): command, instruction, good deeds done according to the prescriptions of traditional Jewish texts, such as visiting the sick, keeping Kosher, and giving Tzedakah.

Nichum Avaylim (H): The Mitzvah of comforting mourners.
Nizkeh LeMitzvot (H): May we have the privilege of doing more Mitzvot.

Olin-Sang-Ruby: one of the summer camps of the Reform movement.

Perutah (H): ancient Jewish coin. The smallest negotiable sum.
Pirke Avot (H): see "Avot."
P'tach: acronym for "Parents for Torah for All CHildren." "P'tach" means "open" — and it is an organization in the United States devoted to providing Jewish education for children with learning disabilities and who are retarded.
Purim (H): holiday celebrating the victory of the Jews over Haman the Wicked during Persian times. The holiday is celebrated with great joy, dancing, masks, and merrymaking.
Pushka (Y): a Tzedakah-box.

Rabbanit (H): a rabbi's wife.
Ramah (H): one of a series of Jewish camps in the Conservative movement.
Rebbetzin (Y): a rabbi's wife.
Rebbi (Y): teacher *par excellence*, not necessarily a rabbi. Also, a leader of a Chassidic sect.
Rosh HaShanah (H): the Jewish New Year.

Sechel (H): common sense, insight.
Seder (H): Passover-night ritual of reciting the tale of the Exodus from Egypt.
Sefardi (H, Var.: Sephardi): Oriental Jew, from Yemen, Turkey, Iran, Morocco and other countries.
Shabbat (H, Var.: Shabbas): the Sabbath.
Shadchan (H): a matchmaker, one who arranges marriages or other encounters between people (by extension).
Shaliach (H): messenger, agent.
Shekhina (H, var.: Shechina): God's divine and immediate Presence.
Shema V'Ezer (H): literally, "hear and help," the Jewish special education program in Washington, DC.
Sherut La'Am (H): program in Israel for volunteers from overseas to do social service projects.
Shichecha (H): a Mitzvah mentioned in the Torah whereby a farmer is required to leave any forgotten sheaves of grain for the poor.
Shiva (H): literally "seven." The seven days of mourning when the mourners remain in their home. Religious services are held, and comforters come to express their words of consolation.
Sit Shiva: to observe the seven days' period of mourning.
Shulchan Aruch (H): major Jewish law code. (Aruch HaShulchan: a different, later law code.)
Simcha (H): joy, a joyous occasion.

Stam (H): just so, just that way.
Stantsia (Y): stopping-off place.
Sukkot (H): Jewish holiday in the Fall.

Talmud (H): immense compendium of discussions, tales, aphorisms, and insights from Jewish academies (Yeshivot) during the first five centuries of the Common Era.
Tchatchka (Y): a toy.
Tikvah (H): hope. Also, the special education camping program at Camp Ramah.
Torah (H): literally "Teaching." Originally meaning the Five Books of Moses, or Pentateuch, and expanded to mean the entirety of Jewish learning.
Tza'ar Giddul Banim (H): the day-to-day burdens of raising children.
Tzaddik (H, pl., Tzaddikim): a righteous person.
Tzedakah (H): the distinctly Jewish method of performing charitable acts. From the Hebrew word "Tzedek," meaning "Justice."

Yad B'Yad (H): literally, "Hand in hand." The younger Conservative youth movement's Tzedakah project for helping the special children in the Tikvah program.
Yahrtzeit (Y, var.: Yohrtzeit): anniversary of someone's death.
Yasher Koach (H): "May you be strong." A statement of well-wishing, encouraging the recipient to continue to do Mitzvot.
Yeshiva (H): school for Jewish study, academy.
Yom HaAtzma'ut (H): Israel Independence Day.
Yom HaShoah (H): Holocaust Remembrance Day. The full name of the day is "Yom HaShoah VehaGvurah" — "Remembrance Day of the Holocaust and the Heroism."
Yontiff (Y, H = Yom Tov): a Jewish holiday.
Yoreh De'ah (H): one of the four major sections of the Shulchan Aruch law code.

Zechut (H): a privilege.
Zeyde (Y): grandfather.
Ziess (Y): sweet.
Zohar (H): the major book of Jewish mysticism.